Bestse

Ba

gives you top-dog advice—and unleashes
all the backstage secrets—on how you can put
your pet's best paw forward and become a

StarPet

It's like American Idol *for your pet!*

Praise for "Bash"

"[He] has such a cult following among Manhattan pet owners that he is known simply as Bash, like a rock star."
—*The New York Times*

"Bash Dibra is recognized as an authority and deservedly so."
—William J. Kay, DVM, Animal Medical Center

"High-profile folks like Mariah Carey and Henry Kissinger
rely on Bash, the trainer who can turn the most problematic
pooch into a model canine."

—*W*

"There's nobody quite like Bash when it comes to dogs. Within a few weeks my two Bichons were behaving perfectly and trotting happily on their leashes."

—Barbara Taylor Bradford

"I think Bash Dibra was raised by wolves."

—Nancy Friday

"Bash did a great job in training Sally, our Border Collie, and in return she absolutely adores him. That, to me, seems like the best endorsement of his training philosophy."

—Matthew Broderick

"Bash not only trains dogs, but truly loves them. And they love him too."

—Sarah Jessica Parker

"Anyone who can teach Spike anything should be sainted."

—Joan Rivers

"[Bash] explains how to understand feline body language, facial expressions, vocal signals, and other instinctive behaviors . . . [and] how to get the most out of human-feline relationships."

—*Publishers Weekly*

"[With *Cat Speak*] Dibra shows how to channel cats' natural instincts and capabilities into desired behaviors."

—*Science News*

"[*Dog Training by Bash* is] great fun to read . . . well-written, accurate, informative, and entertaining."

—*Library Journal*

Also by Bash Dibra

Your Dream Dog
Cat Speak
Dog Speak
Teach Your Dog to Behave
Dog Training by Bash

StarPet

HOW TO MAKE
YOUR PET A STAR

Bash Dibra
with Kitty Brown

POCKET BOOKS

New York   London   Toronto   Sydney

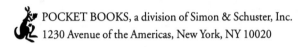 POCKET BOOKS, a division of Simon & Schuster, Inc.
1230 Avenue of the Americas, New York, NY 10020

ISBN: 0-7434-9194-7

First Pocket Books trade paperback edition April 2005

10   9   8   7   6   5   4   3

POCKET and colophon are registered trademarks of
Simon & Schuster, Inc.

For information regarding special discounts for bulk purchases,
please contact Simon & Schuster Special Sales at 1-800-456-6798
or business@simonandschuster.com

Designed by Jaime Putorti

Manufactured in the United States of America

To all pet owners who appreciate the unconditional love and joy your pets bring to your lives and who see your pets as potential stars, as diamonds in the rough. With love and proper training, each and every one will shine like a star, a StarPet.

Acknowledgments

There is no way I can express my gratitude to those whose patience and understanding supported me throughout the writing of this book—my family, my friends, my clients. Special thanks go to my sister Meruet, who took over all business matters while I was otherwise engaged, and to my sister Hope, who is always there for me.

Kitty wishes to thank her family and friends, who understand that lives are put on hold during the writing of a book, and to salute Sean and Rodion, for their invaluable support.

Thanks as well to my creative editor, Mitchell Ivers, for his ongoing guidance, and to José Dennis, for his wonderful illustrations.

And to all the animals in my life—past, present, and future—I am deeply indebted; but most especially to Mariah, my wolf, whose spirit, the true essence of StarPet, remains a part of me, and, I hope, with you, within the pages of this book.

Contents

StarPet

Preface: Mariah and Me

Some young people dream of going to Hollywood to become a movie star.

I dreamed of going to Hollywood to make a dog a star.

You see, for me, it all started when I should have been bitten—but *wasn't*—by a vicious guard dog.

It was post–World War II Europe, the beginning of the Cold War, actually, and my parents had gathered their family—and their courage—and fled the Communist tyranny of our homeland, Albania. But much of Europe then was still in a state of upheaval, and we were detained at the border and imprisoned in a Yugoslavian internment camp. These camps were brutal, former Nazi concentration camps. Our day-to-day life was one of desperation and despair. We lived huddled together in a cold and tiny jail-like cell of a room. Time moved on, but we could not. Our past was taken from us, and we did not know if we had a future. All we knew was confusion and helplessness and hopelessness. There was no sunlight or fresh air, and hunger and hardship were a way of life.

I was just a toddler then, barely able to walk. When I did walk, however, I had one destination, and one destination only: the imposing barbed-wire fence ringing the perimeter of the camp, which was patrolled by guards and their dogs. I was fearful of the guards, but fascinated by the dogs. I was drawn to them, curious to touch their thick fur and gaze deep into their dark eyes. I felt the dogs had something very important to tell me, if they could just be free from the guards, and if I could just be near them.

Soon, my "dogged desire" and inquisitive nature led me to the fenced-in enclosure where these exquisite creatures slept and ate, free from the restraints of the intimidating guards. No one had ever explained to me that these dogs were ferocious, trained to attack—to kill, if necessary—any refugee who tried to escape. In my innocence and longing, I approached the fence of the dogs' enclosure, and stuck my tiny, determined little fist through the wire, hoping a dog would come to me. Always on alert, one of the dogs approached me almost immediately. I was thrilled and instinctively opened my hand. As stunned guards watched from afar, the big dog slowed down, and his teeth never touched my hand. Instead, he lowered his head, sniffed, and gave my hand a gentle lick. By the time the horrified guards caught up with us, I had made a friend and found my future. Wherever they might lead me, dogs would be my destiny.

But that day, the guards scooped me up and away from the dogs, whisking me off to their office and summoning my parents. We were interrogated about what I was doing there and why. Didn't I know the dogs could have killed me? My parents were warned that they must keep me away from the dogs. To make certain that we got the message, the guards donned their protective gear and gave a vivid and terrifying demonstration of how guard dogs attack and the fatal damage they can do.

My distraught parents were furious with me, terrified of what the dogs could have done to me, and intimidated by the guards. Who knew what terrible repercussions might be wrought upon us and our fellow refugees by my behavior? The guards were angry at me because I had somehow, unwittingly, infiltrated their line of defense in the camp's containment of the refugees. I was confused because I had angered both the people I loved—my parents—and the people I feared: the guards. It was as if the guards and my parents had become uneasy allies in their shared quest to keep me away from the dogs. My parents put me under "house arrest"—I was kept indoors, well away from the dogs' area.

But the dogs were my refuge in that dismal refugee camp, and I resolved to be with them. Determined to end my exile, it wasn't too long before I made my break and found my way back to the dogs. Despite the guards' attack demonstration, I remained unconvinced that these beautiful animals were the evil, vicious creatures everyone kept telling me they were. So, when no one was looking, I once again approached the dogs' area and stuck my fingers through the fence and, once again, with my open, outstretched palm, the dogs slowed, sniffed my hand, and gave me several warm licks. My fate with these furry creatures was sealed, literally with a "kiss," once and for all.

And it was then (in a kind of "pet therapy" before I even knew what pet therapy was!) that the guards, because of the dogs, also became my friends. Somewhat mystified by their dogs' response to me, and definitely frustrated in trying to control a dog-happy toddler, they decided it might be better for camp control to allow me supervised "visits" with my dog friends.

So, for the next three years, the guards, the dogs, and I established a happy ritual: I could visit the dogs, but I must go through the guards' quarters first. The guards didn't want their superiors or other camp internees to see me. It would have meant trouble for them in their ranks, and would have been bad for the morale of other refugees to see that I had more freedom than others.

But the fact was, I *did* have more freedom. My friendship with the dogs was my passport, if only for a few hours each day, to a new world of freedom on the other side of the camp's fence—a taste of a world unknown to me; but a world I knew I longed for. A world of daylight and dreams—and *dogs*!

And when I was old enough to understand such things, a Holy Man in the camp told me a story. It's a story I've never forgotten, and it reflects my own feelings about dogs and the bond we share with them.

"You are very lucky, Bash," he told me, "that you have had this amazing experience with animals. The relationship that we have with dogs—this bond we feel—is a gift from God. And it comes from a time in the far, far past, when man lived in the garden, and it was a very beautiful world. Man and nature were in unison in this very special place, where man and animals lived in harmony and could talk together, each in his own language. All understood one another perfectly and life was beautiful. It was nothing at all like this camp.

"But one day man broke God's rules, and God was very, very angry. He gathered all of the animals in the garden and told them that because man had broken the rules, he would have to leave the garden. However, being a merciful God, he asked that one animal remain by man's side. The world outside the garden was a very frightening and lonely place; God wouldn't be there to protect man, who would need a friend. All the animals looked at one another, and not one said a word.

"Finally, a wolf stepped forward and stood next to the man. And when the man and the wolf stepped through the gate of the garden into the wide world outside, the wolf was transformed into a dog. Man and dog have been best friends ever since."

So, like the man and the dog who stepped through the gate together and into a brave new world, I knew that somehow, "my" dogs—these "vicious" guard dogs—would take *me* there, also. Indeed, in a way, they already had—and not just to the other, freedom side of the camp's gate. These dogs had helped me to escape in the same way the wonderful dog stars in the movies help people to escape problems and worries and depression: the escape of the imagination to a wished-for world. The "escapism" that our shared, twentieth-century Hollywood "heritage" affords anyone who can afford a ticket and a bag of popcorn, and that, if only for the run of the film, allows your mind to run away with you, transporting you to a place, that, for whatever reason, is better than your own place in your own world.

Those prison dogs were both my escape and my destination; my desire and my destiny. The dogs hadn't bitten me. They didn't break the skin or draw blood. But they had gotten *under* my skin and *into* my blood. I definitely had "dog fever"—and there was no cure!

Within a few years, the United Nations sent an American committee for human rights, and they won us our freedom, allowing us to relocate to Italy. I will always be grateful to the United States, but I almost didn't want to go—it meant leaving the dogs. But I knew I had to. The dogs had helped me to escape once before, and they didn't let me down this time. For as surely as a benevolent guardian holds the hand of a bewildered child through troubled times, the dogs had gripped my heart and given me courage in a frightening time of world unrest, as well as a determination that dogs would always be a major part of my life.

Indeed, I realize, in retrospect, that the guard dog's first lick of my hand was really my first taste of dog training! Sadly, I knew that I could not take these dogs with me. But I *also* knew that I would never leave them behind. Just as they had been my salvation

★ Mariah the Wolf. ★
COURTESY BASH DIBRA

and carried me through disconcerting times, so they would *continue* to be my salvation. I carried them in my heart that daunting day when I crossed the threshold into my brave new world, and they have remained with me ever since.

And although I never looked back, I *did* return—having realized my dream of making a dog a star; and having that dream come true, in part, thanks to the remarkable wolf who accompanied me on my return: Mariah.

Indeed, it would be more accurate to say that I accompanied *her,* because, like my dogs, Mariah had become a star in her own right. She had starred in a network television movie and had won a coveted contract as the "cover girl" for a major cosmetics company. And finally—having been selected by the International Olympic Committee to serve as the official mascot and goodwill ambassador of the 1984 Winter Olympics in Sarajevo—Mariah had journeyed to Yugoslavia, the land of my childhood refugee camp, where she commanded the world stage.

As Wordsworth poetically observed, "The child is father of the man," and Mariah's stirring performance was a powerful tribute both to the long-dead guard dogs who had taught this child so much and to Mariah herself, who had taught so much to the man I had become.

As surely as the wolf in the story of my childhood changed the course of mankind's history, Mariah changed my life profoundly—not just because of her career successes, but because of her inner self, what she taught me and how she inspired me. She became my muse and my Rosetta Stone, my inspiration and my understanding. With her beauty, she was the model for Revlon's Gypsy Gold ad campaign, and with her inner beauty—her ancestral wolf characteristics—she became the model on which I base all my training.

To the public, Mariah was the symbol of the brotherhood of the eternal Olympian quest for extraordinary athletic accomplishment, unconstrained by culture, unbounded by country. But to me, Mariah was the symbol of the symbiotic spirit of the brotherhood of man and dog, and what we can accomplish against all odds. In my own private Olympic marathon, the guard dogs had been my goodwill ambassadors to my captors, forging our friendship and insuring my passage to a new life in a new country—just as my Olympic goodwill ambassador, Mariah, years later, brought me back again, in liberty and triumph.

And if I can do it, you can do it.

★ Mariah and me. ★
COURTESY BASH DIBRA

I don't mean, of course, that every impossibly insurmountable obstacle can be overcome by a shared human/hound Herculean effort. But I do believe that, whatever your dream—discovered or rediscovered—you can capture it and make it your own. People and pets are a winning combination.

When you first choose your dog, as I outlined in my last book, *Your Dream Dog,* you are embarking on a journey of a lifetime, wherever it takes you. With this book, *StarPet,* I am encouraging you to reach for the stars; to find your inspiration, your muse; to learn all you can; and to emulate that ideal. And, when you do this, and you are the best that you can be, you will be an inspiration to others, whether in your own local orbit or in the hemisphere of Hollywood hounds!

Indeed, I've never cared for the old saying, "You can't teach an old dog new tricks." As you'll discover with *StarPet*, lots of old dogs—and other pets—can learn lots of new tricks! In fact, some of motion pictures' greatest dog and cat stars became accomplished actors at all ages and from every conceivable—and inconceivable!—background.

The legendary Rin Tin Tin, for example, was a young pup near death in the foxholes of World War I Germany before being rescued by a young soldier, Corporal Lee Duncan, and taken to a new life in Hollywood, where he became a leading actor, and delighted in playtimes with his leading actress friend and neighbor, Jean Harlow! Under Duncan's tutelage, Rin Tin Tin soared to stardom with his onscreen heroism and derring-do—earning fame as "The Mortgage Lifter" and "The Dog Who Saved Hollywood," because his box-office blockbusters not only carried Rinty and Duncan to fame and fortune, but also rescued Warner Brothers, drowning in debt, from bankruptcy!

A few years before Rin Tin Tin sniffed around Hollywood, a little nondescript stray pooch, abandoned, frightened, and whimpering, was rescued by Bill Buskirk, then head of the Property Department of the Fine Arts Studio. Buskirk dubbed his furry foundling Props, and the likable little dog soon had the run of the studio. Props especially liked playing with the Triangle Kiddies—an ensemble cast of talented kiddie actors à la the Little Rascals. One day while Props was watching the kids film a scene involving a runaway wagon, the stunt went horribly wrong. Safety wires broke loose, and with little Baby Charles, the star, hanging on for dear life, the wagon careened out of control toward a deep gully, threatening to derail the entire production. Everyone froze, except Props. The plucky pooch dashed out from behind the camera and valiantly flung his little body in front of the wagon. Baby Charles was saved, and so was the picture—and it was all captured on camera. The little dog was soon cast in several box-office hits—most memorably *The Little Yank,* with Dorothy Gish.

And when Charlie Chaplin was looking to cast a dog as Scraps in the immortal film *A Dog's Life,* it was a poignant pup of a dog named Brownie—another stray-to-star story, thanks to Charles Gee, who rescued the little guy—who rose to fame costarring with the Little Tramp.

But not all of the dog stars were young pups, and not all of their costars were people.

Teddy, the Great Dane, was a charismatic canine who was equally adept at comedy and drama, and, in a career that spanned nearly a decade, commanded starring roles well into old age—and paved the way for many other dog stars, including Rin Tin Tin. But Teddy was best known for his costarring comedic capers with Pepper the alley cat. Under the direction of the legendary Mack Sennett, their popularity rivaled even that of Sennett's Keystone Kops.

And Pepper's phenomenal rise to stardom is no less amazing than that of her canine counterparts. Indeed, the Hollywood cliché of a young actress clawing her way to the top was never more applicable.

You see, Pepper literally clawed her way to the top of the movie industry when, as a starving young kitten, orphaned and abandoned by the rest of her motherless littermates, she pawed her way up and out from under the floorboards and onto the sound stage—right during filming! With more than a dozen cast and crew, spotlights, cameras, and other equipment, the scene should have terrified the little kitten. But Pepper seemed to find it mesmerizing—not to mention the lure of friendly voices and the scent of cream for coffee! As with Props, the camera caught history in the making: A kitten was saved and a star was born! And when Pepper was cast opposite her older male costar—Teddy, the Great Dane—the old dog's star took on new luster, and he worked well into his twelfth year, as the affectionate, charismatic film duo turned out hit after hit.

But none of the stars on the Hollywood horizon would have risen so high or shone so brightly if it had not been for the very *first* StarPet, Jean. Jean not only paved the way for the celebrity pet parade to follow; she *also* paved the way for her young master—Larry Trimble—to claim his place in motion picture history as premiere trainer of the greatest dog star ever: Strongheart.

You see, the year was 1912, and no dog had ever performed in

★ Strongheart in a silent movie. ★
COURTESY STAR MOVIES

a motion picture. The industry was in its infancy then, and Trimble wasn't much older! A young boy with a pet Collie named Jean, Trimble loved two things more than anything else: teaching his dog to perform tricks and hanging around the nearby Vitagraph studios where the "moving pictures" were being made. One day, fate intervened. The legendary studio boss Alfred E. Smith needed a dog to perform in his picture, and Larry and Jean were in the right place at the right time! The talented twosome fetched their opportunity and ran with it, acing the impromptu audition and launching young Larry's career—and Jean's stardom. The two of them were trailblazers. He was a trainer-in-training, she was a star-in-the-making. They learned together and forged their own path. And when the final curtain fell on Jean's stellar career, Trimble—by then a young man, and armed with the understanding Jean had given him, and the techniques he had perfected—set out to create the greatest dog star ever: Strongheart.

The year was 1921, the film was *The Silent Call,* and the star was a magnificent German Shepherd. The powerful film captured the undying love of a dog (played by Strongheart) for a wolf (played by Trimble's wolf, Lady Silver), and his death-defying heroics to keep his family safe from the dangers of the wilderness. With barely any *human* actors in the film, Strongheart was in nearly every frame. In the final scenes—when tragedy takes the lives of his young family—Strongheart's portrayal of shocked disbelief, grief, and utter despair has not been matched. Strongheart earned critical raves and public adoration, and his illustrious career fired an entire nation, an entire generation, with a passion for the noble breed.

And so these StarPets—along with their trainers who guided them into the halls of Hollywood history—shine brightly for you to look up to: to hitch your leash to, to find your muse, your mentor. I share these stories with you because, when I first became enchanted with animals in film, I had not even heard of Hollywood, let alone the stories behind these captivating creatures, and how they found their way onto the silver screen. And, when I embarked on my career as an animal trainer, I knew little about the trainers of these animals, and how they transformed their pets into stars. Their lives were a world away from my life, and they had died long before I was born. Indeed, the legendary dog trainer, Larry Trimble, whom I would posthumously adopt as my mentor, was a virtual unknown to me.

Yet as surely as Jean's rising star led Larry to Strongheart, Mariah's rising star, a half-century later, unknowingly yet unerringly led me to Strongheart and Trimble.

You see, as Mariah and I were working on the set one day, an enigmatic old-timer who had quietly observed us—day in and day out for nearly the entire production shoot—finally ambled over to us with the simple pronouncement that watching Mariah and me reminded him of his days as a young stagehand, watching Larry Trimble train an incredible wolf! He then pressed into my hands a worn and tattered edition of a 1929 *Saturday Evening Post,* in which Trimble had penned an article about his work with Strongheart—as well as with a pack of twenty-three wolves! From the historic handler himself, I learned about his philosophies and training techniques, and that an incredible "she wolf"—Lady Silver—was Strongheart's costar, and the creature of whom the old stagehand found Mariah so dramatically reminiscent.

For a young dog trainer, that moment was like finding the Holy Grail—or, in this case, the Holy Growl!

That serendipitous encounter was like stumbling upon an old, undiscovered letter from an ancestor you have admired from afar and longed to emulate—and, as the words come to life, they bring an awakening deep within you that maybe, just maybe, you might have what it takes to follow in his footsteps.

You see, in hindsight—perhaps *hound*sight would be more applicable—I see how my *own* journey unwittingly followed the StarPet path Strongheart and Trimble had forged a half-century earlier.

Strongheart hailed from post–World War I Europe, where he was a guard dog. I hailed from post–World War II Europe, where I was *guarded* by dogs like him!

When Trimble ransomed Strongheart from war-ravaged Germany, he relocated the dog to upstate New York. When my family and I were liberated by an American-sponsored United Nations human rights team, we relocated to upstate New York, where I acquired a dog.

Like Trimble with Strongheart, my dog of choice was also a German Shepherd. And, as with Trimble and Strongheart, my Shepherd and I also championed many philanthropic endeavors during the course of his career.

And finally, just as Trimble had trained an incredible wolf for the silver screen, so Mariah had come to me, and I had been privileged to raise and train her for a very special film.

These revelations were both humbling and energizing. They inspired and encouraged me, not only in my work, but to learn everything I could about the work of the legendary Trimble and Strongheart, and to pass that knowledge on to others who aspire to make their pets StarPets. And, along with that knowledge, to also give—as Trimble unwittingly, unknowingly gave me—the inspiration and encouragement of the legends before us, to follow your dream, and to become an inspiration to others.

You see, my story just shows that, wherever you seek inspiration or search for a mentor—and your shared canine or cat commonalities!—you will find your inspiration, and you may be closer to your mentor than you realize, and closer to realizing your dream!

Maybe the biographies of all our StarPets were written in the stars a very long time ago—and imprinted on their shining souls as they came to earth and into our hearts and homes. Maybe it is up to us to study their stories, to learn from them, and—like a pet training manual for *ourselves*—use their stories to help guide other people and pets. For we may train our pets, but our pets *teach* us— and the *best* teachers are the ones who *inspire* and *encourage*. We may imprint on our pets to influence their training—but *they* imprint on our *hearts* and influence our lives and the lives of those around us, *forever.*

So, as Larry Trimble did with Strongheart, we must—in big ways or small ways, professionally or personally—let our StarPets shine and use their spotlights as beacons of light for responsible pet ownership and shining paths to those who endeavor to follow in StarPet pawprints.

For all StarPets are wonderful and have special stories to tell, but the professional StarPets take their stories to the stage and screen—and that special pet just might be yours!

Discovering Your StarPet

Shakespeare rightly predicted that "the cat will mew and the dog will have its day!" But not even this visionary playwright could have imagined the proliferation of pets today, or their increasing value to the success of motion pictures, television shows, commercials, and print ads.

Let's face it. How many times have you watched a dog in a film and thought, "My dog can do that!"? And perhaps you've seen a cat in a commercial who can't *begin* to compete with your precious tabby? Or maybe you've flipped through a magazine and spotted an especially appealing animal in an advertisement?

Everyday people just like you call me or visit my website (www.starpet.com) to ask whether their pets have what it takes to succeed in the entertainment industry. And you know what? Very often these pets do have what it takes—and so might yours.

For twenty-five years, I've had the pleasure of training what I have come to call my StarPets.

StarPets are the pets who are public stars in their own right, appearing in motion pictures, television, commercials, and print ads—as well as the pets who are the private costars of human

★ Here I am with Matthew Broderick and his dog,
Sally, during a training session. ★
Courtesy Meruet Dibra

celebrities, the companions who share and complement the private lives of very public people. The celebrities on the other end of the StarPet leash include Sarah Jessica Parker, Matthew Broderick, Jennifer Lopez, Carly Simon, Mia Farrow, Mariah Carey, Martin Scorsese, Henry Kissinger, Alec Baldwin, Kim Basinger, and Ron Howard.

And, sometimes, the worlds overlap. Like exuberant dogs who bound into play mode whenever they spot a friend, and find themselves (and their people!) hopelessly entangled in a labyrinth of leashes—Who's walking who?—so the world of StarPets sometimes reads like an old-time Hollywood script, with real life seeming to mirror the reel life of a screwball, mixed-up, madcap (muttcap?) movie! And here, the script might read, "Who's *training* whom?"

This happened when I was training Sally, the wonderful Border Collie who belongs to Sarah Jessica Parker and Matthew Broderick. Sally has high energy, keen intelligence, and a potent personality. She could easily have had a career as a professional performing pooch—not to mention that, with Matthew Broderick and Sarah Jessica Parker as her "people," she was *definitely* well-connected! In fact, Matthew loved to take Sally with him on film sets, where she would entertain the cast and crew alike with her amazing feats. Indeed, with her sparkling talent, she was a featured star in my dog-training workshop video, *Teach Your Dog to Behave!*

Little did I know that Sally would soon be starring in her *own* "workshop," which could have been entitled, "Teach Your Star Person to Act Like a *Dog!*"—and "costarring" her stunning "star person," Sarah Jessica Parker.

·I was working on my third book, *Dog Speak,* in which I was concentrating on the way dogs communicate, and the subtleties of the expressions of their emotions—and trying to impart to my readers the way discerning dog people can understand what is going on *within* their dogs' minds, by correctly reading what is exhibited from *without.* Sally always had an exceedingly *expressive* personality, and, being very extroverted (of course, has anyone ever known an *introverted* Border Collie?), Sally served as a wonderful model for the book.

At the same time, Sally's "star person," Sarah Jessica, was working on her *own* project: She was slated to star in playwright A. R. Gurney's Broadway vehicle *Sylvia,* in which she would play—guess what?—a *dog*!

So, as I was coaching Sally to elicit various emotional responses and expressions for *Dog Speak,* Sally, in turn, was "coaching" Sarah!

You see, Sally was very prolific in dogspeak (which is why I was using her as my "model," of course!), so she was quite the "language coach." Actors frequently use dialect coaches, so why not a coach for dogspeak? Ever the consummate actor, throwing herself totally and studiously into the role, Sarah diligently dogged Sally's every move: her eyes, ears, muzzle, facial expressions, and body language. Indeed, with *Sarah* mimicking *Sally* mimicking *me*, in a kind of "round robin" of "cross-species" Method acting, I gained newfound respect for acting!

Not surprisingly, audiences and critics alike took Sarah Jessica to heart! Miss Parker garnered rave reviews for her finely nuanced performance, and the house was sold out every night for the run of the play. On street corners and in critics' columns, your "average" New Yorkers—aloof and opinionated, sophisticated (and sometimes jaded!)—were all equally incredulous, *dumbstruck,* at Sarah Jessica's awesome acting ability to virtually *transform* herself into a *dog*! And, needless to say, this was probably the *only* time in theater history that a beautiful, talented, accomplished, and award-winning actress was thrilled to be referred to as a "real *dog*"!

With the dramatic proliferation of pets on stage, screen, commercials, and print ads, it was difficult for supply to keep up with demand! It was a good problem to be saddled with, of course, but, nonetheless, a problem. I wasn't a Hollywood trainer, working from a ranch in California, where space isn't an issue. I was in the middle of New York City, where the prime issues of real estate are both lack of space and lack of acceptance of pets! Not so easy for someone whose business, also, is pets!

Serendipitously, with so many of my clients involved in some aspect of the entertainment industry—be it people or pets, behind the scenes or in front of the cameras—I began to find my stable of stars in the soaring penthouses and townhouses of New York City.

Long romanticized as the "playground of the rich and famous," New York was, for me, fast becoming the playground of the rich, the famous, and the *furry*!

You see, I may get a call for a specific type of cat or breed of dog that is not currently "in residence" in my own stable of StarPets but is, in fact, the type of cat or breed of dog I have chosen, bred, or trained for a *client*. And that animal may, in fact, be just the right answer to the casting director's call! Having trained the pet— and, oftentimes, the owner, as well!—I know if the pet can handle the job. And, equally important, I know if the owner can handle being the "handler"! Thus, during a busy season, I might not only engage the animal for an acting gig, but recruit the owner to be his animal actor's handler, as well!

So, with a demand too great for my own animal actors, this sort of informal arrangement started out of necessity for me. I made certain, of course, that these "private" pets—the pets of some very "high-powered" clients—were well-prepared for their high-profile "public" work.

What I *wasn't* prepared for, however, was the enthusiasm of the pets' owners—my clients! I knew the pets would have fun, what with all the attention and hoopla—but I didn't realize my *clients* would *also* be "hooked"! They each wanted to make—or have *me* make—their pet a star!

And so, a StarPet was born!

You see, every dog is a "diamond in the *ruff*," every cat is the "cat's meow"—even a bunny can bedazzle and a pet pig can "hog" the spotlight! If you pamper, pet, and polish it enough, a StarPet— like a genie out of Aladdin's Lamp—can burst onto the scene and create movie magic.

And, although many of my clients are celebrities, you don't have to be a star *yourself* to have a StarPet. Many of my StarPet clients are people just like you, who have learned from my books and video or participated in my StarPet workshops and casting calls. They may not be celebrities *themselves,* but their dogs and cats are bona *fido* and bona *feline* stars, who learned to perform on cue, navigate the blocking of a sound stage, and interact with human costars in the manner a script calls for.

Some of these *extraordinary* pets from "ordinary" households are Wesley, the Brussels Griffon who portrayed "Rags" on ABC's popular sitcom *Spin City* with Michael J. Fox; Jade, the suburban Chihuahua-turned-*show*time-Chihua*Wow* who did a star turn with Reese Witherspoon in an MTV *Total Request Live* video take-off of the hit motion picture sequel *Legally Blonde 2;* and Lucy, who appeared in NBC's *Law & Order* and in HBO's *Sex and the City* with Sarah Jessica Parker.

Just think of me as the Lee Strasberg of pets, who can take your seemingly "average" Norma Jean of a cat and bring out the Marilyn Monroe in her. Or perhaps you have a shy little Marion of a dog on the outside—but on the *inside* there's a two-fisted (four-pawed?) he-man (he-mutt?) John Wayne of a dog just waiting to premiere!

In truth, actually (and in a true StarPet role reversal), that charismatic cowboy had the *canine* brought out of *him!*

Legend has it that John Wayne was nicknamed "the Duke" because it sounded so macho. That, however, is only part of the story. Studio reps had christened Marion John Wayne because his given name was deemed too "prissy." But when publicists knighted him "the Duke" to signify the legendary status of the macho persona of their star, it was a tip of the star's ten-gallon hat to his beloved childhood dog, Duke. The movie legend and his dog were so inseparable that whenever Wayne was called, Duke would show up, and whenever Duke was called, Wayne was at his side! Talk about chemistry!

In our hearts, we know that there is, within each and every pet, a *star.* When you pamper and pet it, practice with it and polish it, that pet can become a star, not just in your own home, but in your community—performing in local plays, parades, pageants, and civic and chamber of commerce–sponsored community events, as well as working in the gratifying philanthropic realms of pet therapy and humane education. And, perhaps, you and your pet might even decide to "take your show on the road" and go professional—all the way from auditions to curtain calls!

And there is no better time to embark on such an adventure than *now.* More than ever before, pets are enjoying the accolades of show business. In fact, when I conceived and built New York City's "Canine Court" (the world's first doggie playground), I did so with the mission that city dogs should have a place to play together with their people and other dogs. If they are aspiring animal actors, they should have a place to practice agility and to rehearse acting routines and movie/TV stunt work.

It is no coincidence that this outdoor rehearsal hall is in the form of a playground.

Shakespearean scholars and theater purists alike will tell you that, since the days of Shakespeare and the legendary Globe Theater, the original word for actors is players, and the original term for acting is play-acting. As Shakespeare wrote in *Hamlet:* "The play's the thing," which is no less true for our *"hairy* Hamlets"!

You and your pet can only embark on the StarPet adventure if you are determined to have a good time. To play. To enhance your relationship with your pet, and to enjoy the adventure. All the work you and your pet do must be based on what comes naturally to your pet, and what your pet enjoys doing.

So just how do you discover your pet's inner, hidden talents? The same way any casting director, acting coach, producer, or critic discovers the talents of a human star! Watch your pet "perform"! No "Method" actor is better at "playing to type" or "living in the moment" than a dog or cat! Even animal *amateur* actors can run rings around the professional human actor when it comes to "the play"!

So, set aside an evening after work or school, and make it an "Evening at the Improv," as you play with your pet, keeping an eye out for what he loves doing most and the uniqueness of his expression.

Turn a lazy Saturday afternoon into a movie "*mutt*inee" or "*cat*inee." As you play with your dog or cat, imagine his special look or physical antics being a part of a film, TV show, or commercial. Does he listen to you? And does he like the playful interaction? Does he look to you for more? For a successful StarPet, everything he does, all the "work," must be based on what comes naturally to him, what he enjoys doing. Just as with people, pets cannot be successful in their work unless they enjoy their work! True, dogs (and some cats!) love having "jobs," and these dogs *love* to "work"—although some cats I know would rather have *you* work for *them*! StarPets must *love* their work—not work for love!

With this book, we will explore your pet's star appeal, as well as your ability to discover his hidden talents, and, with the techniques learned here, nurture your *private* StarPet—granted, an endearing but nonetheless *amateur* StarPet—into a *professional* StarPet!

So, whether you "take your show on the road" and embark on a *professional* StarPet career or you just want your pet to attain a professional *standard,* you must always remember to keep it *fun!* Whether you are working from your own home, backyard, or community—or you take it all the way to New York or Hollywood—remember that you and your StarPet are *"players"* and "the *play's* the thing"!

Quite simply, just remember to always keep the *play* in playacting!

And remember that StarPet is a journey, a journey of discovery, a journey to be shared and enjoyed with your pet.

Legendary literary chronicler of the American experience John Steinbeck, in his book *Travels with Charley,* took a journey across country in an old pickup truck with "only" his dog, his Standard Poodle, "Charley," as company. The aim of the trip was to discover, firsthand, the character of the American people, but Steinbeck found himself, instead, discovering, first *paw,* the exemplary and extraordinary character of the American dog.

"Charley," wrote Steinbeck, in discovery and newfound appreciation of his traveling companion, "is not a human; he's a dog and he likes it that way. He feels that he is a first-rate dog, and has no wish to be a second-rate human!"

The StarPet journey of discovery is similar. We are not out to turn a dog into a caricature of sometimes silly human behavior. I agree with Charley and Steinbeck—and that *other* exceptional student of Americana, Mark Twain, who observed that "man is the only animal who blushes—or needs to!" No, the journey of StarPet is to help guide our dogs to be the very best dogs they can be, whether at home and in their own communities, or in the public spotlight as a symbol for all the wonderful ways pets—both dogs and cats—enhance our lives.

And the StarPet journey should be as fun for you and your pet as the proverbial car ride is fun for the proverbial dog! (Think

Steinbeck and Charley!) In fact, the kind of joy and exuberance with which StarPets throw themselves into their work, as if they were jumping into the family car for a much-anticipated trip, was illustrated nicely by one of my clients, whose dogs acted in summer stock.

My client, Sergeant Brown, was an Air Force man, whose daughters were talented ballet dancers, spending their summers in regional theater. Theatrical endeavors were always a family affair for the Browns (Sergeant Brown always headed the lighting and technical crew, while Mrs. Brown handled costumes and refreshments)—even the family *dogs* sat in on the rehearsals! One year, the premiere summer stock production was *The Wizard of Oz,* and, serendipitously, the Brown dogs were the same breed as Dorothy's Toto—Cairn Terriers! Well, no auditions were even considered. The Brown brothers, Christopher and MacDuff, won the role of Toto—*paws down!—sharing* it, much as the Olsen Twins, Mary-Kate and Ashley, shared their early babyhood days on ABC's *Full House*! But both dogs loved working with all the kids and actors in the show so much that neither dog wanted to put in time, *off*stage, as the understudy!

So, how did Sergeant Brown keep both "dog stars" happy—*and* the production running smoothly? By keeping the family car—engine running—just outside the stage door! You see, as much as the dogs both loved their theatrical life, they *also* loved going for rides in the car! So, if Christopher, for example, was happily performing, reveling in the spotlight, Sergeant Brown—to keep MacDuff from being unhappy about *not* being on stage—would take the theater-happy dog for an "exciting" drive around the neighborhood!

But learning the StarPet craft is a journey within. It is discovering what your pet is capable of (and what *you* are capable of!), and how the two of you, together, can accomplish your goals, have fun along the way, and make your dreams come true! For the adventure, as any dog will tell you, is not just in the destination, but in the ride—and all the adventures along the way!

For human actors, this journey of discovery is called the "Actor's Arc," whether it be the arc of his career or the arc of the character he is portraying.

For *animal* actors, however, this journey of discovery is a little more hairy—pun intended!—and I find it helps my StarPet clients to think of this journey as "Bash's Ark," a kind of cross between the Actor's Arc and Noah's Ark! You see, Noah took the animals in, two by two, and I am taking the two of you—you and your pet— for some specialized, star-bound, in-tandem training.

You see, the Actor's Arc requires Method acting—digging deep within the human actor's psyche. But Bash's Ark requires the Mariah Method, which will teach you how to dig deep within your pet's psyche to discover your pet's talent, and will enable you together—with in-tandem training—to retrieve that talent from the depths of his psyche and put it into the spotlight.

And who knows? Your StarPet may unfurl a rainbow of "reel" rave reviews—and maybe even a pot of residuals at the end of the rainbow!

But, *more* important, you and your pet will have a wonderful, shared adventure—and *shared* adventures are the *best* adventures! And, as you build that special bond with your StarPet through in-tandem training, your pet's *off*stage behavior will get equally good reviews from those all-important critics, family and friends! But perhaps most important—because we love our pets so much—you will garner the loving accolades of your animal actor for sharing such a wonderful adventure.

Along these lines, I am often asked if a StarPet is born or made,

★ Bash with a wolf pup. ★
COURTESY DENNIS MOSNER

but I never get into a debate about it, because every time a puppy or kitten or other baby animal comes into this world, I believe that a star *is* born—and will *always* be a star in the heart and home of his owner.

So, whether you and your pet remain in the "real" world or step into the spotlight of the "reel" world, whether you have a dog or cat, a mutt, mixed-breed, shelter-rescued, or pampered "pick of the litter" champion line from a private breeder, your pet, with you by his side, has the potential to be a StarPet.

However, although a *private* StarPet may be *born,* a *public* Star-Pet, a *celebrity* StarPet, is *made.*

A pet fulfills the greatest role of all for the sometimes struggling human condition: providing unconditional love. A StarPet has the ability to bring that role to the public arena, for the betterment not just of humankind, but of all.

When I was studying animal behavior, I was greatly influenced by the "prophetic" work of the extraordinary eighteenth-century French naturalist Comte Georges-Louis de Buffon, in discerning and documenting the character and place in our lives of the so-called "ordinary" dog.

Centuries before pets were in our homes as family members, in our schools as educators, and in our hospitals as "therapists," Buffon published *Portrait of a Dog*, which put his spotlight on the power of the dog to heal a nation. Great leaders throughout history, and from differing and diverse nations, have all agreed that the standard by which a nation judges its greatness can be measured by how they treat their animals—and Buffon's exquisite and erudite work spoke volumes, not only about the treatment and well-being of pets in society, but also about how pets impart their special talents and affect the well-being of a nation's citizens.

Buffon's celebrated and celebratory work was the triumphant culmination of a two-year journey in which the naturalist—commissioned by King Louis XV to discover the most remarkable (and valuable to mankind) species on the face of the earth—embarked on an intense and detailed study the world over, only to return to the shores of his own continent, and to find his answer patiently awaiting him on his doorstep: his faithful home companion, the dog!

For his near-poetic work in detailing the exquisite, finely nuanced character of the species, King Louis XV co-opted the title Poet Laureate and conferred on Buffon the post of Naturalist Laureate.

In detailing his discoveries in *Portrait of a Dog*, Buffon wrote:

The dog is a species so intimately involved with our own. More docile than man, the dog adapts himself to the gestures, the manners, all the habits of those who give him orders. He takes on the tone of the house where he lives. The dog, faithful to man, will always conserve a degree of superiority over the other animals.

It can be said that the dog is the only animal whose fidelity is put to the test: the only one who invariably knows his master and the friends of the house; the only one who realizes when a stranger arrives, who hears his name and recognizes the voices of "his" family.

Independent of his beauty of form, his liveliness, his strength and his agility, he has par excellence all the inner qualities that could attract attention. The pleasure of attaching himself to a man and the desire to please: he lays his courage, his strength, his talents at his master's feet. He councils and questions. One glance is sufficient, he understands his master's will. The dog has all the warmth of feeling, and, even more than man, the dog has fidelity and constancy. In his affection, he has no ambition, he has no desire for vengeance, he is all zeal, all ardor. More sensitive to memories of kindness than of injury, he is not discouraged by mistreatment.

In chronicling the supreme, soulful symbiosis of the canine species with homo sapiens, this Naturalist Laureate rallied his countrymen to the side of the noble creature who had forever stood stoically at their side. In doing so, he influenced the manners and mores of a nation regarding its pets.

So, even hundreds of years ago, the dog was the leader of the pack in guiding human beings to a better understanding and kinder treatment not only of the canine species but of all species humankind shares this earth with—as well as leading us to a greater understanding of ourselves.

Before *Portrait of a Dog,* Buffon had nearly been forced into exile by the French clergy, who deemed his claim that animals had immortal souls blasphemous. In fact, his twenty-one-volume encyclopedia on animal behavior had even been banned.

In Buffon's native France, in the very next century (in 1895, to be exact), history was made with a poignant documentary capturing the struggles, and oftentimes the desperation, of the human condition. Perhaps it is no coincidence that this historic strip of film *also* happened to capture the very first *dog* on film—and to have the dog's place in our lives immortalized in celluloid for the benefit of people and pets, and all their progeny, everywhere.

Produced by the inventive French brothers Auguste and Louis Lumière, *Leaving the Lumière* was filmed with their revolutionary (at that time) yet still rudimentary hand-cranked cinematograph. The film was shot with the stationary camera and chronicled, documentary-style, the exodus of overworked factory employees—all women—from the Lumière headquarters in Lyons, France. And amid the mass of nameless, nearly faceless, hungering, and hopeless humanity, the camera captured—almost unnoticed and without fanfare—their sentient salvation.

At the end of a long and grueling day, as the workers made their weary mass exodus, there, just outside the gates, waiting dutifully for the dispirited denizens, is one lone, loyal dog.

With his brief appearance at the end of the historic, first-ever motion picture, that one dog—the spirit for the dispirited—still managed to steal the scene.

Pets help us at home, in schools, and in hospitals. They are our eyes if we are blind, our ears if we are deaf, and our limbs if we are weak. They offer us quiet repose in the midst of disquieting conflict. When we find ourselves mired in the grips of inexplicable inertia, they herd us into action with an unavoidable "up and at 'em!" enthusiasm. They are a force of optimism in a world that is often desperate and pessimistic. They imbue us with their joyful ability to "live in the moment"—yet at the same time they are steadfast, never wavering in their diligent and loyal guardianship.

And last, but not least, they *entertain* us. As surely as dogs "force" us out for a walk or a drive in the car, our pets force us to step outside ourselves and see—as they do—what a wonderful gift life is. And when we need to be brought down to earth and become a little more circumspect, they help us to walk a mile in another man's moccasins, or another pet's paws.

So, whether our pets remain stars solely in our homes, or take their newfound talents and skills into our local communities, or actually become working professionals in the entertainment industry, their ability to *entertain*—to touch hearts, to foster joy and love and understanding and laughter—is a gift that can change the world. Lassie did it. So did Strongheart, Rin Tin Tin, and Benji. In fact, the cinematic canine countenance is so powerful that even conjuring it up in animation is awesome in its ability to touch our souls.

Since time immemorial, dogs have saved us by licking our wounds and tugging at our extremities, as they drag our helpless selves to safety. Today, still more dogs (and *cats*!)—StarPets—save us by tickling our funny bones and tugging at our heartstrings as, from stage and screen, they pull our hapless human selves out of our cold and lonely inner prisons and into the shared warmth of their spotlight. The StarPet is a true and trusted friend to the millions of moviegoers who have ever known or owned a pet, and who have ever loved—and, perhaps more important, *longed* for a pet.

CHAPTER ONE

From Street Dogs to Pets

After I escaped the cold confinement of the internment camp, life in Italy was near idyllic for a young boy with a vivid imagination who loved animals. Images of Italy's most famous saint, St. Francis of Assisi, the patron saint of animals, were everywhere: icons in churches, statues in gardens, frescos on village walls. The colorful feast days, when entire villages celebrated the life and times of St. Francis with music, theater, art, games, and picnics, filled my head with visions of an everyday "Peaceable Kingdom." My pets were the village dogs and cats. They weren't really strays, but unlike pets as we know them here in America today, these dogs and cats were left more to their own devices. Much like Blanche DuBois in Tennessee Williams's classic *A Streetcar Named Desire,* these pets depended on the kindness of strangers—the local villagers who embraced them with open arms. I was no exception.

My earliest memories are of playing with these dogs and cats in front of my favorite fresco of St. Francis. This particular one was the largest and most colorful, depicting the defining moments of the life of St. Francis. The series of life-size paintings guided the onlooker through the life of St. Francis, capturing his most memorable times: first, the beloved saint as a young troubadour entertaining in the streets and cafés; next, preaching his famous sermon to the birds; then, imploring the mayors of the villages to pass laws that people must make certain to feed the cats and dogs and other animals on Christmas Day; another, the famous nativity scene; and, finally, the taming of the legendary wolf of Gubbio. That was the fresco that affected me most.

I would take the street dogs and cats and direct them to act the scenes from the fresco. I would have the dogs and cats—grouped in circles with dishes of food—"sit" and "stay" to portray the noble men and women in the cafés where St. Francis entertained when he was a troubadour. For the sermon the little saint preached to the birds, I would try my best to train the street cats *not* to follow their instincts to go after birds and butterflies. I didn't have much success with that, however.

Cats, of course, are "harder" to train than dogs, as you will discover in Chapters 6 and 7, but I think it would have taken the saint himself to train those streetwise cats not to act on their natural impulses! The nativity scene was fun because it required props and costumes, but my favorite scene was the taming of the wolf of Gubbio. To my young mind, the wolf in the fresco looked very much like my dogs from the internment camp, and I wanted to communicate with the street dogs as I had with the camp dogs. Indeed, I found that the street dogs learned their roles very quickly and happily, and always came back for more fun.

When I look back on that time in my life, I realize my childhood games were actually training for my future, when I would train my StarPets for roles in television and films. In fact, depicting each "scene" from the fresco was very much like working from a

TV director's storyboard—which I will teach you to do yourself with your own pets, in the following chapters.

As a young child in postwar Italy, however, I had no knowledge of television, of course, and had never seen a movie. But one day, my mother took me to a museum, which was showing a six-minute piece of film on a loop—running it continuously throughout the day for the museum visitors. I didn't realize it at the time, but it was a piece of history—the first film ever made purely for entertainment.

Rescued by Rover was shot in 1905 by Britain's legendary Cecil Hepworth (who also cast his own family in the film) and directed by Lewis Fitzhamon. A terrific Collie dog (named Rover, of course!) comes to the rescue of the family baby, who, despite the watchful attendance of the nanny, has been kidnapped by gypsies! Entranced, I watched spellbound as the camera followed Rover's derring-do detective work from the time of the abduction to the discovery of the gypsies' hideaway and the tearful reunion of the baby with her family!

I watched *Rescued by Rover* over and over, until my poor mother's patience wore thin and the museum closed its doors. But I wasn't finished with the film. My new childhood game was "Rover."

I endlessly cajoled my poor mother to take me to the museum every day for the run of the film. When the exhibit ended, I was bereft. I began to pester my mother to allow me to go into town with the other kids to see the Saturday matinees. Now I was hooked. Maybe I would find *another* Rover!

Eventually, my mother relented, and the exposure to movies awakened me to a world I'd never dreamed of. That little theater in postwar Italy didn't have access to the modern American films, but that was just fine with me. I saw all the great early films of the silver screen: Laurel and Hardy, the Three Stooges, and all the Mack Sennett funfests, which included, of course, the famous Keystone Cops. But each time the camera's aperture expanded to include animals my eyes really widened and my own horizons expanded: Chaplin's *A Dog's Life,* Larry Trimble's *Strongheart,* Lee Duncan's *Rin Tin Tin, Our Gang* (with Petey!), and all the animal antics of Mack Sennett's irreverent repertoire! One day, years later, I would put together a reel of Sennett's best moments from his movie menagerie for a fund-raiser to benefit service dogs, but at that point I'm not sure I even understood that the dogs were *actors!* These "reel" dogs had a very *real* hold on me. They were my pals, just like my street dogs, who were always there for me.

Twenty years later, I would be directing my *own* dogs in Italian movies.

My father found a great deal of work in Italy, indeed all over Europe. The ancient Romans had built a complex labyrinth of underground drainage tunnel systems. Their work was so ahead of its time that the system had remained in use even up through modern times. But nothing remains in good working order without upgrades, and Italy's system required constant upgrading. Compounding the problem was the fact that the "landed gentry" had built massive estates and villas on thousands of acres of land over these tunnels. Because of this, my father would be called away all over the continent. Wherever the work took him, I had a new opportunity to acquire new skills that still guide me in my profession today.

At each estate, our family would be housed in modest quarters on the compound along with the other workers—the household staff, the groundskeepers, and the gamekeepers. As a child who was drawn to the dogs and horses, I hung around the kennels and stables, mesmerized not just by the dogs and horses, but also by the skills of the kennel masters and stable masters. Hungering for any crumb of attention they might throw me, I eagerly sank my teeth into any odd job they might ask of me.

Eventually, they began to teach me what they could, as well as allow me to try my own uncertain hand at dog training and horse training—even falconry! When the dogs and horses were down for the night—and I should have been in bed, as well—I would sneak out to the barn to try out my newfound training skills and techniques. Nighttime was showtime for the barn cats! With their keen night vision and physical dexterity, these felines were amazing to watch as they controlled the rodent population and played, pawing at fireflies and jumping at shadows.

As I grew older and practiced my techniques and honed my skills, I had the honor and privilege of apprenticing with some of the most renowned trainers and kennel masters in Europe. Many of the kennels I worked in were devoted exclusively to developing and breeding show-quality dogs, and the experience gave me the unique opportunity to get to understand and work with the different qualities and performance skills of almost every breed of dog.

As I continued my apprenticeships, fine-tuning my craft and learning as much as I could about the trade, what I glimpsed inside the great villas influenced me almost as much as my work in the fields outside those gilded walls. You see, inside were beautiful paintings, great works of art, depicting how the great noble men and women felt about the very animals we were training—their pets! Wall after wall came to life with pampered pets captured in paint: the master and his hunting dog, the lady and her lapdog, the "nanny" dog in watchful repose at the baby's cradle, a great Newfoundland rescuing a child and her doll from an overflowing

★ Here I am as a child in Europe with my parents and our dog. ★
COURTESY BASH DIBRA

brook. I was struck by the power of these painted people and their pets to elicit such pathos from the human heart, the ability of an artist to transmit the power of the human-animal bond—and how the landed gentry in the paintings could translate the beauty of that intangible bond to others through art.

As I grew older and my world expanded, my father found work in Alsace, the birthplace of the Alsatian—the German Shepherd— the breed of Larry Trimble's great dog actor, Strongheart. It was also the birthplace of another icon, Albert Schweitzer. Physician, theologian, musician, and author, the acclaimed Dr. Schweitzer was a consummate humanitarian. His legendary work as a medical missionary serving the poorest of the poor in Lambarene, Africa, had won him the Nobel Peace Prize in 1952, several years *before* my family and I arrived in Alsace. Much like Mother Teresa today, he became a celebrity of iconic proportions, a universal symbol of altruism, self-sacrifice, and dedication.

Equally concerned for the welfare of *animals* as for that of human beings, his philosophy of "Reverence for Life" literally came to life in his hospital compound in Lambarene, where he brought life-saving medical treatment, not just to the people, but to their animals as well. And, indeed, when cultural mistrust or misunderstanding threatened to stand in the way of life-saving treatment for the people, he simply allowed his patients to bring their extended families, pets, and farm animals along for the hospital stay, as well. He was a pioneer in pet therapy!

Schweitzer's words and actions inspired people from all countries, all generations, and all walks of life. President Kennedy's Peace Corps was inspired by Schweitzer's work, and so were many of today's animal welfare groups and societies. Indeed, when my family was in Alsace, in the years following the awarding of the Nobel Peace Prize to Dr. Schweitzer, people came in droves—on *pilgrimages*—to follow in the venerable doctor's footsteps.

Schweitzer encouraged people to emulate, in whatever way they could, the philosophy of "Reverence for Life," and uttered the now-famous words that gave clarity to my unfocused dreams: "Every man has his Lambarene!"

Schweitzer's words crystallized my destiny, if not my destination, the Lambarene of my heart. It already housed the incredible guard dogs from my early childhood in the refugee camp. Now it made room for the possibility of sharing what they taught me and what they gave me—and, indeed, what all dogs can teach and give to all people.

So, although I didn't know *where* my Lambarene would ultimately be, I had a vision of *what* it could ultimately be. Perhaps

I would train people's pets, or maybe become an animal doctor. One thing was certain. My Lambarene would be peopled with animals!

Serendipitously, not long after Albert Schweitzer's words provided me with a road map for the "what" of my existence, my destiny, the American committee for human rights from the United Nations, which, years earlier, had ransomed my family from the internment camp, once again came to our aid and sponsored my parents' United States citizenship. Now, I not only had a destination, I had a *glorious* destination: the United States of America! New York, to be exact!

My newfound world was upstate New York. My heart may have been in Hollywood and moviemaking, but Cornell University College of Veterinary Medicine was my immediate destiny. Sadly, however, my father passed away. Now, as the eldest of my siblings, I switched my studies to animal behavior and psychobiology, and worked as a dog trainer to help support my struggling family. Eventually, however, work began to take up more and more of my time.

I needed to support my family, and I was deeply immersed in training and showing dogs with the Bronx County Kennel Club and the Westchester Kennel Club, when I met the famous animal trainer Captain Arthur J. Haggerty.

Captain Haggerty is an enduring legend who supplied trained animals for Broadway shows and hundreds of feature films and television commercials. Indeed, a true legend and show business character, Captain Haggerty's inimitable look is almost as recognizable as his animal stars! You see, Captain Haggerty's place is often in front of the camera, as well as behind the scenes. An actor as well as a trainer, he was the original Mr. Clean in the company's phenomenal ad campaign—and many of the stars whose pictures

Haggerty's dogs are in often ask Haggerty to appear, as well! Discerning fans can spot him, for example, with both his dog and Rod Steiger in *The Pawnbroker*!

So, when Haggerty offered me the opportunity to work for him, I didn't need to think twice.

One of my early movie projects under Haggerty's auspices was training the animals for the Burt Reynolds film *Shamus,* which also starred the lovely Dyan Cannon—not to mention Haggerty himself. Working with Haggerty always promised loads of fun. Although I'd been hired to work with the dogs, the legendary Morris the Cat of 9 Lives fame also appeared in the film, and I had an opportunity to witness the training techniques of Bob Mardwick, the equally amazing cat trainer!

But first and foremost, working with Haggerty gave any trainer—junior or senior—a solid, hands-on learning experience, both from the master himself and from the eclectic group of trainers and animals he put together.

During the course of the *Shamus* shoot, I really came to admire the work of Jai, an incredible Great Dane who had to "attack" Mr. Reynolds in one scene, choreographed by the talented Bob Maida, who was Jai's owner and trainer. Burt does all his own stunts, including those with the dogs.

Reynolds was terrific in working with his animal costars, and his positive experience in that arena stayed with him and served him (and a little dog who was to enter his life!) quite well in the ensuing years. For when Reynolds began directing and producing as well as acting, he scored a real hat trick: His career swung into white-hot high gear with his super-successful *Smokey and the Bandit* series of feature films, and he didn't leave any really important work to chance. When the script called for a dog, Reynolds himself auditioned all the aspiring animal actors! And, in true good-

★ Bash acting out a movie scene as Captain Haggerty looks on. ★
COURTESY BOB MAIDA

guy, time-honored Hollywood-legend tradition, the dog he chose for the role was a homeless shelter dog named Happy. And when the film finished shooting, Burt chose Happy to costar with him at home: Reynolds adopted Happy.

It was then that I began to realize the beginnings of my dream of the far-reaching positive effects of the duality of StarPets: training pets for show business, as well as training the pets of celebrities. I really hadn't thought it out to that degree, of course, but I began to realize that by training celebrities to work with animals on the sets of commercials, TV shows, and films, I could foster greater understanding between celebrities and the StarPets they worked with professionally, which would also foster better understanding and treatment of pets in the entertainment industry itself. And, by virtue of the far-reaching orbit of these Hollywood superstars, they could also have a profound effect on the understanding and treatment of pets by the audiences they touch—not only through their films and TV shows but also via radio, TV, and print interviews, as they share their affection and understanding not only of the animal costars they work with, but also of their own pets, and pets in general.

I was still, however, a long way from Hollywood, but my mind was not. In fact, before I left Cornell, I had to write a paper on Charles Darwin's famous dissertation *The Expressions of the Emotions in Man and Animals*. When Darwin wrote, "The dog expresses joy, affection, pain, anger, astonishment and terror, as well as the subtler and more intermediate emotional expressions, such as perplexed discomfort," I couldn't help but think that Darwin was talking like a high-powered theatrical agent promoting his client for a variety of roles. And then, when Darwin begins to contrast and compare the dog with man—"Even man himself cannot express love and humility by external signs so plainly as does a dog, when, with drooping ears, hanging lips, flexuous body and wagging tail, he meets his beloved master"—all I could think was that Darwin had discovered the scene-stealing secret of moviedom's magical mutts.

Finally, Darwin concluded, "Nor can these movements in the dog be explained by acts of volition or necessary instincts, any more than the beaming eyes and smiling cheeks of a man when he meets an old friend." Darwin knew that the dog is truly man's best costar.

In fact, there is a classic, quirky early Hollywood five-reel animal film called *Darwin Was Right,* produced by William Fox and Educational and Tiffany Pictures in 1924. With an all-animal cast of dogs, monkeys, apes, chickens, and birds, it is considered the rarest of all animal films. I hadn't seen that film yet, but what I *did* know was that Darwin was certainly right about the expressions of emotions in dogs, and I wanted to bring that understanding to as many people as possible. Working in the entertainment industry seemed to be the best way possible. When I finally completed my paper on Darwin, which took quite a while, with all that day-dreaming, I began to return to my childhood dream: to make an ordinary dog so special that it would become a star!

Around the time that the original *Ben* movie premiered and simultaneously made a rat a star and gave Michael Jackson a hit with the movie's title song, I decided that if I was going to study animal behavior any further, it would have to be in a way that was *immediately* applicable to my life and my dreams, which were, quite frankly, to work with the interaction of people and animals, people and pets, the human/animal bond, both onscreen and off-screen, and, of course, to marry that with my need to support my family.

In short, if I was going to work with rats, they would have to be pet rats or movie actor rats. So, with my mother and siblings firmly ensconced in New York, I arrived in Los Angeles, determined to learn what I could about animals and moviemaking.

It was a difficult time to be in Hollywood. The golden age of animal-driven pictures was drawing to a close. Our nation's international turmoil with Vietnam caused great internal turmoil, its repercussions rippling into an extraordinary upheaval of traditional, intergenerational change—and then Watergate opened the floodgates of domestic social turbulence, which made family-fare entertainment (which is where animal actors get the lion's share of their work) passé.

I arrived in Hollywood in these transitional times. Work was

★ Rudd Weatherwax and Lassie. ★
COURTESY KITTY BROWN

scarce and the old-timers bided their time. Although the famed Hollywood pioneers, Larry Trimble and his Strongheart, Lee Duncan and the first Rin Tin Tin, were no longer with us, the old guard was still around: the legendary Rudd Weatherwax, Lassie's original owner and trainer, and Bill Koehler, the original trainer of so many of the legendary Disney Dogs. I had a once-in-a-lifetime opportunity to learn from these brilliant, incomparable, and inimitable legends, and to be a part of their world. These giants would live on forever through their dogs captured on film and through their dog-training techniques, used by generation after generation of trainers.

One of the legends who not only survived the "dry" times of

★ Benji and Frank Inn. ★
COURTESY MULBERRY SQUARE PRODUCTIONS

the seventies, but actually flourished, was the phenomenal Frank Inn, owner, trainer, and handler of the equally phenomenal dog star Benji. In fact, he was able to successfully bridge the gap from movies to television and back to movies again—a difficult feat even *human* actors are rarely able to accomplish.

In those days, Inn had successfully guided the career of an endearing little dog, Benji, from a starring role on the successful television series *Petticoat Junction* to international film star status, shooting to fame with his incredible, groundbreaking hit movie. As with the other legends, I was privileged to learn from, and be inspired by, Frank Inn.

I found encouragement not only from the old masters, whom I so admired, but also, to my surprise, from other professionals on

★ **46** STARPET

the sets where I worked. As time wore on, I found that the animals' human costars, as well as the many professionals behind the scenes, began to approach me. "Can you train my dog to do what you just trained that dog actor to do?" "Can you train my cat to do that?" Soon, I found myself doing as much training behind the scenes, personally, as I was, professionally, for the animal actors in front of the cameras!

But fate intervened and ended my Hollywood adventure. My family needed me back in New York, and I had to be there for them.

My father had brought us to New York from Europe, and my mother did not want to leave. My sister Meruet loves animals as much as I do, and I encouraged her to study veterinary medicine. Meruet wanted to build the family business with me, so veterinary medicine gave way to a three-pronged study plan to become a vet tech/ groomer/handler. Without Meruet's vision, business acumen, and hard work, my business would not have grown to what it is today.

So we set up shop in a modest building in a beautiful and perfectly suited locale that met both my family's personal needs and my professional obligations. On the edge of historic Van Cortlandt Park, Fieldston Pets was a short ride into Midtown Manhattan for industry shoots and celebrity training sessions.

Fieldston Pets soon grew to include my stable of StarPets, a pet shop, and a grooming salon. As my reputation as "dog trainer to the stars" grew, Fieldston Pets grew to include personal one-on-one training. The pets are *never* alone, and our work is 24/7, but we wouldn't have it any other way. Our business is a way of life; our work, a labor of love.

That is what StarPets is all about: life and love. It is what we give to our pets, and what our pets give back, in return, to all of us:

families, friends, and audiences. Everything else about StarPets is just logistics, mechanics: pet supplies and retail pet shop, grooming, and training. All that is lifeless, meaningless without the heart and the soul and the spirit of the business: the animals themselves.

For to any of us who have ever known or owned an animal, it cannot be a coincidence that animal is derived from the Latin *anima*—meaning life, soul, spirit. Indeed, there are as many derivatives as a cat has the proverbial nine lives! From animus (mind), to animistic (spiritual), to animism (the belief that all life has a soul produced by a spiritual force separate from matter)—that is what our StarPets are to the StarPet Agency. Meruet and I may run the business, but it is the animals who are the soul of the business, the animals who animate it, who give it life and vigor and spirit.

When Fieldston Pets was in its infancy, there were three original StarPets who graced our lives, giving us—and what would become our life's work—a defining heart and soul and spirit. These incredible creatures were Orph, the German Shepherd; Mariah, the Timber Wolf; and Muffin, the Tibetan Terrier.

They say that Dog is God spelled backward. If that is true, then Orph, Mariah, and Muffin were my "holy trinity," the canine cornerstone upon which I built the foundation for StarPets.

Orph was my "Strongheart." A magnificent and majestic German Shepherd, Orph was, to me, what the inimitable German Shepherd Strongheart must have been to Larry Trimble. A consummate canine actor, Orph sank his teeth into whatever his role called for, sometimes literally. With a towering talent that surpassed and superseded scripting and directing, he could strike terror in hearts with a boot-quaking show of strength, or make souls tremble with a finely nuanced display of heartfelt (and heartrending) emotions.

Orph came to me as a very small pup to be trained for a very big role.

German Shepherds had always been my breed of choice, and Orph was the choicest of the choice. His conformation and character were of outstanding pedigree, and he had high intelligence. But he also had something beyond intelligence. He seemed to have a remarkable sense of self: an understanding of who he was, his place in my life, his relationship with me personally, as a dog, and his relationship with me professionally, as an actor. He savored his personal life, relished his professional life, and, understanding the difference, flourished in both.

But, even beyond that, Orph also seemed to have an understanding of others around him (other animals, as well as people) and their relationships not just to him, but to one another, outside himself. Orph even, I would go so far to venture, seemed to ruminate on his place in the universe. Orph wasn't just inordinately smart, he was inordinately thoughtful. Indeed, it might not be out of line to say that Orph had an added spirituality to his canine countenance, that he seemed to subscribe to the loftier ideals we mistakenly think only human beings can aspire to.

But whatever that extra something was, which words cannot capture, Orph captured the hearts of those who knew him and selflessly surrendered his heart. He gave his heart—his all—to his family of humans and other StarPets, and especially to my wolf, Mariah. He was gentle with schoolchildren and senior citizens, in his work in humane education and pet therapy. And, of course, he struck a chord with film and television audiences everywhere. Indeed, like Strongheart, Orph never gave anything less than his entire heart, his absolute best.

Whether he worked in film, television, commercials, or print ads, he always gave his all. He came on like gangbusters on the

★ Orph, the German Shepherd. ★
COURTESY MERUET DIBRA

Late Show with David Letterman, with an inspired comic turn as a canine "bouncer" who, in a reversal of refusing entry to "average" Joes into trendy, hard-to-get-into celebrity night spots, *refused* to let Letterman audience members *out* of the studio! And in a series of TV commercials and public-service announcements sponsored by Purina pet food promoting responsible pet ownership, Orph's poignant performance left even his costar, the gruff Ed Asner, visibly moved.

Like Strongheart with Larry Trimble, Orph not only shared my life, he would actually come to define my life. I acquired him for a specific acting job, a role that would require not only a great deal of versatility, with a multitude of emotions and actions, but a singular defining and charismatic presence. When I chose Orph for the role, I thought he could do it; when I began to work with him, I soon knew he could do it.

Orph was chosen for the starring role in the screen adaptation of award-winning dog writer Jerry Mundis's acclaimed novel *Dogs*. In an emotionally and physically demanding role, Orph portrayed Orphan—a scientifically conceived "Super Dog." Rescued from the laboratory and evil scientists by a secret group of caring children, Orph, with the kids in tow, embarks on a superdog life of detective work and derring-do—rescuing people and other animals from the clutches of evil, saving them from misfortune, and averting tragedy.

Orph portrayed Orphan (he was named for his character in the film) magnificently. At an age when most dogs' talents are barely in bud, and still require careful nurturing, Orph's wide-ranging talents were already in full bloom.

Unfortunately, the project never came to fruition. Midway through shooting, the production was beset by unforeseen and, ultimately, insurmountable problems. Completion, let alone distribution, was not to be.

But perhaps the loss of the movie was fate's way of freeing Orph for the role of a lifetime—the role he was destined to play—to "costar" with my wolf, Mariah, and to help me "direct" her.

CHAPTER TWO

From Pets to StarPets

*I*f Orph was the heart of StarPets, Mariah was the soul.

Mariah was, indeed, a very old soul (commingled remains of wolf and human fossils date back over 135,000 years!), but when she came to us, she was just a child star; just *days* old, and nestled deep in the dark woods of Maine, unaware of the spotlight that would soon be hers.

I had been asked by a group of producers at ABC to raise and train a wolf for what would become a landmark in children's educational television history: the highly acclaimed film *The Boy Who Cried Wolf.* They had the boy. All they needed was the *wolf* !

I discovered our star, nursing on her mother's milk in the protective comfort of a wolf sanctuary, blissfully unaware that she would soon become a star!

At Mariah's birthplace, in the tranquil wolf sanctuary in Maine, a group of caring and compassionate biologists were breeding wolves in captivity for a variety of roles. Some were bred to be reintroduced into the wild to replenish endangered wolf populations, others for educational purposes and to restock zoos and wildlife parks.

The wolf I chose was destined to follow in the famed footsteps of Larry Trimble's awe-inspiring wolf, Lady Silver. A half-century before, Lady Silver, costarring with Strongheart, had conquered Hollywood with her mystique and movie magic and had done much to conquer the public's dangerous and unfounded fear of the species. Mariah seemed fated to carry Lady Silver's torch. Through her many public roles and private appearances, Mariah affected audiences everywhere, furthered the human understanding of her species, and insured the safety of generations to follow. I was overwhelmed, exhilarated, and intimidated by the challenge of raising and training this incredible creature. Who (except Larry Trimble, of course!) could know how a wolf might react to living in a house and being raised with domestic pets?

And then I had an epiphany: It was not just what I could teach Mariah, but what Mariah could teach *me,* as well.

But, whereas Trimble amassed a pack of twenty-three adult wolves with whom he lived, as one of them, in a specially built compound deep in the Canadian woods in his amazing and unparalleled star search for Strongheart's leading lady, the quest for my leading lady was no less profound.

Trimble accomplished the incomparable feat of molding a group of unrelated adult wolves from diverse backgrounds into one pack, of which he was the Alpha, and from which he would choose and train an adult female as Strongheart's costar. The course I set for myself, given the intimate nature of the role the wolf was to play with human costars in the film, as well as the time constraints of the film's shooting schedule (preproduction had already begun), was to choose one family of wolves, and from that family choose one newborn pup, which I felt had that star potential, and to live with that one, cohesive wolf family. If I could assimilate myself into the wolf family and gain access to the pup, I felt I could foster its imprinting (bonding) on me. I would become the pup's Alpha, and from that would flow all training.

So, in a true "star is born" fashion, I discovered Mariah, a newborn, only days old, in this wolf sanctuary deep in the Maine woods.

Wolves can be difficult to work with, so I had to choose my wolf carefully. I knew I wanted a female cub, because through my work with dogs, I'd found that males of any breed tend to be more aggressive and dominant than females. This is especially true of wolves, because in the pack hierarchy, a male must constantly fight in order to retain his Alpha position.

Mariah's mother had been born in captivity, and the more time she spent with me, the more she trusted me to handle the young pups in her litter. The pup I chose would have to be young enough to bond with me and have the right temperament to allow me to train it. I chose Mariah exactly as I would choose any domestic dog pup: by observing the interactions of the pup within the litter, as well as their reactions to sudden noises and movements. I also picked up each pup and held it in my arms. The pup that would relax in my arms would indicate it possessed just the right amount of submissiveness. Mariah passed these tests—as she would all tests, obstacles, and auditions in her life—with flying colors.

The next consideration was tougher. It is extremely important for a wolf pup, as with a domestic dog puppy, to spend sufficient time with its mother and littermates to develop socially and behaviorally. However, our case was unique, as it was equally important that Mariah share this time with me. She needed to bond to me. She would be my pup; I would be her Alpha male (the male she would look up to).

So, while Mariah remained with her wolf family for the first six weeks of her life during that critical and delicate developmental stage, I had to be intimately involved, so she would imprint on *me* and come to regard *me* as her family, as well. This was crucial, not only because of our future life together and the film training we had ahead of us, but also because wolves, with their strong pack behavior, have such deep affection and loyalty toward their families that it can be traumatizing for them to be separated, and I wouldn't allow that to happen to Mariah.

To facilitate the process, I spent as much time as I could with her. I wanted to accustom her to my presence and my scent. As she was being weaned, I bottle-fed her daily. Once she was ready for solid food, I prepared her meals and gave them to her myself, sometimes from a bowl, sometimes by hand. This seemingly innocuous pattern of alternating feeding from bottle feeding through weaning and hand feeding was very important. Food is integral to the survival of any species, and our ancient symbiotic relationship with the wolf was probably instrumental to the survival of both species. Guarding our food is an equally strong, in-born self-protective instinct of any species, especially wolves. From a very early age, a young wolf has to guard its food from everyone else, including its littermates, until it has eaten its fill, or it will go hungry.

So, although I bottle-raised Mariah since infancy, when I switched her from bottle feeding to solid food in a dish, her primal food-guarding instinct immediately manifested itself. I overcame this by alternately hand feeding Mariah. The same premise held true for Larry Trimble with Lady Silver. His "breakthrough" with the still-wild, not-yet-named Lady Silver came about, in part, by Trimble patiently offering handheld morsels of his own food. Lady Silver's first step to stardom came with her first tentative steps to Larry as she broke away from the pack to forge her bond with the legendary trainer.

After six weeks, Mariah had forged her bond with me. Unlike Trimble, I cannot lay claim to being the Alpha of a pack of twenty-three wolves, but I was enough for Mariah, and that was all that mattered. She had imprinted on me and I had become her Alpha leader in our modest pack of two! She was totally dependent on me, and I was solely responsible for her, the relationship that, genetically, as a wolf, she needed and expected—an unbreakable bond, identical to the one that develops between man and dog.

After nearly two months of my assimilating into Mariah's world, we packed our belongings and left the woods of Maine for the jungles of New York City. I knew it wouldn't be easy, but I had faith in my chosen star, Mariah. I reminded myself that it is said that, with faith, all things are *possible*—not necessarily *easy*!

I knew as I drove through the darkness of the New England woods that Mariah and I were at a historic crossroads of our lives. I hesitated briefly, as if to somehow seek answers through time and space that the darkness somehow shrouded. I wanted Mariah's new life to be a new dawn for her and for her species, and I looked for a beacon of light.

And then, Mariah, somehow picking up on my sense of being lost and alone, found my gaze and held my heart. And as I gazed into her eyes, at once inscrutable yet understanding, she became, for just a moment, the Alpha of our pack—and guided me back to my sense of self, and her self, and our place together in the life we were embarking upon. And safe in the intimacy of the car, I restarted the engine and drove through the darkness to our boundless horizon. And as Mariah, somehow all-knowing, looked out into the night—as if somehow seeing, divining, the path before us with a clarity unknown to me—I whispered to Mariah (but more, to be honest, to my uncertain self) the final words of Poet Laureate Robert Frost's "The Road Not Taken," in what would become my prophetic Maine mantra, as we drove out of the darkness and into the dawn:

> *Two roads diverged in a wood, and I—*
> *I took the one less traveled by,*
> *And that has made all the difference.*

Fifty years earlier, when Trimble was faced with the daunting task of introducing his newest star, Lady Silver, to his pack of dog stars, as well as to other people in the studio and on the set, it was Strongheart who, behind the scenes, coaxed and coached the wolf to the ways of her new world, sending her on her way to their costarring fame.

And so it was, a half-century later, when it was finally time for Mariah to meet *my* pack of dogs, my Orph stepped into his "Strongheart" role as if on cue, and with an unfailing intuitiveness and unfaltering sense of rightness. If Mariah was born for the role I had chosen her for, Orph was born to facilitate that stardom. As an actor, Orph had already demonstrated that he was teeming with talent, but when I teamed him with Mariah, he displayed a tacit yet tactile tenderness in directing her that surprised even *me*. Orph was both Mariah's director and costar, her special friend and guide. They developed a unique bond, and, like any actress with a good director, Mariah blossomed under Orph's firm but gentle guidance.

Because Orph's presence seemed to calm Mariah and give her confidence (perhaps, in part, because a German Shepherd's and a wolf's physique and temperament are closely related), I made certain Orph was present when I introduced each of my dogs to Mariah, individually. Because wolf puppies are always subordinate to all the adults in the pack, I put my dogs in a down or stay position so as not to overwhelm Mariah, so she could feel comfortable in approaching them and sniffing them. And, because Mariah would lie on her back—belly up, in a traditional wolf/dog submission posture—I occasionally instructed my dogs to lie on their sides, to telegraph to Mariah their acceptance of her. Mariah got the message, and it was wonderful to see her interact with her new pack.

But out of all the pack, Orph was the reigning Alpha male, and Mariah recognized him as such. This helped me enormously in the assimilation and training of Mariah, because as closely as the wolf and the dog are related, the wolf is still a separate species, and, unlike the domesticated dog, a species that remains inherently wild. In fact, it could be said that working with Mariah was a bit like working in a foreign film, or with a foreign actress, and Orph was the translator, my "assistant director," if you will—something of a "canine conduit" to interpret for Mariah my directions.

In that respect, Orph took his role as Mariah's "leading man" quite literally.

In training sessions, when I would ask Orph to go get Mariah, he would find her, pick up her leash, and gently but firmly lead her toward me—or wherever I instructed—and wait, leash in mouth, Mariah by his side, until my next directive. And when, in the woods upstate, I intensified Mariah's off-leash instruction, I connected her with a "coupler" (a short, bridlelike twelve-inch lead) to her "leading man," Orph. Orph, understanding his role in the training, would dutifully allow himself to be "led" by Mariah as she navigated her way through training. If, however, she took a misstep, a wrong turn that might mean danger, Orph would immediately spring into action, not only taking the lead, but also taking the *initiative* in keeping her out of harm's way and leading her back onto the right training track.

I imagine the coupler—coupled with an amazingly intelligent and intuitive Alpha dog such as Orph—as enabling the unerring good judgment of the "automatic pilot" (Orph!) to kick in for the young pilot-in-training, Mariah! This method advanced Mariah's training sessions by leaps and bounds, and she almost literally flew through off-leash training, thanks to Orph. Eventually, Mariah worked without the coupler, following my direction by following her "costar's" lead. I, for example, would give a verbal cue or hand signal to Orph, and he would go out into the field and act out the command or perform the stunt. Mariah would watch, and, connecting the command to the action, mimic Orph's performance. Eventually, I could take Mariah out alone, and she would perform beautifully.

And, not to sound sexist or anthropomorphic, Orph was also the quintessential "director" in dealing with a pack of differing "divas" and defusing their canine competitiveness. While recognizing Orph as the Alpha male in my pack of animals, Mariah, at times, "aspired" to be the *female* Alpha. So, there was, at times, a jostling for that "starring" female lead role of the pack, the Alpha female, and (pardon the pun!) Orph would intervene to make certain it didn't erupt into a "catfight." And, if it can be said that an animal handled a role with aplomb, then that is exactly how the deceptively affable Orph took firm control and handled the potentially explosive situation. Rather than challenging Mariah or fighting her (the natural instinct for the Alpha male in a situation such as this), Orph instead chose to defuse the situation, to deflate Mariah's Alpha, dominant drive by distracting her with, and inducing her to join him in, a *play* mode.

But, as a good costar and director and friend, Orph was always exquisitely and effectively attuned to Mariah's moods. Being a wolf, Mariah "wore her heart on her sleeve." Her primal drives, especially her "fright or flight" instinct, were always just under the surface, ready to take over if she were panicked or stressed or fearful. At these times, Orph, sensing Mariah's inner turmoil, would go to her and sit with her and that would calm her. Working on this, I would then give Orph the command to lie down by her side, and then to stay next to her. This gave Mariah the time and presence of mind to realize that Orph was there, protecting her, and there was no need to flee.

This may sound simple and unnecessary, but, in fact, Orph's influence in Mariah's early training sessions and his prescient presence in her life were invaluable. For, although I did not want to squelch Mariah's innate wolf behavior, I did have to suppress aggression tendencies toward unfamiliar animals, and I had to curb some other behavioral traits as well, such as the extreme flight behavior that would surface whenever she was confronted by unknown people, different surroundings, or new or unusual experiences (all hallmarks of working in show business). Harnessing these wolf behavioral traits was paramount, not just for her career, but, more important, both for her happiness and safety, and for the safety and well-being of others.

But I also didn't want Mariah to be caught between two worlds, belonging in neither. I wanted to give Mariah a kind of "dual citizenship." I hoped to do more than just train her and pay passing homage to her wolf heritage. I wanted Mariah to retain her species' birthright and yet function happily within the confines of *my* species. To do this, I knew I would have to work *with* her wolf traits, not *against* them. No amount of human companionship or socialization can override a wolf's genetic makeup. I would have to train Mariah from *within* her deeply imprinted code. I would somehow have to merge the wolf behavior she was born to exhibit with behavior that was socially acceptable in a civilized world.

Mariah's career soared. After her star turn in *The Boy Who Cried Wolf,* Mariah was never without work. She was featured in PBS's *3-2-1 CONTACT* and won a coveted "cover girl" spot for Revlon's Gypsy Gold ad campaign. And at home she played the role of Alpha female to my pack of female StarPets. But Mariah was definitely not a diva. She seemed to grow into the understanding that fate had thrust her into a position to foster interspecies understanding and to promote humane education and pet-facilitated therapy.

As with all my StarPets, Mariah became a philanthropist, working as diligently for charitable causes as she did for networks and cosmetic companies. Dr. Marlin Perkins, creator and host of Mutual of Omaha's award-winning TV series *Wild Kingdom,* the longest-running animal show on television, tapped Mariah and me to go on tour to benefit the Wolf Canid Survival and Research Center. The tour was a great success in contributing to the public understanding of wildlife in general, and wolves in particular.

Mariah was selected by the International Olympic Committee to serve as the official mascot and goodwill ambassador of the 1984 Winter Olympics in Sarajevo, Yugoslavia—the country of my childhood refugee camp and the incredible guard dogs who started me on the journey of discovery.

They say that you can't go home again—but my presence with Mariah proved otherwise.

As if to prove she understood her place in my life, and the place in my heart of the guard dogs before her, Mariah, ever the pro, and unfazed by the lights and cameras and crowds (thanks to Orph!), held the crowd in the majesty of the moment, inspiring those gathered at Sarajevo for the opening ceremonies.

Back on our own home shores, Mariah continued to spread goodwill. She was asked to participate in Capitol Hill's First Annual

★ Bash with Mariah and Dr. Marlin Perkins. ★
COURTESY MRS. CAROL PERKINS

Celebrity Dog Parade in Washington, D.C., given for the benefit of the Children's Museum. Dozens of members of Congress and the diplomatic corps brought their dogs to meet Mariah, but, rather than "hobnob" with the politically connected pets and "Hounds of the Hill," Mariah chose to leave the spotlight and sit on the sidelines, giving all her attention to a quiet, wheelchair-bound gentleman. No amount of cajoling could make Mariah budge. Mariah had never disobeyed my commands. At first, I was taken aback, but, upon closer observation, I began to respect her refusal. The man had reached out to Mariah, and his companions

★ **62** STARPET

★ Mariah and I are greeted by President Reagan's White House press secretary James Brady. It was Mr. Brady's first public appearance after the Hinckley shooting. ★
COURTESY KITTY BROWN

had become quite excited. It turned out that Mariah had bonded protectively—indeed, as if a sentry, a sentinel—to the then–White House press secretary James "The Bear" Brady. It turned out that the Celebrity Dog Parade was Mr. Brady's first outing since he had been paralyzed in the assassination attempt on President Ronald Reagan, and something about Mariah touched him. And perhaps Mariah, in return, sensed this. In fact, Mr. Brady's family and doctors were so pleased with his response to Mariah that they decided on the spot that a dog would be a wonderful addition to his life.

Soon after Mariah's visit, Mr. Brady acquired a beautiful Labrador Retriever, and his renewed interest in animals led to his pioneering and continuing participation in horseback-riding therapy, which has proven so beneficial that, in the ensuing years, there has been an extraordinary proliferation of pet therapy and riding programs. I like to think Mr. Brady's meeting with Mariah was instrumental in reawakening his childhood love for animals. It certainly reconfirmed my lifelong belief in the importance of animals to the spirit and well-being of people—and it reaffirmed my resolve to continue this work with Mariah.

Mariah dedicated much of her later years to promoting pet-facilitated therapy and humane education. I found myself happily touring the country, with Mariah, in an educational capacity to raise public consciousness about the true and good nature of wolves, and their place in our lives and on this planet. We taught seminars on these subjects at the American Museum of Natural History, the City University of New York, and the University of Michigan, which hosted a kind of "stewardship school for endan-

★ Bash and Mariah at an endangered species seminar
at the Horace Mann School in New York. ★
COURTESY KITTY BROWN

gered species," where the field station and biological center became a lightning rod for important conferences among noted biologists and animal behaviorists from around the world.

One of Mariah's last projects was at New York's Mercy College, where, as an adjunct professor, I was developing a pet therapy curriculum for their veterinary technician and medical students. Impressed with her work, the Mercy College Animal Behavior Society invited Mariah and me to a seminar at the wooded retreat of one of legendary architect Frank Lloyd Wright's homes in Garrison, New York. The estate had a dramatic quarry and pristine waterfall. The students were to observe unconstrained wolf behavior, which was just fine with Mariah. Off-leash, Mariah was free to explore the brooks, fields, and forests in all her wolf glory. Not surprisingly, Mariah reveled in her "schoolwork" and soon found a favored place: a cathedral of trees.

Following Mariah along with the rest of the students, I was intrigued by how the architect had "built" a cathedral out of the forest. But not in the traditional way, mind you. No, this cathedral had been induced to take up residence in the wild forest by a clever, thoughtful, reverent way of planting, designing the trees so that, as they grew, their combined forms—in a kind of arboretum of architecture—became, with limbs uplifted in artful, prayerful choreography, the shape of a cathedral's steepled and vaulted ceiling, reaching to the heavens.

And it was then, in the waning sunset—in the gloaming—that I glimpsed Mariah. Captured in the dying spotlight of the last rays of sunset, her regal wolf stature standing strong and secure—and at home—in the cathedral of trees, I was struck anew by the blessing of her noble life, and the life's work she had wrought from me.

At that moment of stillness, Mariah, portraitlike, stood as beautiful and dramatic as Sir Edwin Landseer's famous "Monarch

★ Mariah, Bash, and actress Paula Trueman on the set of
The Joe Franklin Show. ★
COURTESY KITTY BROWN

of the Glen." Every artist has his muse, and, like Landseer's heralded stag, Mariah had been mine. Seeing her stand out amid each
individually distinct tree that had its own special place in insuring
the wholeness and integrity of the "architecture" of the cathedral
of trees reminded me of the importance of sometimes *not* "seeing
the forest for the trees." Because it often happens that in the shap-
ing and nurturing of one individual life—be it a tree or a wolf—
the success of that one single tree, or that one lone wolf, can do
more for the life of a forest or the salvation of a species than a de-
tached treatise observing the inanimate "whole" of the entity, but
forsaking the unique individuals that infuse enduring life to the
whole.

Mariah's singular presence in her very public life helped eradi-
cate the dark fear from myth and legend, which for centuries has
unjustly maligned wolves and targeted them for extinction. She

also taught *me* and, in teaching me, allowed me to continue her work, not only for her own species, but for her species's direct descendant, the dog.

In our fourteen years together, Mariah became the Rosetta Stone I needed to help me decode the *fourteen thousand* years of genetic evolution cloaked within the dog of today. She allowed me to better understand dogs, to put that knowledge to work to foster better understanding between people and their pets, and to strengthen the symbiotic human/animal bond.

When Mariah was nearly twelve years old, I felt it was time for her to slow down and retire from her sometimes hectic public life. As much as she loved people, and her work, and the public arena, I felt it was time for her to extinguish the torch of public service and rekindle her kinship with nature. I wanted her to retire to our country property in upstate New York, where, so often in her youth, she had run like the wind.

Indeed, during those idyllic years of *both* our youths, it seemed as if running together, learning together, living together, we had run even faster than the wind—outrunning mortal boundaries and transcending time and space and species.

Mariah lived for three more years, and died peacefully—her life complete—of natural causes, in her sleep, her soul at one with the wind.

If Orph and Mariah were the heart and soul of StarPets, then Muffin was the spirit of StarPets—and a very blithe spirit he was indeed!

Joyful, bouncy, and bright—and full of play—this life's-a-party pooch personified the StarPet credo: "Always keep the play in play-acting!"

In fact, it's been said that the dog is the "God of Frolic," and, if that is true, then Muffin reigned supreme as a delightfully delicious, down-to-earth doggy deity!

But this God of Frolic was also not above getting down and dirty! In fact, when I first met Muffin, he was no altar boy, let alone deity! For although Muffin had the innocent face of an angel, he was the furthest thing imaginable from a canine choir boy!

More devil than deity, more delinquent than dogstar, Muffin came to me in dire need of discipline.

He belonged to a wealthy Park Avenue socialite who had thrown up her hands in disgust and despair at the despicable behavior of her Tibetan Terrier. He was already five years old, but was stuck in the worst case of terrible twos I'd ever seen. And, although I'm always on the lookout for new talent whenever I meet a new client, I must confess that, when I met Muffin, I did, in fact, see star behavior—just not the kind of behavior any star's publicist would want the media to get hold of!

You see, Muffin wasn't an actor, but he definitely acted out!

Muffin wasn't a star, but he was a real bad actor! His abominable behavior was a real tour de force as he took on the role of all the young and popular bad-boy actors and rock stars for whom it seems to be the de rigueur, these days; to trash their posh hotel rooms! Indeed, the worse their behavior, it seems, the greater their popularity, as both frenzied female fans and panting-for-exclusives paparazzi pursue these hot young stars with equal relish!

So, although Muffin didn't have any motion picture or MTV credits to his name, he *still* had succeeded in making a name for himself—a very *bad* name!

In the grand tradition of bad-boy actors and rock stars, Muffin had totally trashed the socialite's antique-filled, designer-decorated, perfectly appointed Park Avenue pied-à-terre! Muffin had a great many issues and problems, and he took out his frustrations by shredding to pieces a hundred-thousand-dollar sofa and urinating all over a half-million-dollar rug! And, if that wasn't enough, in a kind of in-your-face rock star rebellion, Muffin also barked incessantly, day in and day out, and all night long.

But there are no bad dogs, only bad behavior—and I knew Muffin wasn't a lost cause. My client and I agreed that I should take Muffin back to my place for a week's worth of intensive, one-on-one training and behavior modification.

It was a daunting job, but I had faith in Muffin. I was certain that lurking somewhere deep within Muffin's heavy-metal-like, nerve-shattering ode to *bad,* behavior there was a golden, lyrical hymn to *good* behavior!

And I was right. During my week of personal tutoring, I found

★ Muffin and me. ★
COURTESY BRUCE PLOTKIN

Muffin to be a model student. In fact, I discovered that Muffin had an angelic personality to match his angelic appearance. Indeed, I felt Muffin had everything—and more—it took to be a StarPet. His cute, huggable, shaggy-dog good looks would make him a perfect model, and his engaging and ebullient personality would make him a dynamite StarDog!

But Muffin was not a professional StarPet, and he was not a shelter dog I could *rescue* and *make* a star. He was a personal pet, living a sheltered and pampered life on Park Avenue. My job had been to rescue him from his bad behavior, to save him for and return him to that coveted canine lifestyle he risked losing by his troubled behavior and his owner's misunderstanding and frustration. I had rescued many pets over the years who were refugees because of similar circumstances—troubled behavior on the pet's part, combined with misunderstanding and frustration on the owner's part, almost always add up to a homeless pet, abandoned on the streets or to a shelter. Muffin was special (indeed, all dogs are special!), and I was glad I could "right" the situation and return him to his rightful home. Still, I knew I would miss him.

So, imagine my surprise when, upon contacting Muffin's mistress to work out travel logistics for what should have been his happy homecoming, Muffin was turned away!

In Muffin's absence, his mistress had put her staff to work and gotten her household in order, and Muffin no longer fit in to that order. My client was certainly nice enough to me about her decision. "Would you please keep the dog?" she asked. But it was a decision, nonetheless, that she had already made.

Muffin had been rejected.

But that was the one and only time in his life that Muffin would ever be rejected! And how many actors can lay claim to that?

That was not Muffin's only claim to fame, of course, but it gives you an idea of the enduring career and track record he had in the entertainment industry.

Indeed, in an industry in which it is notoriously difficult to get a job or earn a living—where actors can barely stay afloat without drowning in despair of ever working—this cheerful, bubbly, and buoyant little dog somehow managed not only to stay afloat in the industry, but to continually rise to the top!

Muffin was in great demand in the industry. He took his commitments seriously, but he had fun on the job, and it showed. Not only did it show, it was contagious. And that lightheartedness, that sense of fun and play, that effervescence and incandescence, drew people to him and drew audiences to the screens that captured his persona. People wanted to be close to him, to be a part of him. And if they couldn't be close to him or be a part of him, they wanted the next best thing. They wanted something he was part of—and that is what made Muffin an advertising agency's dream. With his golden halo of curls and unerring sense of how to carry a scene or sell a product, Muffin was truly the "golden boy" of television commercials and print ads.

Muffin may have been booted from Park Avenue's "white glove" high society, but Madison Avenue's advertising elite embraced him with open arms. Muffin made (relatively) big bucks, at least for a little dog, who at one time faced homelessness, and in true StarPet tradition, he always donated a portion to benefit homeless dogs and cats and pets less fortunate than he.

Muffin worked tirelessly (although he would let you know that it is not "work" when you are doing something you love so much), and his extensive résumé ran the gamut from movies to TV shows to commercials and print ads, as this gregarious, giddy gamin of a play-actor dog romped his way through a variety of roles. His

★ Muffin on a photo shoot, singing. ★
COURTESY BRUCE PLOTKIN

charm and charisma sold Bayer children's aspirin, Hershey's syrup, Butcher's Blend dog food, Ken-L Ration burger, Cycle dog food, Ridgeway clocks, Montgomery Ward catalogues, and Sony Walkman.

Out of all Muffin's ads, however, I think the one that most captures this precocious pooch's perennial playful persona is the ad campaign he did for Friendly's ice cream, with the tagline, "Get friendly with someone you love."

Muffin was a friend, a pal, to all. He offered, whether onscreen or in person, his friendship and love, and it was real. It's been said that that indefinable something that, upon entering a room, puts one actor in the crushing embrace of adoring fans, while other actors (equally talented, if not more so) can enter a room and remain totally unnoticed goes beyond talent and personality and good looks and charisma. It is the ability of the star to make you feel

★ Bash preparing Muffin for the commercial. ★
COURTESY MERUET DIBRA

that, in a room full of people, you are the most important person there, you grab his heart and attention, you are all he sees or cares about. You feel he sees right into your very soul, and, in return, perhaps you have been blessed with, however fleetingly, a glimpse into the soul of a star.

This was Muffin's appeal.

One day I got a casting call from the producers of the soap opera *The Edge of Night* to supply a dog for a day's shoot—just a day player, really not much more than window dressing, ambience. Muffin was the dog for the job.

Muffin's winning audition for *The Edge of Night* had poised him on the edge of stardom. Muffin reported to the set for his first (originally slated to be his only) day of work and found a place in the script and in Hollywood history books: Muffin became the first dog ever to appear on a soap opera.

Upon meeting Muffin, with his soulful eyes and winsome ways, the producers realized immediately that this appealing dog had the unique ability that seems inherent only to that rare breed, the soap opera actor. And that ability is the tear-jerking talent of somehow transcending the screen and reaching out to the audiences at home, holding their hearts in the palms of their hands—or, in Muffin's case, the pad of his paw!

Huddling with the senior writers, the producers rewrote Muffin's "walk-on" so it would become a catalyst to move forward the "love story" of the two main stars, Allen Fawcett and the delightful ingenue Lori Loughlin.

Where the original script had simply called for Muffin to walk across the beach in a long shot, as background to the young lovers as they strolled hand-in-hand along the water's edge, the *revised* storyline called for Muffin to portray a frightened and abandoned little nondescript mutt of a dog, with no one to love him and nowhere to turn. Allen and Lori were to come across him by chance, and, deeply dismayed and anguished by his plight, try desperately to save him. The young lovers' rescue attempts would be futile, however, and Muffin's character was to succumb to exhaustion and exposure.

But the producers hadn't counted on the potent personality of this plucky little pooch!

As Muffin played his "deathbed" scene to the hilt, lying listlessly with his head between his paws (a trick which you will learn to train your StarPet to perform), his mournful eyes pleading into the camera for *someone, anyone,* to save him. Thousands of fans across the country wrote and called the network, pleading with the network to save the dog!

The producers—seeing that they had a full-fledged star on their hands, were more than happy to oblige the fans. But what were they to do? The scene where Muffin's character had supposedly died had already been aired! Indeed, that was the scene that had caused such an uproar! The poignant deathbed scene had left Lori Loughlin and audiences inconsolably bereft, as Allen tried helplessly, futilely, to comfort his weeping love. "You'll feel better in the morning," he assured the grieving girl, holding her tightly, as the show faded to black.

But Muffin's popularity demanded that his character live, so the ingenious writers, in what has become classic soap opera style, simply fetched the little dog back from the dead! So, in the following episode, *Edge of Night* fans watched Muffin—having made a miraculous recovery!—bound joyfully up and out from his deathbed and into the arms of an ecstatic Lori Loughlin!

Muffin successfully parlayed a one-shot, "day player" appearance on a major television drama into a three-year ongoing role, earning him a place of affection in the hearts of loyal fans everywhere, and respect and admiration in the eyes of his peers and the industry insiders with whom he worked.

The key to Muffin's stardom and success was more than his awesome acting talent. It was also his ability to assimilate smoothly into an ensemble acting cast and his ability, off-camera, to adjust with appropriate behavior to life on the set (which you will also learn about later).

With Muffin, life on the set of *The Edge of Night* was one big party. Full of mirth and merriment, Muffin was always the life of the party, and if there wasn't a party, well, when Muffin entered the

★ Lori Loughlin and Muffin. ★
COURTESY KITTY BROWN

room there soon would be a party. Muffin's first Christmas with
The Edge of Night was spent Christmas shopping with Lori Loughlin at the magical toy store FAO Schwarz. The outing began as a
publicity shoot for the show, but Lori enjoyed the holiday outing
so much, she made a day of it with Muffin, and the two of them
went shopping all over the city!

As is often the case with the casts and crews of many soap operas working so closely together day in and day out, year in and
year out, the cast and crew of *The Edge of Night* became something
of a family.

And, as with true family members, there was a special bond
among them, and Muffin was no exception. Personally, they all

genuinely liked one another and cared for one another, but professionally, as an actor—when it is necessary to deliver your lines and feed your costars their cues (and time is money, don't forget!)—sometimes you need some extra motivation, and, if you happen to be a dog actor, that often means a little liverwurst along with the lines! And sometimes, the only scenes shot from the day's filming that actually make it into the "can" are headed directly to the Hollywood "Bloopers" shows, or *America's Funniest Home Videos*!

This happened when Lori Loughlin and Allen Fawcett had their first meaningful love scene. Lori was lying on the sofa with her leg up (her character's leg had just been operated on) and her other leg was dangling, barefoot, down by the edge of the sofa,

★ Lori Loughlin and Muffin, costars in *The Edge of Night*, admire a stuffed dog in FAO Schwarz. ★
COURTESY PROCTER AND GAMBLE

where Muffin's character was to be lying quietly, faithfully, at Lori's feet. This was to set the stage for Allen, sitting attentively next to Lori, to proclaim his love for her.

Well, it had been a long day's shooting. Things just hadn't gone smoothly during the rehearsals for lighting, wardrobe, and blocking, and the cast and crew were forced to retake, reshoot, scene after scene. It was not the fault of the cast. Everyone, including Muffin, had met their marks and delivered their lines and action. All were beginning to get tired and frustrated, and Muffin was beginning to get bored. He knew he had done his job well, and he was frustrated that he had to keep retaking the scenes.

So, to alleviate some of Muffin's boredom, and to let him know that he was, in fact, a good dog, I decided to give Muffin some liverwurst—his favorite treat. But the liverwurst also served a more important purpose—to help Muffin keep to his mark. To keep Muffin occupied and focused on his mark during this sensitive integral scene, I smeared the liverwurst on the bottom of the couch, Muffin's mark.

Well, my time-honored StarPet dog-training ploy should have worked, but it didn't! In fact, it backfired—big time!

We started filming, and everything seemed okay, but it turned out that Muffin couldn't get to the liverwurst on the couch. Lori's foot—bare foot, I must remind you—was in the way of the liverwurst! Muffin could smell the liverwurst, but he couldn't get to it, and it was driving him crazy! So, what does he do? He starts nibbling and nudging at her foot to get to the liverwurst! The cameras continued rolling—time is money, don't forget!—and Lori did her best to carry on with the scene. The cameraman, seeing what was happening, tightened up the shot a bit so the camera wouldn't capture all that Muffin was doing. That allowed Lori to move her foot out of the way so Muffin could get to the liverwurst, but once he did, and he finished it, he wanted more! Muffin, in a search for the most elusive liverwurst ever, then began licking Lori's toes, nearly tickling her to death! Throughout all this, Allen, despite seeing the barely contained laughter in Lori's eyes, and feeling her body inwardly contort into tickle-induced spasms, somehow continued his monologue of heartfelt love!

Thanks to great ensemble work with both the cast and crew (and dog actor and dog trainer!)—along with the help of some well-placed lines, liverwurst, and laughter!—the scene was salvaged, money was saved.

Muffin forged new territory not only with his groundbreaking role on *The Edge of Night,* but also, in his spare and charitable time, by taking on the groundbreaking role of pet therapist in what was then a new and pioneering quest, pushing the boundaries in discovering just how much pets could help people in all capacities—including medicine.

Muffin was already adept at using his celebrity for charitable causes—something StarPets has always championed, and what has become known in the industry as cause marketing—and this newest, most innovative realm was no exception.

Fresh from leading a star-studded, star-spangled July Fourth parade in Edgartown, Massachusetts, to raise funds to build and operate an animal shelter for the famed and historic enclave of Martha's Vineyard (this event became a prototype for, years later, a launching of "Paws Across America"), Muffin was ready, with his usual unflagging, indefatigable spirit, to champion the cause of pet therapy.

Muffin had already pioneered what was then a new breakthrough in canine companionship, wherein an ordinary, beloved household pet can be trained to handle any emergency, efficiently and safely. Much as the American Humane Association would later train dogs for their Hearing Dog Program to aid the deaf, and the Delta Society would train service dogs to aid the disabled in their Pet Partners program, Muffin was trained to respond to the individual needs of an owner in crisis (usually elderly, ill, or disabled), to take life-saving charge in an emergency by calling for medical help or police protection by running to and tugging an alarm switch. Whenever the pet discovered that outside help was necessary, the pet would activate the alarm, which would call a predetermined party—hospital, police, fire department, neighbor—through a central command station. If a disabled or elderly person were alone with a medical emergency, the pet could mean the difference between life and death. And, by the same token, the forced entry of a locked door would send the dog running to trigger the alarm for the police. The premise here was that this kind of service dog is far superior to a traditional attack dog, who often cannot distinguish between a burglar and a friend stopping by for a surprise visit!

Muffin distinguished himself with this work and he was a natural, when—along with Mariah and a host of StarPets, medical professionals, animal behaviorists, and state legislators—we initiated pet therapy programs throughout New York City, New York State, and beyond.

I can honestly and unabashedly say I thoroughly expected Muffin to shine in this arena, to be a real star—and not because of his acting celebrity, but, rather, because of his soulful, supportive empathy and determined, engaging cheerfulness. So I was thoroughly dumbfounded to discover that not only Muffin's personality, but Muffin's celebrity had contributed to the healing and improved health benefits. And that contribution was powerful.

Every "shut-in" or home-bound person Muffin visited, every patient, every nursing home resident Muffin attended to, *all* of them greeted Muffin—through the power of his talent and TV—as a longtime personal friend, returning home for a family reunion! And that recognition factor—that feeling of being visited by a special friend—worked beneficially on *both* ends of the pet therapy visits. For as much as the visits of pet therapists are undoubtedly *positive* (they lower blood pressure, for example, and foster communication skills and alleviate loneliness), oftentimes, when the visits come to an end and the pet leaves, the letdown, the disappointment, can undo some of the good work.

But, with Muffin, patients welcomed him warmly as an old friend who had visited them often (via the television), so when it was time for Muffin to leave, the patients knew they would see him real soon—the very next day on TV! The patients had *more* of Muffin than most private pet therapists could give, and by virtue of following his exploits on *The Edge of Night,* patients' communication skills and interactions with one another were also greatly enhanced.

Muffin always wanted to make everyone happy and turn every visit into a party, so he often brought along other old friends to visit the nursing home residents—cast members from all the patients' favorite soap operas.

Muffin took the StarPet credo—"The play's the thing!"—to heart, and made sure that not only would *he* have fun, but *you* would, *too!*

This attitude was illustrated nicely during one of Muffin's humane education stints. Muffin had cajoled a shy, alienated little girl who was fearful of dogs into joining her classmates in the dog-initiated day of fun; as the day drew to a close, the once-scared young student gave Muffin a heartfelt hug, and announced that Muffin's name was spelled Muf*fun*—because he was so much *fun!* Taking her Muffin-inspired word game one step further, I assured

★ Muffin demonstrates how to hold an object in his mouth. ★
COURTESY BRUCE PLOTKIN

her that she was right, and that was because good times are fun only if they are *shared;* and there is no "I" in fun, just "U"! The ultimate "God of Frolic," Muffin was a real "missionary of fun"— collecting canine converts wherever he went! At the end of that special, heartwarming day, I gave Muffin a special, heartfelt "Thank-U!"

Muffin was a cross between two inimitable *human* show business legends: Will Rogers, approachable and friendly, like Muffin; and Mickey Rooney, like Muffin, small in stature but strong in spirit, with his boyish charm and enthusiasm exhorting his friends, "Hey gang, let's put on a show."

Muffin was always ready to put on a show—or to show someone a good time!

With Muffin, it didn't matter if it was a professional job or a personal outing. He turned every professional venture into a personal adventure. To Muffin, success wasn't based on what his fame and fortune brought him, but, rather, on what he brought to his family and friends. An approving nod from his family, rather than a critic's accolade, was his fame; his friends were his fortune.

Muffin never gave of himself half-heartedly. With Muffin, you always got more than you asked for. If you asked him to give you his paw, he'd sit up with barely contained exuberance and give you both paws. If you asked him to lie down, he'd lie down, roll over, and leap joyfully into your arms! He was a quick study both of human nature and of the medium that reflects and portrays it, television, and that is what made him so successful in both. In the studio, he would often pick up his cue and run with it—whether it was in the script or not!—and, more often than not, had the bewildered directors happily rewriting the script to follow Muffin's right-on-target successful show business instincts! This same unerring instinct carried Muffin through his personal life and vastly improved the lives of those he touched in his charitable work, especially in the realm of pet therapy. He always seemed to know, unscripted, unaided, and unasked, just how much to give and when to hold back. Muffin never stopped giving.

Even at the age of fifteen, Muffin never entered his "twilight years." He was eternally exuberant, optimistic, and young, and he refused to let any of us—his friends, family, and audiences—let go of our childhood dreams. And, if we did, Muffin would fetch each and every one of them and—digging deep within our hearts— plant an *entire* "field of dreams."

Muffin lived life to the fullest—and he wanted us to, as well.

I have no doubt that, as the sun set on that last day of summer, and this God of Frolic was called home to meet *his* God—and all the dogs who had gone on before him—he bowed down with his most fetching, most fervent *play*-bow, and said: "Hey gang! Let's put on a show!"

So three very distinct creatures—Orph, Mariah, and Muffin—became the cornerstone of StarPets. Through their public performances and private philanthropy, they imbued our lives, and the lives of those they touched, with their heart, their soul, and their spirit.

We may train dogs, but dogs *teach* us. Dogs may come to us when called, but they are actually responding to a higher calling. Dogs may shadow us when we command them to heel, but we, in fact, live in the shadow of their upstanding good character.

So, when I think about the early "glory" days of StarPets, the glory is not mine. Mine is simply the reflected glory of that which is, truly, Orph's, Mariah's, and Muffin's—and all the StarPets' who followed them.

In the words of poet William Butler Yeats, "I think where Man's glory begins and ends; And say my glory was I had such friends."

Our roster of celebrity pets continued to grow, working happily and steadily in front of the cameras in all areas of the entertainment industry—stage, print ads, film, television, and commercials—while, "backstage," our roster of the *private* pets of celebrities *also* grew, and included the pets of such notables as Henry Kissinger, Lee Radziwill, Andy Warhol, William Paley, Calvin Klein, Carly Simon, Mia Farrow, Alec Baldwin, and Kim Basinger.

Still, young trainers like me—wherever our work might take

us—continually learned from Rudd Weatherwax's handling of Lassie, both onscreen and offscreen, onstage and backstage. When Weatherwax traveled to New York with Lassie, for example, he made certain to bring along one or two of Lassie's "playmates" to give his dog star a sense of home and family during their travels. Indeed, I almost felt like "one of the litter" when I learned that Lassie's *favorite* pal was the diminutive (but big in talent!) dog star (Yorkshire Terrier) of the hit TV series *The Lou Grant Show*—which also starred Orph's friend and costar, Ed Asner!

While Weatherwax and Lassie were in town promoting their latest film, Lassie's "mom"—the delightful June Lockhart—and I were both working to promote the cause of pet-facilitated therapy into the mainstream media. June, combining her celebrity and lifelong love of animals, was starring in the daytime drama

★ Ed Asner with Orph. They appeared in a public information spot on television. ★
COURTESY RALSTON PURINA COMPANY AND ED ASNER

General Hospital, while, simultaneously, taking on the post of celebrity spokesperson of the American Humane Association's fledgling-but-soon-to-soar groundbreaking work, the Hearing Dog Program. This phenomenal program trains dogs to aid the hearing-impaired much as traditional guide dogs aid the blind.

Across town, Muffin was appearing on *The Edge of Night,* as well as working with another soap opera actress, Paula Trueman, from *One Life to Live,* promoting pet-facilitated therapy in nursing homes. With a strong, single pet therapy message, our loosely knit band of brothers, June, Paula, and Muffin, joined forces with industry insiders, most notably the editors at *Soap Opera Digest* (the Bible of daytime television) and the producers of *The Guiding Light,* to promote the importance of pets in our lives and further the knowledge and appreciation of pet therapy dogs, "hearing ear" dogs, guide dogs, and service dogs.

Lassie's and my paths crossed twice more in New York. Before Animal Planet emerged, Fox-TV's FX channel produced a marvelous, mixed-bag, mixed-mutt of a pet show called *The Pet Department.* It was very different from any other pet show— informative, entertaining, campy, and edgy—but what I enjoyed most was that it was *live.* When you combine live television with animals, it's a proven *hilarity*! It was fun to be involved with the program at its inception, especially when it hosted a rare appearance by Lassie.

A few years later, when I was involved in the production of my second Super Dog Variety Show to benefit the Delta Society and its Pet Partners program, we were privileged to host a guest-starring appearance by the one and only legendary Lassie! Sadly, Rudd Weatherwax, the inimitable Old Master, had passed on, but the shining Weatherwax torch had been passed on to Rudd's son,

Robert, and, in his capable and caring hands, the torch has not dimmed.

As *"dog trainer to the stars,"* my job entails not only making certain that pets understand and follow their roles in their family "drama," but also insuring that, if there is more than one pet in the family, the "costars" get along! And sometimes, I am asked to "cast" the perfect pet to complete a family ensemble.

This happened when a lovely, talented young raven-haired beauty named Ana-Alicia was leaving her role on the ABC hit soap opera *Ryan's Hope* to go to Los Angeles to star with Jane Wyman and Lorenzo Lamas in a new prime-time soap opera, *Falcon Crest.* She had a marvelous little Poodle/Pekingese mix named Chica, but Ana-Alicia had always dreamed of, always longed for, German Shepherds. Until her success on *Falcon Crest,* she had to be content with a dog that would fit in the small New York City apartment of a struggling young actress—enter the eight-pound Chica! Ana-Alicia loved and cherished Chica, of course, and she would always be top dog, but now Ana-Alicia wanted to incorporate the dogs of her dreams into her life, as well.

And that was my job.

Ana-Alicia wanted a pair of German Shepherds that would have a single-minded trust, instinct, and devotion in serving a myriad of Ana-Alicia's complicated needs! First and foremost, the dogs must have an understanding that little eight-pound Chica, who was already elderly, must be treated gently and respectfully— ever and always the top dog! Second, the dogs must also serve, not just as beloved and pampered house pets (which, with Ana-Alicia as their mistress, they certainly would be!), but also as guards of her sprawling estate. And, finally, from guards to *guardians,* these dogs would have to gently welcome and protect, and lovingly treat as playmates, the children Ana-Alicia hoped to have in the not-too-distant future!

A tough bill to fill, to be sure, but I was just as sure that I had not bitten off more than I could chew. And I knew that was true, not because of an ego-driven faith in my own abilities, but rather, because of my faith in the breed and the knowledge of their abilities, not mine! The first step, of course, before any training could possibly occur, was to find the right dogs for Ana-Alicia. I knew they would have to be the best of the best, the crème de la crème. If I was to mold, to sculpt the instincts and tendencies of these dogs into behavior finely and intuitively attuned to the parameters of Ana-Alicia's life, only the right dogs, a very special class of dogs, would qualify as "students"—and they had to be students that would graduate with honors!

I was looking for outstanding character and temperament, high intelligence, arresting beauty, and stand-out conformation. I found all this—and more!—from a top breeder whose dogs were of champion lines, imported from Germany.

With Ana-Alicia's hectic shooting schedule, it was agreed that the young pups—as adorable and irresistible as they were—should stay with me for their first, tentative "baby steps" of nursery and kindergarten schooling (housebreaking, basic on-leash training, and so on). I wanted this accomplished quickly, so the pups would still be young enough to bond totally with Ana-Alicia, as well as to "look up to" the tiny Chica as their Alpha leader!

When the time came for the young pups to make their Hollywood debut, my sister Meruet accompanied them across country to help them settle in. Meruet had been integral to the pups' training on two counts. First, Meruet has a love for and way with the breed that rivals that of any trainer, and, second, as Meruet was a female, as well as (serendipitously!) resembling Ana-Alicia, with a slim build and long dark hair, I felt that the pups might more easily transfer obedience and allegiance from Meruet to Ana-Alicia, thus facilitating the all-important assimilation.

Things went smoothly on all counts, and Ana-Alicia's childhood dreams were finally fulfilled. The dogs were named Helden and Ersenen, meaning much loved and longed for—and that, they truly were.

Not long after Helden and Ersenen went out west, I followed for some all-important follow-up for Ana-Alicia and her dogs. Things went swimmingly—literally! Ana-Alicia never let fame go to her head, but she did let it go to her heart, and that meant doing anything she could to make animals happy—from the sublime to the aquatic! You see, Ana-Alicia might have turned up her nose at the notion of spoiling herself (she thoroughly disliked that whole notion of "movie stars, swimming pools!" kind of life)—but *animals* were another matter altogether!

So, just as she had opened her property to homeless cats and personally looked after them with medical care and housing, so she decided that on hot Hollywood summer days, the dogs should be able to take a refreshing swim! Of course, not only was there a regulation-size swimming pool for the dogs' enjoyment, but they also had to have something to swim *to.* So, for her dogs (not for herself!), Ana-Alicia went Hollywood! What she wouldn't do for herself, she did for her dogs! She built two charming little grass-covered islands in the middle of the pool, and (thinking of everything) included a footbridge for the little Chica! The engaging little dog didn't care for *swimming,* but loved to follow the Shepherds all around—barking and bossing them, and telling them where they could and could not go, and where they could and could not swim! Like a little drill sergeant, the littlest Alpha leader drummed her very big sense of self into the hearts and minds of those magnificent, majestic (and sometimes mollified, thanks to Chica!) German Shepherds! Mine had been a job well done!

Helden and Ersenen had not only assimilated beautifully, they had flourished and enhanced the life of the one—and her growing family—who had so longed, for so long, to love them. They adored and respected Chica, and Chica adored being adored and respected! They loved and were reverential to Ana-Alicia's mother when she came to live with the young star, and they deferred their Alpha roles to Ana-Alicia's new husband when she fell in love and married. And, finally, when Ana-Alicia had children, Chica, all-important and full of herself at the impressive old age of twenty-

★ StarPet dog Goldie appears in an "advertisement" for Geoffrey Bone. ★
Courtesy Ilene Rosenthal Hochberg/Dogue

one, became a grande dame of a nanny—and Helden and Ersenen became precocious playmates and dutiful guardians.

Chica, Helden, and Ersenen all lived long, full, and rich lives, and they enriched the lives of Ana-Alicia and her family.

On subsequent trips to Los Angeles, I was delighted with the work Ana-Alicia continued to do, behind the scenes as well as in front of the cameras, for animal welfare. As celebrity spokeswoman for the American Humane Association, she worked hard to promote animal welfare, and teamed with Robert Urich (star of hit TV series *Vegas* and *Spencer for Hire*) in a series of high-profile campaigns to promote healthy diets for dogs. We came full circle when she costarred with Angela Lansbury, with whom one of my dogs, years earlier, had shared the screen! And, on one of my last visits out there, for a *Tonight Show* appearance with Jay Leno, we also squeezed in the Patsy Awards, the American Humane Association's animal Oscars (Performing Animal Top Star of the Year), where Ana-Alicia toiled as a presenter, along with hosts Bob Barker and Betty White.

Not long after I returned from Los Angeles, I had the opportunity to revisit the land of my formative years, Italy, where once I had pretended to direct movie dogs with my cast of stray street dogs. I returned to direct a real dog in a real picture when an Italian movie producer and director, Gianni Bozzacchi, asked me to direct his dog in a film. Bozzacchi maintained a lovely villa in Rome and a commanding penthouse in Manhattan. I first met Bozzacchi when he summoned me to train his high-spirited Husky, "Mac" (short for Macaroni). Perhaps because he was a director himself, Bozzacchi took a keen interest in Mac's training, but I had no idea that the man who had made so many Italian human stars would want to make a *dog*—indeed, *his* dog!—a star!

The picture was to star Jerry Orbach (the late star of NBC's hit series *Law & Order*), Scott Baio, Christopher Plummer, enduring Italian film star Virna Lisi—and, with a blind eye to "nepotism," the *producer's* dog, Mac! The Husky isn't my dog of choice for movie work—the breed can be unpredictable and inattentive, and not always the best at taking direction, preferring to keep to their own schedule, not the production schedule! But Mac did well, actually, and was quite the actor! Indeed, his handsome, Husky good looks really lit up the screen! I was grateful for Mac's newly discovered latent talent and his onscreen success. I don't know how I would have been able to "break it" to a powerful Italian movie producer (and, at this point, *friend*) that his dog couldn't act!

★ "Beauty and the Beast." Supermodel/actor Carol Alt and Pinca. ★
COURTESY STEVE HILL

My next Italian adventure was a film called *Chantilly Express,* and it starred the stunning supermodel-turned-actress Carol Alt. In person, Carol was as down-to-earth as her onscreen persona was effervescent and ethereal. Perhaps because this beautiful and talented actress was *also* the daughter of a New York City fireman and wife of a professional hockey player, Carol threw herself into her role with as much grit and guts as beauty and talent—and that was good, because her costar was a fearsome-looking Doberman Pinscher!

My Doberman Pinscher was actually a very *sweet* dog, but she was *also* a very accomplished *actress.*

Pinca, as she was known both personally and professionally, had cut her teeth in the training ground of the venerable daytime dramas, as many actors do, to hone their craft and make the big-league leap to film. And Pinca was no different in following that time-honored thespian tradition. She had a season's contract on ABC's *One Life to Live,* starring opposite Michael Storm, and she enjoyed her work immensely. Because of the nature of her soap opera role, the script often called for her to snarl and growl. Pinca was very good at that—she had very capably strutted her savage stuff in a Black Sabbath MTV video!—and she enjoyed doing her work and accomplishing a job well done.

But what I suspect she enjoyed even more, as she was quite the comedienne, was sneaking up on her fellow actors offscreen and displaying—sans script—her pearly whites! I swear she did it just to see their split-second, frozen-in-fear reaction—before breathing a sigh of relief in the knowledge that she was actually teasing them!

I kid you not, and I am not being anthropomorphic.

Pinca *did* have a sense of humor, as well as a sense of human nature, and she was very smart. During the run of her contract for *One Life to Live,* she became quite close to the director and fellow actors, and they all had a friendly, easygoing working relationship. In fact, Pinca always produced her trademark "pearly whites" gnarl at the snap of a finger, right on cue. And she was so good that she often frightened the actors until they realized she really *was* a professional actor, and, to her, it was just a game!

Pinca, like all my StarPets, understood that she was just "play-acting." And she did her best, offscreen as well as onscreen, to keep the *play* in play-acting! Pinca also realized the effect she had on the actors, as well as the effect the *director* had on the actors. Pinca was so good at "snarling" on cue that the director often teased his actors that he wished *they* could act as well on cue—it would certainly save time and money! It was a continuing joke, of course,

★ Bash's Doberman Pinscher, Pinka, with actress Kirsten Frantzich and actor Michael Storm in scenes from ABC's soap opera *One Life to Live,* 1986. ★
Courtesy ABC, Inc.

but it did put a little pressure on the human actors to keep their performance on a par with a Pinscher—and Pinca delighted in being at the center of the on-set fun!

So Pinca joined Carol Alt and the cast of *Chantilly Express,* having "cut her teeth" on *One Life to Live* and ready to "sink her teeth" into her motion picture debut!

Carol could more than hold her own on screen with Pinca's fear-inducing portrayal of a bloodthirsty hound, but Carol wasn't prepared—nor was the rest of the cast—for Pinca's sense of humor, of fun and games.

Pinca was, as most actors are (and dogs are, as well, come to think of it!), a student of human nature. And, working in the Italian film, it had not gone unnoticed to Pinca that the flirtatious pinching of people's behinds elicited hilarious reactions! Soon, Pinca had taken to innocently walking up behind people and mischievously goosing her chosen victims' bottoms! The expressions on the people's faces (especially that of the beautiful Carol Alt, who was a big star in Italy, and used to the enthusiastic attention of her Italian male fans!) were hilarious—and doubly so when they discovered that the notorious pincher was a Pinscher!

Another movie in which Pinca's trademark pearly whites twinkled brightly with Hollywood stars was *The Exterminator,* with the beautiful British actress Samantha Eggar and Robert Ginty (*The Paper Chase*). In this movie, however, some of her star appeal was actually shared in triplicate with Strider and Sweepea, who were two of Pinca's canine colleagues in my stable of StarPets. Much like the Olsen twins, Mary-Kate and Ashley, in their fabled role-sharing on the hit TV series *Full House,* Pinca shared her acting duties with Strider, a stunning, striking stunt dog of a Doberman, and Sweepea, a dear and delicate darling of a Dobie.

Because the requirements of the role were complex and far-ranging, I used three Dobies to portray the one Pinscher, using the techniques I had acquired from Rudd Weatherwax's approach to Lassie's acting, wherein he had several Lassies for different scenes that required different aspects of character portrayal. One Lassie was accomplished with a certain set of stunts, another Lassie might execute an effortless repertoire of shape-training, while another excelled in the ever-important emotional closeups.

Pinca, Strider, and Sweepea were a topnotch trio in this approach. Pinca, ever the star, brought a trademark intensity to the picture, with her star-turn show of teeth and closeup, and finely nuanced stunt work. Strider, with rippling muscles and a powerful persona, was the full-blown stuntman of the group. He would leap into the air to grab the hidden, padded sleeve of a human stunt-man to portray a deadly attack dog, or jump from a moving car to capture a criminal. His strength and stamina conveyed an on-the-edge-of-your-seat, hold-your-breath excitement in his stunning long shots of stunt work.

And, last but not least, Sweepea's specialty was simply what her apt name implied: being her sweet, endearing, sometimes silly self—but her secret was, in tandem with a good cameraman and a succinct sound man, to portray the most vicious dog you would ever, never, want to meet! You see, Sweepea was very sweet, loved everybody, and loved to kiss her costars! (You know, they say that

★ StarPet dog Topper appears in an "advertisement" for Georgio Arfmani. ★
COURTESY ILENE ROSENTHAL HOCHBERG/*VANITY FUR*

the insulated, imaginary world of making a movie on a set or on location tends to foster romance between the film's stars!) Seriously, though, Sweepea was a real love, and we used that—along with a smear of liverwurst!—to turn movie know-how into movie magic. You see, with a little dab of liverwurst smeared on an actor's neck to add intensity to Sweepea's loving, licking kisses, combined with an overhead, top view from the camera, and added background sound effects of snarling, biting, and fighting, the cast and crew could create a nail-biting, nerve-wracking killer scene!

Along with all the television and movies, I still kept my fingers in the traditional world of the show dog, striving to meet the rigorous standards of conformation and obedience in the ring. Unlike the entertainment industry, where you can improvise if a well-rehearsed scene goes awry, or a groundswell of fan support can keep your career afloat, in the show ring, it's all between you and the judges, and the strictest of standards must be adhered to.

The dog who not only kept my fingers in the business, but holding blue ribbons as well, was a wonderful, incomparable German Shorthaired Pointer, Eli, who was bred to be a champion and followed that destiny admirably. In his genetics, his makeup, his personality, in all respects, Eli was a champion. He had a remarkable and inimitable way of moving, holding a position. His stance, bearing, and gait all commanded attention—and respect. And he won the respect of Westminster judges when they deemed him a champion at the heralded Westminster Dog Show in New York City's venerable venue, the historic Madison Square Garden.

Eli was not content to rest on the laurels of his Westminster win, however, so we moved on to the field trials, where he exhibited, in exquisite canine choreography, his textbook-perfect ability to point at birds. Eli was a champion in the field, and, as bird dogs

Eli becoming a show champion at Westminster Kennel Club, Madison Square Garden. ★
COURTESY L. EDMONDS

honor the point of the lead dog, so the judges, in awarding Eli his championship, honored his award-winning point!

Eli continued his quest for the hat trick by throwing his hat, this time, into the ring of obedience trials! Once again, Eli excelled, this time at demonstrating intelligence with well-trained obedience and performance skills. Eli was a true performer, and he became the StarPet of his time—a show dog with beauty, personality, and intelligence. He was a natural showman, and when he married his natural, inborn talent with theatrical technique, he launched a satisfying career in print ads, commercials, and movies.

But you don't have to be purebred with centuries of good breeding or have a pedigree with a genealogy of ancestral champions to be a

StarPet. In fact, many of the brightest stars in my stable of StarPets have been very charismatic canines with very contemporary genealogy! But where they may be short on pedigree, they can be infinitely tall in talent. Their known relatives at a family reunion couldn't fill a room, but their stellar résumés could fill a rehearsal hall, and their credits could crowd a critic's accolade-filled review!

CHAPTER THREE

StarPet Stars

*O*ne of the best examples of the StarPet is Mike the Dog.

Mike was a one of a kind (in both body and soul!) shaggy dog, who had been abandoned—unloved and unwanted—on the mean streets of New York City. But, thanks to a remarkable woman who became a friend and client of mine (New York film and television actress Judy Jensen), Mike went from being unloved and unwanted to being much loved and much wanted—not only by Miss Jensen, but by casting directors and film producers everywhere! Mike was a classic rags-to-riches, true Cinderella story (Cinder*fella*?)—and Judy was his Fairy *Dog* Mother!

But there was nothing magical—except the magic of love in Judy's heart (and that, sometimes, is the greatest magic of all!)—that transformed this dog from rags to riches, from heartbreak to Hollywood. It was very real love, tough love, in fact—and the hard work of doggie discipline and totally committed training to back it up!

You see, Mike had been living on the streets during his formative years—the first three or four years of his life—and he was a very damaged dog, both physically and emotionally, when

Judy's tender heart went out to him. Undaunted, Judy took him in and nurtured him back to health. And, once Mike regained his health, he also regained his good looks! Bathing and grooming revealed, to her surprise, a cute, scruffy black and white dog—very appealing, with the kind of huggable looks the camera loves!

But, despite his looks and Judy's love, Mike was far from camera-ready. In fact, his behavior was so bad that he was deemed untrainable period (let alone star material!) by the countless animal behaviorists and trainers Judy hired. Still, Judy would not give up on Mike. An actress all her life (as a child actress, she logged several seasons with TV's legendary *Patty Duke Show*), Judy knew that, in the business, success rarely comes on the first few auditions, and so it was in real life. Innate talent can only take you so far. In anything in life, discipline, hard work, and training is a must.

So, late one night, exhausted, undaunted, and unaccompanied (no one wanted anything to do with Mike!), Judy rushed to the nearest bookstore (do bookstores have an emergency entrance?—she certainly needed one!).

Bookstores may not have emergency entrances, but New York City is (like kindhearted people with problem dogs!) the city that never sleeps, and Judy found a bookstore open for business. Luckily for both of us (and I say that because I feel very blessed to have been an integral part of Mike's and Judy's lives!), Judy chose several of my how-to training books, and the rest, as they say, is history. From rescue to rehab; from a raring-to-go undisciplined mutt to a refined and dedicated StarPet—the luminous love story of Mike and Judy is a beguiling biography of an astounding StarPet journey.

With only my book in one hand—and Mike's leash in the other—Judy made astounding advances in training Mike. And the road was an arduous, uphill path, with many obstacles. Don't forget, experts had advised Judy to have Mike put down.

But not only would Judy not put Mike down, but, rising to Judy's love and encouragement, Mike himself—somehow infused with Judy's undying belief in him—refused to be kept down, and, indeed, rose up to the heights she believed he could attain, and went on to light up the screen and bring life to many film and television roles.

You see, once Judy realized the success that a layman could achieve from working with my books (and, as an actress, understanding that working one on one with a specific director or acting coach can mean the difference between success and failure), Judy decided to forget the books and go right to the author, the director, the professional, and see just what Mike was capable of and just how far his career could go.

Judy contacted me, and we jumped right into one-on-one personal training for Mike.

Mike and Judy were a joy to work with, and he had a stellar career that spanned more than a decade. Most of you would recognize him from his commercial stints for Burger King, Wrigley's chewing gum, and Cheerios, but he also appeared on MTV, *Late Night with Conan O'Brien,* and NBC's critically acclaimed *Law & Order.* And I, myself, personally, enjoyed hiring Mike for work on my projects.

A few years back, Mike and I turned the prolific shopping network QVC-TV into DOG-TV, when we hit the airwaves in a frenetic, freewheeling, minute-by-minute, movie-mutt marathon, selling my training video, which, by the way, Mike just happened to star in! It was certainly a role he was born to, having been trans-formed—by Judy's tenderness and my techniques—from the Master of Mischief to the Master of the Mariah Method. Talk about truth in advertising!

Also on QVC-TV was my old friend and client Joan Rivers. Miss Rivers was hawking her incredibly successful line of signature jewelry, as well as (of course!) bragging about her beloved York-shire Terriers, Spike and Veronica, who—like Mike and me—shared the stage with their mistress. I hadn't seen Joan since we appeared together on ABC-TV's *The View*, where I conducted Veronica's first puppy training session. Young Veronica had been a quick study, and I was pleased to see that both she and Spike be-haved themselves beautifully on QVC-TV.

Our time at QVC-TV was a great deal of fun. Mike loved everyone—both the on-camera hosts and hostesses and the behind-the-scenes crew—and everyone loved him. In fact, our performances there were like one big playtime—proving that it's not just the animal actors who must keep the play in play-acting!

But Mike's *greatest* role, for which he will live on—and that en-sured that, thanks to Mike, millions of other dogs will live on!—was as spokesdog for the national rescue group, the North Shore Animal League.

Mike was hired to portray a homeless shelter dog, looking for someone to love, and to love him in return. The ad was designed to show what wonderful pets homeless and abandoned dogs (what-ever their breed or nonexistent breed) can become, and Mike did his job beautifully.

Indeed, I am certain that Mike, like so many pets who have suf-fered from abandonment and homelessness, never forgot the expe-rience of his near-death early beginnings, his body emaciated, his spirit both beaten and defiant. I never cease to be touched and

★ Bash and Mike with Joan Rivers and her two dogs
Spike and Veronica at a QVC show. ★
COURTESY KITTY BROWN

amazed by the aptitude for gratitude these stray dogs seem to have within their souls.

And Mike was no different. Mike was forever grateful to the angel that was Judy, who saw beyond his outward appearance and actions and focused instead—underneath all the grime, and behind the bad behavior—on his inner goodness and his inner light, and, with tenderness and tenacity, took it upon herself to be his guardian angel and guided him to the light of love, the light of knowledge (how to behave!), and the spotlight of a fulfilling career in show business!

With Judy, Mike grew in both stature and spirit. With the selfless dedication of his "adopted" person, Mike blossomed from being virtually unable to help himself to helping the thousands of other helpless creatures who daily find themselves in the same desperate straits from which Mike was saved.

Mike's poignant portrayal in the North Shore Animal League's commercials and print ads of this "Every Dog" character was representative of every homeless dog everywhere, and contributed mightily to the nationwide adoption of these wonderful creatures. It can truly be said that Mike gave life to the role of a lifetime, which, in turn, gave life to others less fortunate than himself.

Mike loved his life and appreciated his good fortune. He was blessed with good and bountiful times, and he made the most of those times, seeming to understand the old adage that "time waits for no man"—or dog!

Having made my profession by straddling the worlds of animal behavior and show business, I am continually struck by how similar the two can be—and how it often happens that what an actor aspires to is what a dog has already accomplished. Actors who worship the Method school of acting, for example, consider it sacred to foster the ability to live in the moment—while living in the moment seems a talent most dogs (StarPets or otherwise!) are born with, and wise old dogs understand that this is not only the key to *thespian* theology but the secret to life itself.

In his lifetime, Mike became both a good dog and a good actor. He truly lived in the moment, and the moments were many and memorable. And when those moments marched inexorably on, until all that was left was the memory of the magic that was Mike the Dog, his heart may have stopped beating, but it never gave out. It continued to give life to the homeless dogs everywhere on whose behalf he spoke—and, by way of his beloved mistress, Judy Jensen, gave life to a shaggy dog who was destined to step into his pawprints and follow his lead.

You see, as Mike's age finally began to catch up with his

adorable antics, Judy and I felt it was time to think of retirement—but that idea never caught on with critics and casting directors. Mike was much loved, and his work was in great demand.

Around this time, Judy was alerted to an abandoned, stray little dog who needed a home. Well, the odds were pretty good that big-hearted Judy would take in the little dog—but what were the odds that this stray little mixed-breed mutt would look *exactly* like the inimitable Mike?

Whatever the odds (and I'm sure they were astronomical!), Lucy, as she came to be called, looked exactly like Mike on the outside, but on the inside, as Judy tearfully told me on the phone one evening after a particularly exasperating day of putting up with exceedingly bad behavior, Lucy was absolutely nothing like Mike! As so often happens with clients when they acquire (through whatever means) a second pet, it is human nature to expect the younger or newer pet to automatically acquire the good behavior and easy relationship that they had forgotten had taken time for their first pet to mature and grow and settle in. And, if you've been blessed with an incredible dog like Mike, it is even harder to remember, and to begin again, and to, at least temporarily, "lower the bar" or lessen the standard by which you judge and treat your new pet.

Love should be the only "litmus" test, and with that, all lessons will be learned—as wise old dogs like Mike know—all in good time!

And so it was with Judy and Mike and Lucy. Mike loved his life too much to go into retirement full-time; but Judy lessened his professional commitments, and (as all celebrities should with young ones who look up to them!) Mike became a pawsitive role model for Lucy, saving her from a life of behavioral delinquency, and saving Judy's sanity, as well!

Soon, with Mike's guidance, not only was Lucy a well-behaved dog at home, but she began to fill Mike's golden pawprints professionally, as well.

Although Mike did not live to see the day, I am quite certain he celebrated—from a choice seat in a celestial audience somewhere—Lucy's newfound celebrity as she appeared on the HBO hit series *Sex and the City*! And, in a casting coup that teamed Judy and Lucy professionally, as well as personally (and, to this day, I can't help but think that Mike "directed" this destiny with a kind of divine doggie intervention!), Judy also appeared in the same episode! Lucy was finally on her way, and Judy—although never forgetting Mike—looked happily forward to a shared future with her newest canine costar!

But not all the stars in StarPets are dogs. Just as in my boyhood, where my cats lived and worked in the land baron's barn, performing their skillful ratting and other tricks under my admittedly clumsy, childish "tutelage," so today (and with far more sophisticated training skills!) I am blessed to work with a captivating coterie of charismatic cats, who have captured a special place within my stable of StarPets.

Those of you who have read my book *Cat Speak* are by now "old friends," and you know that, although the bulk of my books have focused on dogs, cats have always been very important costars in StarPets and in my life.

Indeed, just as the proverbial cat seems to get into the proverbial everything (around the house, in the garden, up a tree), so my cats also seemed to get into everything—including up a tree. But, in my case, I didn't need to call the proverbial fireman to rescue my cats—I needed to call a publicist to manage my cats!

You see, my cats, far from being chased up a tree by dogs, instead followed close on the tails of my *DogStars*—clawing their way (as they say in showbiz lingo) into every branch of the entertainment industry, from print ads and commercials to theater, television, and movies!

In fact, the old saying, which I have never cared for, "Curiosity killed the cat," should be changed to "Curiosity *made* the cat!"—because a cat who is curious is a cat who is smart, keenly aware of his surroundings, and not afraid to explore and try something new, or to have an adventure. And these are all characteristics of a cat who has what it takes to make it in show business and to embark on the StarPet adventure!

One special cat who made her species' traditional trait, curiosity, work for her in this decidedly *un*traditional business was Bebe. Bebe was a beautiful black cat, sleek and savvy, poised and full of panache. She had an air of mystery about her—as if she could see things unseen or divine the hidden meanings in life's mysteries.

And so it was, when the top-rated children's television series *Sesame Street* was casting for a cat actor to star in a special film to be shot at New York City's famed Metropolitan Museum of Art, this fanciful feline won the role of a lifetime. In fact, this was the role of *nine* lifetimes!

For as prolific an actor as Bebe was, with many television roles to her credit, this terrific role turned out to be a real star turn for Bebe—portraying a little (human) girl who, on a trip with her classmates to the Metropolitan Museum of Art, turns into a magical cat. But this wasn't just any ordinary magical cat. (I guess when you are a member of such an extraordinary species as the cat, as they like to continually remind us, there are degrees of extraordinary!) No, Bebe's character was a time traveler cat. Secretly sequestered amid the rare artifacts and antiquities of ancient Egypt was a centuries-old Egyptian cat mummy—a portal to the mysterious past. And when the little girl spies a nearly hidden scroll next to the cat mummy, and recites its inscription, she is turned into a cat herself—and leads her school friends on a time-traveling adventure back to the days of ancient Egypt, when the cat was worshiped as almighty and all powerful.

Needless to say, Bebe had a field day working with all the child actors in the production of that fanciful field trip! The great English actor Anthony Hopkins, in answering an interviewer's question about how he chooses his movie roles and film scripts, never once mentioned the nuances of the role he was to play! Self-effacing and self-deprecating, the Shakespearean-trained star was puckishly honest. He replied that, in reading the script or film treatment, he does not turn to the page with his character's description but checks instead on the movie's location—where it's being shot! And, if it seems to be a fun or exciting or relaxing place he's never been before, he signs on for the film! I am sure that for Bebe—or any feline thespian—nosing around the vast Metropolitan Museum of Art, full of centuries-old artifacts, is a cat actor's dream!

Another terrific cat was Turkey, my white Turkish Angora. Just as Bebe, my all-black domestic shorthair, always seemed to be cast in roles that called for the proverbial black cat—night scenes, mystical scenes, sinister scenes, and thriller moments—so Turkey always got the calls for the angelic cats, the sweet cats. Turkey appeared in many soap operas and commercials, and he was always called upon to play the roles of the adorable family cat.

Turkey and Bebe were two of my most prolific, hardworking cats. In fact, they seemed to sense that they were top cats around the house, always jousting for the Alpha position. Nose to nose and paws to paws, their careers were in constant competition—but it was always in good fun! And, at least on Turkey's part, good, clean fun! You see, Turkey's fur was so pure and pristine white, and his personality was so sweet and malleable and manageable, that he made a good clean living getting bathed in ads for pet shampoos, as well as working the trade shows for groomers!

So, between the two of them, Bebe and Turkey were "top dogs" in their field, having the dueling dichotomy roles of good cop–bad cop or good guy–bad guy all sewn up! Indeed, I used to joke that if we ever cast an all-cat version of a Wild West Show, Bebe would be the "bad" guy in the proverbial black hat, and Turkey the proverbial "good" guy in the proverbial white hat! And what a job for the wardrobe department *that* would be! Countless miniature cat cowboy hats and neckerchiefs? Forget a New York City haberdasher! I'd have to do it *myself*! Bash Dibra—Cat Trainer and Haber*Basher*!

★ StarPet cat Turkey appears in an "advertisement" for Scratch watches. ★
Courtesy Ilene Rosenthal Hochberg/*Vanity Fur*

Although Bebe and Turkey led the way, none of my cats were content to sit quietly on the sidelines. Nicky and Mia-Cat, for example, were beautiful Siamese cats and *very* talkative. Their unfailing ability to speak on cue kept them engaged in contract conversations for many commercials and television roles.

Winnie, on the other paw, was a soft-spoken Persian cat, who let her beautiful blue eyes and true-blue personality speak for her! With her exotic looks, and calm, almost Zenlike demeanor, Winnie was a terrific model, not just for print ads, but for live runway work. She walked the catwalk with many (human) supermodels for elite designer showcases. Winnie was also a spokescat. She toured with me to publicize my book *Cat Speak* and worked the cat show circuit, promoting not only the book, but also responsible pet ownership. Her social skills also made her ideal not only for public appearances, but for pet therapy in nursing homes as well, and she also appeared regularly on television news shows, such as the CBS *Early Show,* to promote both pet therapy and humane education.

But Winnie was equally happy at home. She was a real *family cat.* In fact, she loved everyone—including the family *dogs!* And, in a major departure from what is considered "normal" cat behavior, Winnie not only "tolerated" children, she adored toddlers! She allowed them to do just about anything to her—playing the "role" of real-life "stuffed animal" with patience and tenderness. Indeed, Winnie was maternal, almost, with the little tykes! In fact, in the complete opposite of the dog's instinctive food-guarding trait, Winnie would "invite" her "playmates" over to her food and water dishes, as if to suggest a "tea party." Winnie-the-Pooh had nothing on Winnie-the-*Cat!*

From Bebe and Turkey to Nicky and Mia and Winnie and beyond, all our StarPet cats have been rescue cats, from abandon-

StarPet cat Russo appears as "that catmopolitan male,
Burmese Reynolds."
COURTESY ILENE ROSENTHAL HOCHBERG/*CATMOPOLITAN*

ment, shelters, or rescue groups—or strays that just happened to
show up on my doorstep. But *all* had a zest for life—and a zest for
the *lights*! Whereas most cats are enchanted playing with bugs underneath the porch light, *my* cats were bitten by the *acting* bug,
and, whether they were kittens or "oldsters," they were all enchanted with the footlights and playing in the spotlight. Two of
these special cats especially represent how pets can become Star-
Pets at any age, whatever their background and questionable résumé!

Vinny, a black domestic shorthair, came to us when he was just
a newborn, orphaned and desperate for a home and a strong dose
of tender loving care! And Vinny gave as much as he got. He was a
real love. He loved everybody, and everybody loved him. In fact,
he was barely out of kitten milk replacement when this lovable little orphan found a home in the pages of magazines and advertisements! His kittenish appeal continued long after he grew into
"cathood," and he became fast friends with all the StarPet brothers

and sisters—including the dogs—he had grown up with. He especially loved my German Shepherd Inga, and she took a special interest in his career, as they worked in many scenes in several projects together. In fact, working with Inga gave Vinny a "leg up" in the business. Vinny earned a reputation as a real trouper, who could be counted on to liven up *any* scene with *any* species of costar—from the smallest cat to the largest dog, and any *human* actor in between!

Skeeter, on the other hand, was a beautiful calico cat, who, far from being a kittenish ingenue, was—as actors of a certain age who no longer want to advertise their age say—capable of playing a wide age range! Chronologically, Skeeter may not have been in her prime for show business, but she was certainly in her element! Acting was obviously in her blood, because she sure knew how to make an entrance! A feral cat, Skeeter literally swaggered out of an alley and brazenly into our lives, appearing unannounced at our front door, as if out of nowhere! It was as if she knew we ran an animal business, and she was determined to be part of the action! And she was right! In fact, almost as if asking to be made a star, she would sidle up to you and wrap herself lovingly around your shoulders! Talk about sucking up to the director! But a star indeed she was, both at home and on the set. She was very sweet and loved everybody, and as with Vinny, that included the dogs! Indeed, when it came to guarding the premises, Skeeter was one of the guys—holding her own with the Shepherds and Dobermans in that department! And, with her photogenic tricolor calico coat, she was a triple threat to the commercial cat competition, scoring audition after audition for print ads, commercials (she became known as the "Whiskas Cat" for the cat food giant), and magazines!

Vinnie and Skeeter were real character actors, and with their oftentimes zany, unabashed sense of fun in working with any costars, including dogs, I longed for a venue that could showcase their abilities à la Mack Sennett's historical all-star animal revues. Indeed, Skeeter—right down to how he entered our lives—reminded me of Mack Sennett's incredible Pepper, the Cat, whom he had successfully paired onscreen with Teddy, the Great Dane! Like my Skeeter showing up out of nowhere at StarPets' doorstep, so the legendary Pepper was *also* a stray who one day just appeared at the studio and took a liking, not just to Teddy, but to the movie industry, as well!

My history, Skeeter's history (and those of all her fellow Star-Pets), was still in the making. A first step toward realizing my vision of showcasing costarring dogs and cats came when the Carnation company invited my family of StarPets to represent the "family" of Carnation Pet Products. Each individual Carnation pet product, cat food or dog food, canned or dry, would be represented by an individual spokescat or spokesdog. I tapped Skeeter, Bebe, Turkey, and Nicky to head the cat contingent, while Muffin and Blondie led the doggie debut! Businesswise, that ad campaign, mixing cats and dogs (along with their assorted culinary accoutrements!), was the perfect merger of product placement with pet placement! For me, personally, however, the Carnation campaign nurtured the germ of my Sennett-inspired idea that was about to blossom.

Serendipitously, around this time, a new client came into my life. Ilene Hochberg was a young, talented, and savvy businesswoman, with a beautiful West Highland White Terrier. Her flair and finesse for business rivaled that of any Fortune 500 executive and were surpassed only by her creative entrepreneurial skills and, more important, her love for her incomparable Westy! She wanted very much to make her Westy a StarPet, and, with unbounded enthusiasm, she unabashedly threw herself into my work—and my world—as well! We spent delightful days in training and at dog shows, literally and figuratively tossing balls in the air both for the Westy and for potential business projects. Happily, one of the ideas Ilene—with a tenacity matched only by that of her Terrier!—retrieved and ran with was to produce a series of Mack Sennett–like satirical pet parody magazines: *Vogue* became *Dogue, Cosmopolitan* morphed into *Catmopolitan,* and *Vanity Fair* segued into *Vanity Fur*! These coffee-table magazines became instant, phenomenal bestsellers.

With Ilene providing both the business acumen and the venue, I happily set about providing the cast of StarPets for this all-animal revue. All but one, that is! For the first book, *Dogue,* there would

★ Here I am with two StarPet stars of *Catmopolitan* and *Dogue.* ★
COURTESY BRUCE PLOTKIN

be countless pets modeling many designer-inspired fashions (and my clients were all clamoring for top placement for their pets!). But Ilene and I both knew that there could be only *one* cover dog, and that spot was all-important. For not only is a book judged by its cover, but a magazine is sold by the appeal of its It Girl—its cover girl—er, *dog*! And who more appealing to appeal to consumers than a fabulous Westy?

With panache and poise, charisma and cachet, StarPets of all breeds and types sashayed in full-dress regalia (and behavioral!) satire throughout the pages of pun and fun! From *Dogue* to *Catmopolitan* to *Vanity Fur,* pets peopled the pages with catty comments and mutt mockumentaries on the specious human claim to embody all things beautiful and smart, trendy and art, high society and high end, merchandising and hypnotizing.

Dogue, Catmopolitan, and *Vanity Fur* stand alone in the marketing merger of pets, publishing, and entertainment, and ignited an international trend that, to this day, sees no end. Indeed, throughout my many Paws Across America–fueled entertainment venues and charity events, the all-animal revues and people/pet "Make Your Pet a Star" segments (which have been showcased everywhere from *People* magazine to television's *Inside Edition* and ABC *News*) continue to be the most popular, for both fun and fund-raising!

But the StarPet time in the spotlight—as fun and exciting as it is for the pets and their people—is overshadowed (and we wouldn't have it any other way!) by the work these incredible animals do behind the scenes, and the light they shed on the people, pets, and places that need to have their time in the sun, and their time in the fun, in the spotlight. Indeed, some twenty-odd years ago, when the field of pet-assisted therapy was barely a glimmer on the horizon, the StarPet took on the role of the therapy pet, initiating the dawn of a new day, where healing was facilitated, miracles were made, and a revolution was begun!

Senior citizens in wheelchairs and recreation rooms in nursing homes may seem an unlikely venue for a revolution, but so it was. And so it was, equally unlikely, that a tiny Chihuahua, Goldie (dog), and a small Persian Blue, Chicky (cat)—each weighing no more than a few pounds, their bodies barely bigger than a stick of dynamite—more than pulled their weight and packed a wallop of a dynamite punch in leading the brigade that broke through barriers and bureaucracies in certifying and allowing pet-assisted therapists to work in nursing homes, hospices, and hospitals throughout New York City and New York State.

The borough of the Bronx in New York City has more nursing homes per capita than any other region of the United States, and, as the Bronx literally borders my own backyard, I knew that this fledgling area of adjunct medicine could vitally enrich the health and well-being of many of our loved ones—on both ends of the leash! So—having developed some of my own techniques years before, in a precursor to pet-facilitated therapy, and using Muffin as my therapy dog—when the head of the School of Veterinary Technicians at New York's Mercy College invited me to become an adjunct professor to develop a pet therapy curriculum, I jumped at the opportunity. Here at last was a way to put theory into practice, medicine into the mainstream, and hope and happiness into the hearts of the patients, their loved ones, and their caregivers.

To accomplish this, I developed an approach that, within the realm of academia, merged the medical arts with the theatrical arts, medical students with StarPet therapists. The veterinary and nursing students would have the opportunity to, in tandem with their scholastic, on-campus studies, conduct research and field work within a network of nursing homes. My students would accompany my StarPets (both dogs and cats) and me into these different nursing homes to medically monitor and document for publication at an academic research level the results and effects of these (then) revolutionary pet therapists! And the results *were* revolutionary—and oftentimes near miraculous! A case in point involves Goldie herself.

Goldie may have been a tiny Chihuahua, but she had a heart as big as a Great Dane! Indeed, in the entertainment industry, it was her heart that was her hard sell! Her gentleness and sweetness made her a much-sought-after costar for children and oldsters alike, and her appealing demeanor sold many Disney products. But it was her work in the nursing homes that helped to sell the

★ Bash with StarPets Ziggy (bulldog) and Winnie (cat). ★
Courtesy Meruet Dibra

very real medical benefits of pet therapy to mainstream medicine, health-care facilities, government agencies, and legislators.

Therapy dogs and cats give the kind of unconditional love that only a pet can give. They are totally nonjudgmental in their acceptance of people and give the kind of touch contact so missed by individuals who are often removed from loved ones. What's more, they often bring a person who has lost his sense of reality back to the present. And, in tandem with the pet's handler, a therapy dog acts as a social catalyst and provides a common ground for conversation and communication. It may sound simple, but it sometimes proves to be near-miraculous, as it was with Goldie at the helm.

Goldie and I were paying one of our regular visits to the nursing home when the facility's recreation director informed me that there was a new resident in the group, who was suffering from an advanced stage of Alzheimer's disease. Unable to remember anything, she hadn't spoken in months. The patient's husband, who was visiting, sadly confirmed this, adding that his wife had once been a very active and accomplished woman. Indeed, she had been a concert pianist, an eye surgeon, and fluent in six languages! He also told me how pleased he was to see Goldie, as his wife had always loved animals.

With Goldie in my arms—and armed with the patient's background information—I held little Goldie in front of the woman, as I asked her husband what languages she had spoken. He told me she had been born in Greece, and I had grown up in Europe myself and knew a little bit of quite a few languages and dialects. Knowing that Alzheimer's sufferers often respond more to the long-ago past than more recent times, I decided to try the language of her childhood. I ventured a soft *"Te kanis,"* which means "hello" in Greek. Her eyes were downcast, but she began to pet Goldie, and, as my greeting seemed to sink in, she looked up at me, her eyes clouded, but her face breaking into the most beautiful smile. Then, as she continued stroking Goldie, she tentatively returned my Greek greeting: *"Te kanis!"* It was a whisper, and barely there, but, undeniably, she was there!

As if understanding her role in this tender tapestry of life, Goldie, ever-so-slightly, as if not to break the fragile thread of communication that could become a lifeline to medical treatment, leaned almost imperceptibly into the woman's arms.

Picking up on Goldie's cue, I readied my next line, deciding to deliver it in still *another* language. *"Désirez-vous le chien?"* (Do you want the dog?) I asked her, this time in French. With that, her eyes widened, and the clouds seemed to dissipate, if only for a moment, and were replaced with a radiance of understanding, and of understanding being loved. *"Oui, je désire le chien!"* she acknowledged, and gently but decisively drew Goldie closer, holding her with an intensity not just of gentle dog cuddles, but the heartfelt embrace of a life being saved.

With that, the husband, who, along with the health-care workers, had been frozen in disbelief and silence, found his voice. "Look! She's talking!" he shouted in amazement. And everyone, including the medical professionals, laughed and clapped with the heady optimism that they might just have witnessed a medical breakthrough, the lifeline to which they could anchor their medical and therapeutic treatment.

Goldie had done her job superbly. A bridge had been forged, and now it was time for the professionals to take over. With therapeutic reconstruction (working from her childhood on, by using the languages she had learned when she was young), they were able to rebuild her ability to communicate!

A door had been opened, not just in the patient's understanding, but in the understanding of health-care professionals and legislators. And with Goldie's "paw-hold" in the door, there was no holding back. The pet therapists' work had been proven and embraced. Legally, however, pets were still not allowed to visit in nursing homes. So, we decided to create a movement to change the laws governing the regulation of nursing homes. And we did this by forming an intergenerational coalition of medical arts and theatrical arts to bring a proven standard of adjunct therapeutic medical care to those citizens who are too often the unseen, unremembered members of our collective family.

With therapy pets and medical teams in the forefront, the movement also garnered the support of the young medical students who had worked so hard in the groundbreaking study, as well as that of the many soap opera actors who had shared their own brand of therapy. Muffin's human costars from *The Edge of Night,* as well as other daytime dramas, were invaluable to the pet therapy, as the patients who watched television every day regarded these big-hearted stars as "members of the family." And, for some residents, these caring stars were their *only* "families."

But even a cause as wonderful and deserving as pet therapy had to work hard to get the necessary media exposure and attention of the government officials who can make a difference. And this is especially so in New York City, with so many people and movements in all fields vying for that all important "one shot."

In 1985, the visionary, then–Bronx borough president Stanley Simon took our vision and made it reality. He issued a proclamation endorsing and encouraging Pet Therapy Week in the Bronx—the first such proclamation in the United States.

Pet Therapy Week was launched with great fanfare and ceremony at the Grand Concourse County Center, where government officials and nursing home officials sat side by side with nursing home residents and their therapeutic pets!

This historic event ignited great media presence and press coverage, and, with that coverage, the venerable *New York Times* created the next "star" of the movement, unwittingly contributing to a citywide—and what would become a statewide—landslide of the tumbling "No Pets Allowed" barricades. Sitting calmly in a wheelchair-bound patient's lap, was Chicky—my very best pet therapy cat.

Chicky was a beautiful Persian Blue with shining copper eyes. She was very smart, had a wonderful personality, and got along well with *everyone*—both children and adults; dogs as well as other cats. She would have been wonderful in show business, but, unfortunately, a congenital, chronic eye condition marred her good looks—at least by the industry's standards. Chicky, however, didn't let that get her down. In fact, she made her deformity work for her on the far more important stage of pet therapy! Chicky did a great deal of pet therapy—oftentimes in a theatrical threesome that included my dogs Goldie and Kimberly! The three of them really knew how to "work a room"—whether it was a studio or a nursing home recreation room! In fact, they kept the patients in stitches—and I only mean that in the best possible way, with the universal medicine of love and laughter!

But Chicky was more than just a fun and smart cat. In fact, she seemed downright insightful in the way she interacted with the residents of the nursing home. I think her own eye ailment (it was not contagious, but it was also not treatable), which may have cut her out of roles in show business, actually allowed her to carve out a special role for herself that allowed her to connect with the nursing home residents, who battled their own share of adversity with chronic medical conditions and ailments. Indeed, that one "bad" eye facilitated Chicky's own personal brand of pet-facilitated therapy, which seemed to embrace the "buddy system," as well. It was an eye-opener for the residents to see the plucky Chicky carry on so beautifully despite her condition, and they adopted the empowering sense of fortitude and optimism that, if *Chicky* could do it, they could do it!

And so it was that, as she sat there on the lap of her patient, just doing her job, Chicky was captured on film and immortalized on the front page of *The New York Times*. Forever working behind the scenes with her philanthropy, Chicky had, with the click of a shutterbug's camera, become a leading *feline*thropist—inspiring then–New York City mayor Ed Koch to proclaim, the following year, Pet Therapy Week in the "greatest city in the world!"

I was honored to be instrumental in the success of this movement, and continued to create the marketing language to both the medical and professional communities, as well as the legislative communities, to continue to rework and revamp the regulations that would allow for the change in law. This, once and for all, would facilitate the advancement of pet-facilitated therapy. To this end, we were joined—across the board—by professionals and paraprofessionals, representing animal shelters, medical groups, and senior citizen facilities. Together for a common good, this crusade, launched from my humble "Center for Pet Therapy" years earlier, developed into the New York Council on Pet-Assisted Therapy, and, under its banner and auspices, the movement picked up even *more* momentum. Then-governor Mario Cuomo signed a proclamation declaring New York State Pet Therapy Week—opening the way for the development of a subsequent statewide pet therapy program.

And so it was that a Chihuahua with the heart of a Great Dane, and a cat with one bad eye (but exceptional vision!), opened the eyes of people everywhere to the strength of the heart in facilitating healing. They led a pet crusade into history, and their legacy continues to pave the way for others to *continue* to make history.

Indeed, it may have seemed a little daunting at times (a lot daunting, actually!), a kind of "David and Goliath" task! But it turned out to be not such a Herculean effort, thanks to New York's incredible leadership. We may have had giants to deal with, but they were gentle giants, benevolent giants, and, ultimately, visionary giants. As I have noted before, philosophers and statesmen alike, from disparate origins and countries, have opined throughout history that "a nation's greatness can be measured by how it treats its animals."

Twenty years ahead of their time in publicly and officially acknowledging the benefits of pet therapy to mankind, the great and visionary statesmen of the state of New York took that observation one step further—"A nation's greatness can be measured by how it allows its animals to treat its people!"

And so the spotlight shone brightly on the twin StarPet endeavors of show business and philanthropy, and people everywhere wanted to make their pet a star—or a therapist! I was gratified by the response of these talented and good-hearted people and pets, but good intentions alone were not enough to qualify for either field. Some standards, some type of testing (and then instruction), had to be developed to handle the groundswell of "recruits"!

Toward this end, much as I had worked with Mercy College in developing the pet therapy curriculum, I joined forces with the American Kennel Club to help advance the Canine Good Citizen Program (CGC). With Jim Dearinger, who was the director of obedience and vice president of the American Kennel Club, and later with Dr. Mary Burch, we promoted the CGC program that has become increasingly accepted as the standard for responsible pet behavior, not only across the nation, but in many other countries as well, including England, Australia, Japan, Hungary, Denmark, Sweden, Canada, and Finland. This program is open to *all* dogs, not just purebreds. You can learn more about this program in my book *Dog Speak.*

And because Chicky, my Persian Blue, inspired countless *felinethropists* to follow in *her* pretty pawprints, I worked with the Cat Fanciers' Association (CFA) to develop a comparable program for cats, called the Cat Fanciers' Association Feline Good Citizen (Feline Lifetime Partner/Companion) Award/Test. This certification promotes responsible pet ownership and care for cats, and their work as goodwill ambassadors and therapy cats. And, with the popularity of cats rivaling that of dogs in so many areas of life—from show business to pet therapy—this certification program is definitely an idea whose time has come.

In developing and promoting the AKC's Canine Good Citizen and in creating the CFA's Feline Good Citizen, I realized that we had a golden opportunity to help animal shelters promote responsible pet ownership, as well as the "adoption option" in choosing a pet. You see, each year, 15 million dogs are abandoned, and ultimately destroyed, because of behavioral problems. It's an overwhelming and tragic statistic, and is even more heartbreaking because it doesn't have to happen. Dogs are abandoned because they are unruly dogs, problem dogs. Only the "best" dogs have a chance at adoption. A dog or cat who is understood, well-trained, and well-behaved will remain with a home his entire life and never be abandoned. If people are thinking of getting a pet, they should visit their local shelter and adopt one. No pet is untrainable, and all pets deserve a good and loving home. Visit your local animal shelter and save a life!

Toward this end, I approached my old friend and colleague, the legendary dog expert and champion of animal welfare reform, Roger Caras. At that time, Roger Caras had just taken over the reins as president of the American Society for the Prevention of Cruelty to Animals. I had known Roger since our days together at the prestigious Westminster Dog Show in New York's Madison Square Garden. In those days, I was showing and handling dogs and he was handling the entire show! From hosting to broadcasting his own inimitable and popular "color commentary," Caras's

★ ASPCA Dog Walk: From left, Bash, Sarah Jessica Parker, Matthew Broderick (with Sally), Al Roker, and Roger Caras (with Beethoven). ★
COURTESY DIANE COHEN

★ ASPCA Dog Walk: Brooke Shields, Bash, and Matthew Broderick. ★
COURTESY DIANE COHEN

professional persona—at once both enlightening and entertaining, and eminently approachable—was *also* who he was *personally*, and I had no qualms in approaching Roger with our proposal.

We wanted to create an event that would not only benefit shelter programs sponsored by the ASPCA but also, within that framework, create an awareness of and an effort to change the organization's decades-old, financially hamstrung operational policy from a kill shelter (that was a city ordnance) to a *no*-kill shelter. Caras *also* saw the need, and agreed, but it was a daunting task. We felt that such a grand vision necessitated an equally grand presence to attract the media attention needed to ignite public support and fuel much-needed funds to convert the shelter's mission to no-kill, and to propel the initiative to a national campaign. To this end, we created the premiere ASPCA Dog Walk, which created such a groundswell of citywide public (and pooch!) support that over ten thousand dogs (with their people in tow!) showed up to champion the cause that none of their pooch peers should ever be homeless or die in a shelter. To this day, the ASPCA Dog Walk is one of New York City's most popular annual fund-raising events.

Another annual consciousness-raising fund-raiser that I had the opportunity to premiere was the American Cancer Society's Pause-for-a-Cause Dog Walk. After we premiered the first annual ASPCA Dog Walk, I was asked to come aboard the American Cancer Society's effort to launch a similar campaign. The American Cancer Society wanted to unite with New York City's prestigious Animal Medical Center in raising funds (and awareness) to help fight cancer in both people *and* pets. With the tagline, "When was the last time you and your dog saved a life?" the Dog Walk Against Cancer's debut was both poignant and profitable (many of the two-legged and four-legged walkers were themselves living with cancer, or cancer survivors), and, ultimately, triumphant: Like the ASPCA Dog Walk, the American Cancer Society's Dog Walk was a financial, media, and public success, and, to this day, well over a decade later, the two events are annual "mutt and media driven" Manhattan milestones.

Another Manhattan milestone for mutts and medicine followed close on the heels of the ASPCA and American Cancer Society events—but hailed from clear across the country! The Delta Society is a national nonprofit organization founded in Portland, Oregon, in 1977 by professionals and academics in the human and veterinary medical fields, who, like myself, strongly believed that animals have the power to heal. With that belief, their mission was to improve human health and well-being through mutually beneficial contact with animals. Through their revolutionary research and inroads in academia, the Delta Society became a national clearinghouse of knowledge for scientists, academics, and professionals in the fledgling field, as well as an "outreach" program of sorts for the loose but potentially powerful network of pet owners, volunteers, health-care professionals, and service dog owners who understand (or daily live with) not only the need for service and therapy dogs themselves, but, perhaps *more* important, the need for the *recognition* of service and therapy dogs. And that was where I came in.

The Delta Society had created a Service Dog Center and Pet Partners Program in Renton, Washington. The Service Dog Center served as an umbrella organization and referral center, directing people with disabilities to appropriately trained service dogs (dogs trained to alert their people to sounds, guide them around obstacles, retrieve dropped articles—even do the laundry and withdraw cash from an ATM machine!). And the fledgling Pet Partners Program was to provide training and screening for people and their pets, who, together, visit nursing homes, hospitals, and other institutions bringing love and companionship. Because of my own background in academia and my network of professionals and paraprofessionals who had conducted similar research and forged comparable programs, I was familiar with the wonderful work of the Delta Society. And that was the problem. My professional colleagues and I were familiar with the Delta Society, but the rest of the nation and the general public, by and large, were *not.* The Delta Society needed to create a strong fund-raising base to support a campaign of national awareness to get these service dogs and pet therapists trained and into the lives of the people who so desperately needed them.

To do this, the Delta Society approached me, and we decided to make my home base, New York City, the launch pad to broaden the Delta Society's national horizons. Little did we know that the Delta Society would grow from a blip on the radar screen to a shining and constant star. I was privileged to work with then–executive director Linda Hines, and once again with Dr. Mary Burch. With the Delta Society, Dr. Burch was the volunteer chairperson of the committee that developed standards for therapy dogs participating in the Delta Society's Pet Partners Program. We worked closely in the exploration and development of guidelines to select, train, and evaluate animals, including shelter animals, so they can enjoy new lives in service and therapy roles.

But my main mission was to put the Delta Society on Manhattan's fund-raising map, which had the power to thrust the Delta Society into the mainstream—and we did so, not only nationally, but *internationally.* Thanks to the largesse, time, and talent of my client Mrs. Victoria Newhouse (New York socialite and wife of Condé Nast chairman S. I. Newhouse), and her work with her pet therapy Pug dog, Nero, the "movers and shakers" of New York City made my mission, the Delta Society's mission, their mission, embracing it with open hearts and open pocketbooks.

We created a four-day fund-raising extravaganza that ran the gamut from elite society soirees in Park Avenue salons to a hootenanny with folk legend James Taylor (and his dog!) to academic conferences and training seminars in New York City's Sheraton Center Hotel, which received national and international attention.

But the crowning event was the star-studded Super-Dog Variety Show at the Danny Kaye Theater, hosted by the quintessential New Yorker: the urbane, erudite, and entertaining George Plimpton, who held our audience of New York's glitterati in the palm of his hand! Having forged a career in discovering, exploring, and celebrating the human spirit and talent of awesome accomplishment against all odds—and being a dog lover, to boot!—Mr. Plimpton was right at home on the doggie dais in honoring the canine spirit and talent that allowed awesome accomplishment against all odds: the award-winning service dogs and therapy dogs (chosen by a judging panel that included Lassie and the Weatherwax dynasty and comic strip canine icon Marmaduke, and his artist/creator, Brad Anderson, serving as honorary Pet Partners!).

As it was a fund-raiser, I pulled out all the stops and engaged my time-proven, crowd-pleasing formula of fun and fund-raising: StarPets helping pets helping people! With a manic, madcap mix of live performance pets with the animal archives of Mack Sennett's Canine Capers, Charlie Chaplin and Scraps, and Gene Kelly and Fido, the Super-Dog Variety Show was a fitting fireworks-display ending to the beginning of a new, national chapter in the history of the Delta Society. In fact, our own emcee, literary lion George Plimpton, later published a witty and whimsical book about a veterinarian and pet advice columnist *(Pet Peeves)* inspired by the Super-Dog Variety Show!

Working with so many different and diverse groups to help save animals, and to *also* help animals save people, I saw the need to develop a cohesive hands-on (paws-on?) organization with a nationwide reach, to connect people and pets with a common goal within their own community. With service and therapy dogs fighting for acceptance in so many areas of society, and with "high society" having me train their pets to pass their near-impenetrable old guard coop boards for admittance into residences that have traditionally disdained pets, I realized that, en masse, we needed to mainstream pets into all areas of society—and that no pet should be left behind in a shelter. To meet this need, I created Paws Across America, a national campaign to promote responsible pet ownership, and, on a regional level, to provide hands-on goodwill and support to local, pet-related groups stressing the proper care and training of our pets.

Perhaps because I grew up without freedom and without hope

and without a home, I feel a special kinship for animals who find themselves, through no fault of their own, without freedom, without hope, and without homes. And, as America reached out, across the ocean and across a continent, to rescue my family and me, to give us freedom and hope and a home—so I understand what a difference an extended hand can make, not only to the pets themselves, but to the *people* who need help in helping the pets. So, by connecting people and pets—hands and paws—across America, the mission of Paws Across America is to provide a blueprint of a morale-boosting, fund-raising campaign from conception to seed money, from development to fruition, to assist charitable and philanthropic programs on grassroots, local, regional, and national levels to flourish.

Paws Across America took its first, unofficial (and, at that time, *nameless*) puppy steps during America's Bicentennial, when Muffin, as grand marshal, led marchers to raise funds for a much-needed animal shelter in Massachusetts's historic Martha's Vineyard, and, twenty years later, continued its progressive pet parade into my own "backyard," New York City's Van Cortlandt Park, with "Pets, People, and Park," a fund-raising event showcasing how pets and parks enrich people's lives. Sponsored in part by the Friends of Van Cortlandt Park, and intended to benefit the park and all the people and pets who enjoy it, Pets, People, and Park became such a popular annual event that, although it was local, it enjoyed—and benefited from—national media coverage.

As matching funds were raised for the park, the pets who enjoy it were not left out. With the help of the New York City Parks Department, we founded "Canine Court"—the world's first dog playground and agility course—putting the historic park on the map once again. You see, as then–New York City parks commissioner Henry Stern, who opened Canine Court with his dog,

Boomer, noted, not only did Van Cortlandt Park house the world's first dog playground, but it was *also* home to America's first (and still thriving) golf course! A few years later, Canine Court had its place in New York City's history officially sealed, when it earned a place of honor and recognition at the New-York Historical Society's exhibit Petropolis, which chronicle the 250-year history of pets in this great metropolis!

As we marched into the new millennium, Pets, People, and Parks—with the help of Paws Across America—morphed into Paws Walk 2000, a citywide event sponsored by major companies within the pet industry to unite, hand to hand and paw to paw, every member of the pet industry and animal welfare world, from veterinarians to animal shelters to groomers and trainers and man-ufacturers of pet products, to promote responsible pet ownership and to create inspirational and educational adopt-a-thons, as well as the instruction and implementation of responsible stewardship of parks, so that generations of people and their pets can create, inherit, and enjoy their *own* Canine Courts!

During this time—on the eve of the new millennium—I met with a small band of visionary veterinarians to help promote a rev-olutionary idea whose time had come: That no pet owner, faced with a life-threatening veterinary emergency, but lack of funds, should have to say goodbye to a beloved pet because of an inability to pay for life-saving veterinary care. These veterinarians vowed that no one should face the unbearable and heartbreaking dilemma of losing a beloved animal companion because of finan-cial hardship. The anguish of being unable to provide life-saving veterinary care when a person and pet are most vulnerable is dev-astating. Thus, with the endorsement of the Veterinary Associa-tion of New York City, and the generosity of the Brand

Foundation of New York, New York SAVE (Save Animals in Veterinary Emergency) was born.

NY SAVE's mission is to provide funding for immediate life-saving emergency care, as well as for treatment of medical conditions that cause pets undue suffering and will become life-threatening if left untreated. This mission is fulfilled by the largesse of the wonderful veterinarians at local veterinary hospitals who are members of the Veterinary Medical Association of New York City, as well as the growing number of philanthropic-minded individuals and volunteers who have aligned themselves in this new and noble endeavor.

United in our belief that NY SAVE was not only an idea whose time had come, but an idea that should be mainstreamed throughout New York City, and perhaps blueprinted in cities across the country, I invited NY SAVE to participate in Paws Across America's Paws Walk 2000. Not surprisingly, Paws Walk 2000 provided a pathway of accessibility and publicity to NY SAVE. Both people and their pets—and the press—were intrigued and supportive. And we needed the support, because the pathway of accessibility had also brought the people and pets who needed the attention of NY SAVE. If NY SAVE was an idea whose time had come, Paws Walk 2000 had opened the gates for the people and pets to come for help.

The caseloads became overwhelming. We didn't want to turn anyone away, but we needed help ourselves if we were going to be able to continue to help others. We decided we needed to ratchet up our fund-raising efforts, and we needed to do so quickly. I decided to call up my old friend George Plimpton, who had so graciously and generously helped my efforts with the Delta Society. Ever the gentleman (and pet lover!), Mr. Plimpton did not disappoint us. He was as gracious and generous as ever. In fact, his magnanimity was such that, in support of NY SAVE, he invited us into his home to shoot a NY SAVE documentary, even appearing on camera in an eloquent and stirring endorsement of the fledgling group.

George Plimpton's presence in the NY SAVE film became the gift that kept on giving, as the beautiful little film debuted in many fund-raising venues (including a costarring effort with enduring daytime diva Eileen Fulton and Rags the Dog from *Spin City*) and garnered much attention, support, and funds. Once again, celebrities and pets, film and philanthropy, entertainment and charity, were a winning—and very New York—combination.

And because—like the great city it serves, whose hostess with the "mostess," Lady Liberty, welcomes the world's tired, poor, and huddled masses—NY SAVE embraces and uplifts those people and pets who are the most in need, and for whom there is nowhere else to turn, I felt we needed a venue that effectively represented not only the heart and soul, and the scope and outreach, of NY SAVE, but also the heart and soul, and scope and outreach, of the towering city it serves. And although NY SAVE is a local group of veterinarians and volunteers serving a single city, it has to be remembered that our hometown is like no other hometown in the world—and we would need a place large enough to house not only the show, but the intended guests, including their pets! It would be a garden party like no other, and no other garden but New York's famed Madison Square Garden would do!

The Garden also hosts the Ringling Brothers Barnum and Bailey Circus, as well as rodeos and equestrian events, and is the home of the prestigious Westminster Dog Show and the International Cat Association show. Having worked the arena regularly at the Westminster Dog Show, as well as the International Cat Association show (hosting seminars and StarPet talent shows and auditions), I knew that the Garden was a venue that could handle my vision.

My vision was to unleash Paws Across America to corral a herd of corporate sponsors within (but not exclusive to) the pet industry, in a united effort to march NY SAVE and a contingency of like-minded organizations (animal rescue and welfare groups, shelters, and hospitals) and supporters into Madison Square Garden for a pet-friendly funfest of entertainment, contests, celebrities, and activities for the entire family (*pets included!*) that would *also* be, for animal welfare, both conscious-raising and *coffers-filling!*

With entertainment by both human celebrities and StarPets (along with our ever-popular "Make Your Pet a Star" talent show, casting call, and workshop), sporting events (agility shows and courses), educational and medical seminars (including pet therapy and service dogs, as well as dogs with disabilities), adoption centers, and hundreds of exhibitors and vendors with all sorts of pet merchandise, products, and food, this family funfest of entertainment and education to benefit the welfare of animals, and which welcomed pets on the stage, in the arena, and in the audience, was truly an original, one-of-a-kind event, with the logistical ability to entertain thousands of New Yorkers and their pets.

The Original New York Pet Show was slated to make its historic debut in Madison Square Garden the weekend of October 27 and 28, 2001.

But on September 11, 2001, history was forever changed, when an aerial terrorist assault on New York City's World Trade Center destroyed the Twin Towers and decimated much of lower Manhattan.

New York is a city celebrated for its diversity, and on that day all

New Yorkers banded together, mobilizing all forces to assist their city and its citizens in every way possible. As the scope and breadth of the disaster continued to spiral astronomically, almost all veterinary hospitals remained opened and fully staffed, and FEMA (the Federal Emergency Management Agency) assigned a task force of specially trained disaster relief veterinarians to Ground Zero to provide on-site advanced care and assistance to local veterinarians and medical mobile units already at the epicenter.

As this tragedy of unfathomable proportions unfolded on the world stage, New Yorkers—from firefighters to police officers to search-and-rescue dogs; from paramedics to paraprofessionals to therapy dogs; from extraordinary working dogs and their handlers to "ordinary" pets and their people—united to do whatever they could to help the legions of affected people and pets.

Still reeling from the unspeakable tragedy, but beginning to steady ourselves with the steely resolve that is as uniquely New York as are our steel canyons, New Yorkers started to go about the business of living in the greatest city on earth. So, we decided that The Original New York Pet Show would go on, but with an added aim.

The Original New York Pet Show wanted the world to see that the mantle of hero is draped not just on the stark silhouette of the fire hats of New York's Bravest and the soothing blue uniforms of New York's Finest, but also on the distinctive orange vests of New York's Faithful: the Search-and-Rescue Canine Corps. These dogs performed their heroic acts in the shadow of death, and they did so selflessly, without hesitation, and without a thought for their personal safety. They executed their missions tirelessly and to the point of exhaustion. And, like their human colleagues, some made the ultimate sacrifice, giving their lives in service to others.

So we invited these dogs and their handlers to a special awards ceremony within The Original New York Pet Show. It was an honor for *us* to honor *them*. And, although in the weeks and months to come, more accolades would be showered upon these deserving dogs and their handlers, ours was the first. We felt it was important to show the world that America was still there. New York was still alive. And, more important, our *spirit* was still alive, and would guide us—along with the gallant dogs—in healing, in helping, and in honoring. And because the stage at Madison Square Garden—"The World's Most Famous Arena"—is truly a *world* stage, these heroes, New York's Bravest, New York's Finest, and New York's Faithful, were rightly recognized, not just for their place in history, but for their place in the hearts of all New Yorkers.

How is it that these wonderful dogs—these incredible pets—always get under our skin, into our blood, and lodge firmly deep within our hearts? As I've shared with you here, my own captivating coterie of canines and cats have marched through my life and into my history—I sometimes guiding them; they more often than not guiding me—but always, always by my side, and always and forever in my heart.

What is it about our StarPets that strikes such a deep, responsive chord within us? What is it that keeps children—as well as adults—strapped to their seats in spellbound silence during a ninety-minute Strongheart or Benji film, with absolutely *no* human dialogue? How do these StarPets seduce us so? What makes these mutts so mesmerizing? These cats so captivating? Is it merely that star quality, that charisma—or is it something much deeper?

CHAPTER FOUR

Training Your StarDog

*I*n our hearts, those of us who love dogs have always known what the Holy Man taught me in the refugee camp so many years ago—dogs are our oldest and dearest costars!

And in 1979, science finally caught up with the humble Holy Man—and gave credit to dogs and their proponents everywhere—when scientists literally unearthed an astounding (but, to dog-lovers, not surprising), groundbreaking archaeological discovery. Embedded deep within the sacred ground of Israel—the cradle of many of the world's religions, and the birthplace of many of mankind's prophets and saviors—was a very special ancient tomb, dating back to 12,000 B.C. Deep inside lay the fossil remains of an aged human being—and a four-month-old *puppy*! Ensconced reverently together for over fourteen thousand years, the poignant pair were nestled side by side, an elderly hand resting gently on the puppy, as if to point to a hoped-for shared eternity.

"The puppy," according to the verdict reached by scientists writing in the prestigious British journal *Nature,* "offers proof that an affectionate, rather than a gastronomic relationship, existed between it and the buried person."

This finding proves what the Holy Man felt was so important to acknowledge—that we and our dogs share a distinct, evolving dynasty and a dramatic, enthralling destiny.

Just as our ancestors, the primitive nomadic tribes and the wild wolves, costarred throughout history in an eons-long action-adventure tale—indeed, in a symbiotic serialization of sorts, like the old-time movie series or modern daytime dramas—so our costarring characters have grown more complex and, with that, our relationship has *also* grown and deepened.

Eons ago, both our ancestors, the wolves and primitive nomadic tribes, began to learn from one another and to rely on one another. With their strong survival instincts, these two very social species banded together and moved beyond *competition* to survive, to *cooperation* to survive. And, as they did so, their territorial boundaries began to fade.

These tribes were of a hunting-and-gathering culture, and they began to follow the wolf packs and their prey in quest of their own game. In turn, the wolves often followed the nomads, scavenging food from the tribes' discarded game carcasses. As primitive man began to understand the wolf, he also began to understand how the wolf could *help* him. These nomadic tribes are thought to have raided wolf dens, capturing pups and then raising the ones that showed the greatest promise of being tamed. In doing this, man soon came to realize that by breeding certain wolves that shared similar traits, those traits could be improved upon and put to the service of man. Thus, some were bred to guard the dens of early man, others to chase game for hunting, and still others to herd. Eventually, through generations of rudimentary selective breeding, line breeding, and inbreeding of the wolf, the modern dog breeds began to take shape.

All over the world, different cultures, clans, and kingdoms bred dogs for a myriad of specific needs, all of which aided and improved the lives of these early civilizations. And, as these cultures began to flourish, so, *also,* did their class distinctions, and the roles of dogs *also* grew.

Dogs were no longer kept just to serve man, but also as *companions* to man. A well-bred and blue-blooded nobleman especially wanted an equally well-bred and blue-blooded dog. The sport of the hunt, of course, was a very important part of the life of the gentry, and the quest for the best hunting dog became as competitive as the sport itself. Contests and competitions to show the finer points and skills of these dogs became popular. Soon, the aristocracy had championship events to demonstrate the abilities of their guarding, herding, and working dogs. While kings and nobleman competed with their magnificent Deerhounds and Wolfhounds, the queens and noblewomen watched the competitions with refined little dogs on their laps. These small dogs were as much status symbols as the giant hounds competing in the shows. They were bred to be lapdogs for nobility, a sign that royalty did not have to work—and neither did their little dogs! Living in the lap of luxury meant having an elegant little dog sharing your throne!

These events created an early kind of sporting club, which soon evolved into kennel clubs. A championship dog was a prized asset for a nobleman, bringing both status and wealth. People naturally wanted to breed the best with the best—champions—and this line breeding developed the high gene standards that are continued in the breeds of today.

So the dog shows of yesteryear developed into the dog shows of today—for conformation, obedience, and field trials. And just as the different breeds were bred and worked and shown for specific temperaments and abilities, so these different temperaments and abilities also began to show themselves for another kind of show dog: the performing dog, the entertaining dog. Oh, these dogs weren't bred for specific tricks and acting abilities, of course, but the different temperaments and abilities of the different breeds began to be recognized and encouraged in the "theatrical" venues of early entertainment.

Gypsies, for example, were well-known for their ability to train horses and dogs, and, as their nomadic lifestyle led them from hamlets to villages to towns, they often entertained the locals with popular performing pooches. Known for both intelligence and agility, poodles and poodle types were the gypsies' dog of choice, and their amazing antics—in full theatrical dress—were exceedingly popular, and the precursor to circus show dogs (think pirouetting poodles in pink tutus!).

Around this time, true nomadic theatrical troupes—the vaudevillians—began to tour from town to town and city to city, making music and laughter and *history*. For even when the fledgling motion picture industry began to share the stage with vaudeville, vaudeville was still king, and Broadway ruled. In fact, many of the early motion picture stars were plucked from vaudeville's fertile stage—fodder for Mack Sennett's and D. W. Griffith's fabled films.

And the performers weren't just people. Equally adept (if not better!) at performing audience-pleasing pratfalls were dogs—and packs of performing pooches prowled the vaudeville circuit, nosing people out of the spotlight and fetching top billing for themselves!

Vaudeville's most famous dog act was called "The Bricklayers." The brains behind the Bricklayers was the legendary Leonard Gautier. Just as the gypsies' favored performing dog was the poodle, picked for the intelligence and agility the gypsies felt the dogs would bring to the performance, so Gautier had his reasons for casting certain dogs in his act. The Bricklayers was an *all-mutt* review, and all were rescued from animal pounds. Gautier insisted that mutts with large, bright eyes showed they were more intelligent than any purebred, and that rescued dogs, who had known life on "both sides of the tracks—mainly the *wrong* side of the tracks!"—could bring an added element of theatrical acting to the troupe!

And, on the other side of the Atlantic—an ocean away from Broadway, but only a heartbeat away from a shared, enduring love for dogs—London boasted a new and novel Broadway-caliber theater for dogs only! Named after the venerable and venerated dog novelist of *The Call of the Wild* fame, the Jack London club was a theatrical venue that hosted all-star dog revues only! The adorable antics of these dogs were hugely popular among the sentimental, dog-loving Brits, and the theater remained active until well into the mid-twentieth century.

Meanwhile, back in New York, a vaudeville brother-and-sister dance duo—Fred and Adele Astaire—were poised to leap from the Broadway stage onto the Hollywood sound stage. But when Fred landed in the pictures, he had a new dance partner—the inimitable Ginger Rogers. And as the two "cut the rug" in sublime, symbiotic choreography that infused the madcap musical comedies of their day with an unmistakable air of sophistication, they *also* cut a wide swath in motion picture history, with such hits as *Top Hat, The Gay Divorcee,* and *Broadway Melody.*

An interesting footnote to that dog-eared page of Hollywood history—and perhaps "*paw*note" would be a more appropriate term!—is that the director who guided Astaire and Rogers through so many of their fabulous films, Mark Sandrich, had a cousin who was *also* a director, but a director of an entirely different sort altogether! His "muses" were his *mutts*!

You see, while Sandrich directed the dancing feet of Astaire and

Rogers, his cousin, director Zion Myers, was nipping at his professional heels, directing canine choreography that parodied the Astaire/Rogers pairing, as well as other movie stars and film hits of the era.

Myers's filmography of the 1920s and 1930s reads like a dog lover's dream. Among Zion's furry film fare are 1924's *A Dog's Pal*, 1930's *Who Killed Rover?*, and, from 1931, three stellar productions: *The Two Barks Brothers* (a comic canine homage to the four Marx Brothers), *Trader Hound* (a lampoon of the MGM African adventure *Trader Horn*), and *All Quiet on the Canine Front* (from the classic *All Quiet on the Western Front*).

But movie fans were most entranced with the takeoffs on the enchanting Astaire/Rogers dance films. One of the biggest hit musicals of the era, *Broadway Melody*, soon became, in the hands and paws of Zion Myers and his dancing dog actors, the lop-eared lullaby *Dogway Melody*!

I often use the analogies of Astaire and Rogers and the director cousins, Mark Sandrich and Zion Myers, to highlight the successful symbiotic relationship between a director and his actor (either human or canine) and, especially, the incredible accomplishment of the successful StarPet.

You see, unlike a human actor, a StarPet not only has to attain a perfect marriage of talent and technique, but also has to first learn the language of the director, as well as acquaint himself with the foreign land he finds himself working in: the theater, photographer's studio, or television or motion picture sound stage. Along with the three P's in training (Patience, Persistence, and Praise) and the three C's (Care, Compassion, and Concern), the StarPet must *also* learn the three A's (Adjust, Assimilate, and Act). This is very important, because before your dog can begin to professionally *act*, he needs to adjust to the situation and assimilate into his surroundings—something human actors (thanks to the accident of birth into their species) already have a leg up on!

So, in short, a StarPet working with a human star is akin to Ginger Rogers dancing with Fred Astaire. Oh, Astaire was supremely talented, no question. Not only was he gifted, some historians even refer to his genius. But a tip of the (top) hat must *also* be given to Ginger Rogers, because, as it is often said, she did everything he did—but backward and in heels!

So, as you learn to train your StarPet, you must pay deference to his difference. Just as we and our dogs are alike in many ways, so our dogs—still likable and lovable—are different from us in many ways. Just as Ginger, backward and in heels, approached the dance from a different direction than did Fred, so our dogs approach the art of acting from a different perspective. And, like a good director, as you are your dog's director, if you can plumb the depths of your dog's psyche, and understand him and bring out the best in him, you can widen his (dog) actor's arc, to achieve boundless horizons.

To do this, Bash's Ark incorporates what I call the Mariah Method. As we discussed in earlier chapters, the Mariah Method is a kind of Method acting for dogs. As the dog is directly descended from the wolf, the Mariah Method is the key to gaining access to, and understanding of, your dog's nine inner drives, which are based on the wolf within the dog.

The Mariah Method

Ever since the modern movie classic *Dances with Wolves* captured the public fancy, I often point to the famous scene in the film where Kevin Costner's character catches the wolf's eye, and the two begin to engage in playlike dance.

As any dance aficionado will tell you, all the complicated choreography of the most beautiful ballets are drawn, unbelievably, from only five basic dance positions. So, also, all great symphonies incorporate the same eight notes of an octave. And so, too, in the art of animal acting, your StarPet, your dog, brings all his engaging, endearing, enigmatic talents from deep within his wolf-based psyche of just nine basic wolf-inherited behavioral traits. And, just as all human actors are unique, with different strengths and weaknesses, so the same holds true for your dog star. Some of these traits may be breed-specific, such as typecasting a Golden Retriever to retrieve and carry an object, or directing a Cairn Terrier to ferret something out of a hole, but all dogs, including the all-American "mutt," can be singular sensations in the spotlight!

So, in training your StarPet, try to imagine your dog's behavior as an incredible canine choreography, with the wolf as the master choreographer—and you've just been handed the conductor's baton!

When you can identify and understand these nine basic behavioral traits from which all canine choreography flourishes, you and your StarPet will be truly in sync. And when you can direct a perfect marriage of talent and technique within your StarPet to bring out his *best* performance, you will have a wonderful working relationship that would rival even Strasberg and Monroe or Scorsese and DeNiro.

The stage is set for you and your StarPet.

The Nine Inner Drives

There are nine inner drives derived from the wolf that underlie dog behavior. They are pack behavior, dominance and submission, socialization, aggression, territory, food-guarding, chase, flight, and vocalization.

1. PACK BEHAVIOR

Mariah's need to follow a pack leader was deeply ingrained, and I was the leader she chose to follow. I vividly remember that when she was a pup, her need of social confidence and security was crucial to her well-being. One day, I received a call from an advertising agency that handled the Revlon cosmetics account, wanting Mariah to be the cover girl for Revlon's newest perfume, Gypsy Gold. The ad would be shot at a studio on Madison Avenue in Manhattan. I knew Mariah and I had our work cut out for us. I brought Mariah into Manhattan, but before hitting Madison Avenue, I detoured first to Central Park, where I walked her around to build her confidence. To a wolf, the hustle and bustle of Madison Avenue—with crowds of people on the move and with cars and buses racing with horns blaring—can be an unnerving, if not altogether frightening, place. It can readily trigger another drive we will discuss later—flight—which could endanger her. By first walking in Central Park, she gained a sense of security and was comforted by having me, her pack leader, lead the way and show her around. (This is a method Trimble also used with Strongheart, feeling it was important to have Strongheart, whenever he felt confused, instinctively turn to him.) So, like Strongheart with Larry, this enabled Mariah to walk Madison Avenue as if she had been doing it for years. Because I was with her, she exuded a confident and calm demeanor and was very responsive to my commands. All this made for an ideal photo shoot.

Watching Mariah easily navigate the crowded streets and handle the photo shoot like a seasoned pro impressed upon me how a pack leader or owner of a dog can instill confidence and stability in a dog faced with an unfamiliar environment. Dogs of today look for the Alpha in their owner to guide them, to give them the security of knowing that they have a leader and they are part of a pack.

All dogs have inherited the social pack behavior of the wolf. Specific, complex relationships exist within a pack of wolves. When you understand pack behavior, you realize how important it is for you to form a close relationship with your dog early in the dog's life and become, once and forever, the dog's leader.

A wolf pack consists of a multitiered hierarchy. At the top is always a dominant male and female, known as the Alpha pair. All of the other wolves in the pack are submissive to the Alpha pair. In turn, there are several tiers within the pack below the Alpha pair, with the wolves on each tier in a position of dominance over the wolves in the tiers below.

Wolves by nature band together, have strong family loyalty, and often establish strong bonds with other wolves. They bond together to facilitate hunting for food, protection, raising pups, and companionship. If a wolf is somehow separated from the pack, he will suffer from separation anxiety. A lone wolf is a distressed wolf. Because your dog, Fido, is also a pack animal, Fido feels the same anxiety when you go out, leaving him alone. Because he feels lonely, rejected, and anxious, he will often take his feelings out on your furniture and anything else he can find in the house to destroy. It is very important for you to establish yourself as the dog's leader.

To do this, you need to be kind, firm, consistent, and affectionate all at the same time in your handling of your dog. Do that and your dog will quickly come to accept you as his leader. Again, you need to be affectionate and kind, yet strong and uncompromising, so that your dog will not get mixed signals and will look up to you.

2. DOMINANCE AND SUBMISSION

When I was raising Mariah, it was very enlightening to observe how she interacted with my other dogs. Orph, a huge German Shepherd, was the reigning Alpha male of my pack of dogs. Mariah recognized that he was the Alpha male, and she was submissive to him. In encountering Orph, Mariah would first go down on the ground with her head and ears back, tail down. She would then slowly turn over on her back and expose her belly and neck to him, a submissive and vulnerable position announcing that she wished to be accepted into this pack. Not only was she accepted, but as time went on, Mariah grew, and she became the Alpha female of the pack.

Mariah presented herself to my other animals through body language proclaiming her status as the Alpha female. To appreciate this, just imagine what the other dogs saw and what she was telling them. She stood tall with her tail held high, her ears completely straight, her eyes bright and open, her body radiating confidence, in essence saying, "Here I am. I am the Alpha."

As the Alpha of your family of animals (whether you have one animal or ten), you need to reinforce your leadership role on a regular basis and never allow your dog to prevail in a challenge to your authority. With a wolf pack there is a continuing struggle for dominance. This means that you have to constantly reinforce your leadership role.

A submissive wolf always lowers his body when he meets a more dominant animal. Bear this in mind when you meet a strange dog. If you crouch down in front of him, he may try to dominate you by showing aggression.

3. SOCIALIZATION

The most engaging and endearing trait of the wolf behavior is their socialization. When I lived with my animals in upstate New York, I would often let Mariah, along with all my dogs, play freely within the safe confines of my fenced-in property. This was our special family time, when we played and socialized. Invariably, with the dogs running around in the fields, out of the corner of my eye I'd see Mariah hiding. I would pretend that I did not see her, and she, in turn, thinking I was unaware of her presence, would run up and playfully hurl her body against me like a hockey player throwing a body check. This was a very affectionate game that wolves in packs play. It can best be described as a kind of combination of the children's games of tag and hide-and-seek. Wolves always take time to play, making it an essential part of pack life and their social structure. Dogs today, much like their wolf ancestors, love to play, but they also *need* to play. Indeed, any dog who is kept isolated from canine or human companionship—who never enjoys a game of toss the ball or tug the bone, or experiences the joy of a playful relationship with its owners—will be an unhappy dog. This unhappiness can manifest itself in behavioral problems. For instance, excessive barking or aggression are signs of boredom and discontent. Therefore, interaction with others is crucial.

So you, without even realizing it, are part of this centuries-old wolf pack social structure. In these deceptively ordinary moments—when for example, you play hide-and-seek with your dog—you accommodate your dog's innate drive to socialize. It is through such games that you and your dog truly bond.

4. AGGRESSION

Socialization is fun to experience and observe. Other drives are less endearing, such as the one Mariah exhibited in establishing her position as the Alpha female of the pack. I must say that observing her aggression was upsetting to me. I had in my family of dogs a female Doberman Pinscher named Sweepea. When Sweepea went into heat (estrus), Mariah viewed this as a challenge to her. Within a wolf pack, only the Alpha female is allowed to breed. Mariah instinctively became very aggressive to ensure that Sweepea would be an outcast and not a threat to Mariah's position as the Alpha female and to her relationship with Orph, the Alpha male. In trying to rectify the problem, I could not alter Mariah's ingrained aggressive instinct. Therefore, I had to remove the challenge she perceived by removing her need to respond to it. The solution was simple: I had to spay Sweepea.

Still, aggression, as unsettling as it may appear to us, is necessary for a wolf's survival. It helps pack members establish their territory, maintain their rank in the pack hierarchy, protect their food supply, and drive away would-be predators. It is a deeply ingrained instinct. In both wolves and dogs, it is triggered by various causes, such as threats to their territory, food, offspring, and, perhaps most often, fear. But in our socialized world, aggression is unacceptable behavior, and there is absolutely no place for it in the life of a domestic dog. Thus, we need to remove the causes that trigger aggression.

5. TERRITORY

Mariah really took this behavioral trait to an extreme level. This was most evident when I would have all the dogs out for a group playtime in upstate New York. The males would routinely inspect the perimeters of the property—which, with all the fields and woodlands, harbored lots of interesting scents, I'm sure—and mark their territory by urinating, as would the females. Mariah, in order to make sure that everyone understood she was the Alpha, would go and mark every spot previously marked by the dogs. She had to have the last word, and that word was, "I am in charge, and these are the boundaries of my territories."

This aspect of pack life—the need to define and protect territory within which to live, raise pups, or hunt—is very important. In the wild, each wolf must establish its own territory. To survive, the wolves give clear warning to other packs: "This is home—you stay out!" A dog urinates to mark its proprietorship of a neighborhood. In fact, the dog's sense of smell is so acute, it can distinguish one drop of urine in ten thousand gallons of water. (Yet they still stick their heads into the toilet bowl, just to make sure their noses do not deceive them!)

Territorial behavior is also displayed by barking to alert others in the pack that there are intruders, and by using aggression to keep intruders at bay. Sound familiar? A dog exhibits this behavior each time it barks when a stranger approaches its property, or growls if another dog approaches its master or the boundaries of its home territory.

As wolf packs travel through or around their territory, previously laid scents provide them with a detailed set of clues. It's like reading a newspaper. They can immediately tell which individuals have been there before and in what direction other pack members have traveled. They can also detect the presence of a stranger who may have intruded within their borders. Dogs today leave scents so other dogs will smell them and read their messages. Often an owner out walking his dog may be annoyed and frustrated when he sees something off in the distance or is heading to a destination that he thinks his dog will find interesting, but the dog is insisting on sniffing in every nook and cranny. Don't be annoyed and don't get frustrated. Your dog's sense of sight is much less powerful than her extraordinary sense of smell. You find your dog's obsession with sidewalk smells boring, but for your dog, this is the chance to "read" the neighborhood gossip sheet. And don't forget, each new day brings a new edition of *The Territorial Tattler.*

6. FOOD-GUARDING

Normally, wolves' nature is to protect the food they have. They will growl or display aggression to keep an interloper away from the food. In the beginning, whenever my dogs went near Mariah while she was eating, she would growl and bark into the dish and warn them not to go near it. This was not acceptable to me. So, I modified Mariah's behavior by feeding her by hand to convince her that it was not necessary to guard the food. I was there to feed her, and I would never take the food away from her. This gave Mariah a strong sense of security that her food would never be taken away. Eventually, through this behavior modification training, all the animals, including Mariah, respected each other's territories to the point that when they finished eating, they could check one another's food bowls without an aggressive confrontation. With dogs, you must establish a positive atmosphere early on, so the need to guard food never develops.

7. THE CHASE

Mariah and I would frequently go off on long, solitary walks together without my dogs. We enjoyed the companionship, although she would walk a few yards ahead of me. Often, when we were startled by the presence of a rabbit, Mariah would stop dead in her tracks, as would I. Invariably, the rabbit would panic and start running. This flight would trigger in Mariah chase behavior—it automatically kicks in—and instinctively she would take chase after the rabbit. At full speed she would bound, zigzagging through the field after the rabbit, stopping only after the rabbit leaped into a rabbit hole, safely beyond Mariah's reach.

The instinct in wolves and dogs is to chase and pursue anything that runs from them. That is why you should not attempt to run from a strange dog or one you're not sure of, as you may unwittingly be encouraging the dog to chase you. If you stand still, you stop the chase behavior from kicking in. Similarly, a pet dog that is being chased by an unknown person or dog will naturally flee.

8. FLIGHT

One scary moment occurred when Mariah and I were walking in the woods, never imagining that strangers would be there hunting in the off-season. When they began firing their rifles, I was frightened that they might see Mariah, panic, and shoot her. Fortunately, her natural instinct for self-preservation kicked in, and she took flight. It was a case of flight or fight (for survival), and in this case, flight prevailed. You've probably observed this behavior in your dog in response to firecrackers or other loud noises. When a dog is startled by the backfire of a passing car, the first thing he does is try to flee. That is why, no matter how well-trained your dog is, it is imperative to keep your dog on a leash when cars are nearby. Even the best-trained dog may panic and flee right into an oncoming car.

9. VOCALIZATION

To my mind, a truly awesome behavior characteristic of wolves that Mariah demonstrated is howling. People always think that wolves only howl at the moon. In reality, the wolf is howling to call and locate the members of its social pack. That is why Jack London's book was called *The Call of the Wild* and not *Howling at the Moon*. The lone wolf is howling *"Where are yoouuuuu?"* and the pack howls back to the lone wolf, *"Here we aaarrrrreee!"*

I find this to be one of the most endearing and amusing behavioral characteristics of wolves. Upstate where Mariah and I lived, most people had crowing roosters waking them up. I had a howling wolf. Mariah was my alarm clock. Her howl was the most beautiful sound you could ever imagine. It was her way of communicating to me that she wanted to start her day. "Where was I?" she wanted to know. Although I didn't return a corresponding howl, I did go to her, assure her of my presence, tell her what a good girl she was, and then begin our morning ritual. I would let her loose, and together we would walk in the woods. This gave her social contact, a chance to play and to partake of our pack ritual. I have often seen this behavior in dogs. When left alone they will howl, telling you to come back and socialize with them. It is instinctive for dogs to want to communicate with other dogs. Dogs that are left alone outside, in particular, may find the need to find another canine to "talk" to, or just to vocalize, "Here I am. Where are you? I'm all alone!"

The Four Basic Steps of On-Leash Training

These four steps will give you the "edge," the "director's edge" that you, as your dog's director, need in order to bring out the best possible performance from your StarPet. Just as my client actor/director Ron Howard receives accolades from Tom Hanks and other major stars he has directed because, having been an actor, he, as a director, has a special understanding of the actor, so you, as your dog's person, know and understand your dog better than any other director. And, as Howard can think like the actor he is directing, so you must think like the dog you are directing.

So, to give you, your dog's director, the "edge" you need, you must first know how to give clear direction.

1. Focus. Get your dog's undivided attention.

2. Command. Let your body language and verbal commands tell your dog exactly what you expect of him.

3. Response. Look for an action response from your dog that is consistent with the command given.

4. Praise or Correction. Give the reward of lavish praise when your dog has done what you ask of him and a quick, clear correction when he's refused or just hasn't understood the command, followed by praise when he finally gets it right. But when your dog doesn't get it right the first time, check yourself carefully to be sure your commands are clear and concise. You'll see that "correction" is not synonymous with "punishment." That's not a word in my training vocabulary. Punishment creates a fearful dog and completely destroys any chances of a close dog/actor, owner/director relationship. Correction is simply a clear corrective action that shows the behavior is not acceptable and won't be tolerated.

STEP 1: FOCUS

Listening—you to your dog, he to you—is the key to the relatively new art of StarPets! And, since the dog is our *oldest* costar, he *wants* to take his cue from you, but you have to know how to direct him!

Within the wolf pack, all other pack members focus on the Alpha, attentively awaiting his command. Now it's up to you, the owner, to assume Alpha authority and convey your wishes to your dog in a clearly articulated way. Before you give the first training command, get your dog's complete and undivided attention focused on you and you alone. Call his name, clap your hands or thigh, give a whistle, or make strange noises—anything that makes him prick up his ears in the now-familiar alert position that tells you he's listening. The presence and use of the control collar and leash will reinforce his expectation that something new and exciting is about to happen.

STEP 2: COMMAND

Nature has programmed your dog to expect visual signals, the body language of the wolf pack that communicates not only your commands but your authority and reliability as well. Your dog's genetic heritage also has given him finely tuned hearing that makes him respond to clearly spoken verbal commands, the human equivalent of the Alpha wolf's short, sharp bark that says, "Follow me." Both are equally important elements in training and acting.

The cardinal rule is: Keep your commands simple, short, and clear. Short, easy words such as Heel, Sit, Stay are the basic language/script of obedience training. Don't use your dog's name; it dilutes the impact (plus, you don't know what the name of your dog's character may be in the script). And, when accompanied by reinforcing signals (cues), an upward hand gesture for "Sit," a hand flashed before the dog's eyes for "Stay," or a pat on the thigh to accompany the word "Heel," these words tell your dog exactly what behavior is expected of him.

STEP 3: RESPONSE

Use simultaneous verbal commands and clearly displayed gestures that get a response from your dog. Whether you get a correct or incorrect response may depend as much on you as on your dog. If your messages are mixed, your commands unclear, or your gestures muddled, don't be surprised if the dog doesn't get it. Always keep in mind the clarity of wolf language. Within the wolf pack, gestures and vocalizations are unmistakable. Your own commands and gestures must be equally easy to read so that your dog knows your intentions beyond any doubt. If he doesn't understand the command, he can't respond correctly, and his correct response always should be appropriate to your command. If you say, "Sit," using the correct accompanying gestures and the right signals with the leash and collar, sit is what he must do. Your job is to repeat the exercise, with verbal commands and gestures, until the right response comes, always praising your dog when he is right, but correcting him when he is wrong.

STEP 4: PRAISE

Praise, in my opinion, is the most important reward any dog can receive. Dogs just love to make you happy, and when you shower them with praise, they know they've done their job and done it well. Besides, there's no better reinforcement for establishing a lifetime of perfect responsive behavior than consistent praise for a job well done. It makes your dog eager to learn more and helps him remember the lessons longer. Praise is also important in building your dog's confidence, and phrases like "good dog" let him know he's done a good job. Plus, on the set of a film, or backstage at a theatrical production, crews will be working—prop men, electricians, stage managers, and so forth—and they may, quite literally, be barking out commands! That sort of distraction is a given in the industry, and nothing should distract your dog from his work. It is also important that your dog understand that the loud commands or negativity from other professionals on the set are not directed at him. This is why keeping him focused and praising him for a job well done are so important.

OR, CORRECTION FOLLOWED BY PRAISE

When your dog is a working professional, time is money, and both cast and crew must work together within the strict constraints of the shooting schedule. Therefore, as with any actor, it is very important that your dog respond promptly, and, ideally, on the first take.

How do you correct your dog when he refuses to carry out your command?

With tough love, keeping the emphasis on love. You must establish beyond any doubt your position as Alpha leader by correcting undesirable behavior swiftly and with clear commands and gestures. Here, timing is everything. A sharp "No!" accompanied by a quick correction of the leash and collar will show your dog that his behavior was unacceptable. Repeat the command and the gestures. When your dog responds correctly, take the time to praise him lavishly. Your dog will be happier, and an abundance of love won't spoil your dog. He'll be happier, and anxious to please, to finish the scene on the first take. And the strength of the praise should outweigh the correction.

BUT NEVER PUNISHMENT

A responsible Alpha leader never hits a dog. Striking a dog constitutes punishment, not correction, and far too many well-meaning people confuse the two. Hitting a dog will only make the animal "shut down" and become fearful of you and unresponsive to your commands. Even worse, it destroys the essential bond of trust that creates a strong and loving relationship between a dog and its master—the bond that lets the two of you work as a team, as actor/director, "the arc," is broken. Striking or yelling at your dog can show him he's been "bad," but it cannot teach him where he's gone wrong and therefore is worthless as a teaching tool. The only thing your dog will learn from that kind of punishment is to fear you and dread the training process. The wise, strong Alpha leader knows how to demonstrate, through tough love, that objectionable behavior won't be tolerated, but will be corrected promptly and in a positive way.

Motivation

For personal training, the **three P's, Patience, Persistence, and Praise,** are the best way to teach a dog the difference between good habits and bad behavior patterns. When you train a dog, you ask the dog to respond to a command, the dog does it, you reward him, praise him, and it's over. But in the professional world, the world of show business, more will be asked and expected of your dog. We may ask him to do a couple of takes—or fifteen, even! And, even if your dog is performing his stunt beautifully, more takes may be required for the technical crew—for sound checks or lighting checks. Or maybe a human actor flubbed his lines! But, whatever the reason, oftentimes the professional dog, despite a perfect performance, is asked to give another take.

Now the dog is puzzled. "I did a good job. Why do I have to do it again?" And this is where you, as the owner/handler/coach/director, have to tell him, "You didn't do anything wrong. Let's do it again."

For professional motivation, praise is not always enough. And you have to find the extra motivation that will motivate your Star-Pet when he is working.

FOOD REWARD

Sometimes the motivation is a food reward. You are telling your dog, "I know you're tired because I've asked you to do it once or twice, but I need that look that is fresh and perky—as if it were the first take. Therefore, I'm going to give you this treat to do the action again!"

In general, I am against using food rewards as a training tool with dogs, especially in basic training. A dog can be too distracted to pay attention to food, or decide that he isn't hungry. Also, food is not allowed in obedience competition or field trials.

However, as with all rules, there are certain exceptions. In dog shows, for conformation *only* (not obedience or field trials), handlers often hold a food treat in one hand. It serves as a focus point so the dog will appear alert and calm as it looks at the hand that's holding the treat.

For print work, food reward can help your dog to focus, and to hold alert positions and expressions. This also works well for commercials. For instance, on one occasion, my dog Muffin was taping a TV commercial and had done a scene ten times. He had performed perfectly, but each time something had gone wrong—

the lighting was off, a camera broke, an actor missed his cue, and so forth. At that point, the director said, "OK, I need two more takes." Muffin was worn out, and his attention span had been exhausted. The only way to perk him up for two more takes was to give him a nice food treat, which brought his energy level back up. Another time food is used in show business is when we want a dog to act as if he belongs to an actor and really loves him. The dog may never have seen the actor before, but if the actor has an especially wonderful food treat in his pocket, the animal will look up at him expectantly and beseechingly as if they were best friends.

CLICKER TRAINING

During training, I use a "clicker" as a sound motivator. The clicker is a simple child's toy, about the size of a car key. It can be plastic or metal, and "clicks" when pressed between your thumb and forefinger. If the dog performs well, I give a click to confirm that he performed well, and then I follow up immediately with a treat. When it's not possible to give him a reward at the exact instant he performs the stunt, the sound of the clicker is a promise that he will get his treat as soon as possible, but, in the meantime, it signals, "That's great, but keep on going!"

Props

Just as a human actor's body is his instrument, so, too, is an animal actor's. And, just as a human actor often uses props, so, too, does an animal actor. And, with the dog star, these same props help to train the animal actor to implement the action—and acting—the script may call for.

There are two pieces of equipment you will need in order to train your dog: a collar and a leash. If two dogs each have a collar and leash, why does one dog perform flawlessly, while the other has a hard time? The answer lies in the proper equipment. Just like the tools of any trade, these accessories have become pretty much standardized over the years, and can be purchased in any pet-supply store. Still, one has to be educated in the use as well as the application. Some are for training, some are for show, some are for restraint, and some are just for everyday use.

THE COLLAR

Training collars come in many forms. Those most frequently used are made of woven nylon, rolled leather, or flat metal chain links. Each type comes in varying widths and strengths for dogs of different sizes. Chain-link collars provide very good control. They are strong and the links make a distinctive metallic "clicking" sound as they move together when the collar is tightened. This sound can be an additional training aid for some dogs and serve as a reinforcement for a command. (For future advanced film work training, which we'll discuss later, this sound somewhat mimics the clicking in clicker training.)

At this time, it's important to mention that the traditional buckle collar is *not* a training collar. It doesn't allow for the reinforcement of proper behavior, and an untrained dog can easily slip out of this kind of collar. The buckle collar is best used with a well-trained dog, and as a "costume or prop" for theatrical work.

There are also collars on the market with studs and prongs that restrain a dog with pressure on its neck. These should only be used in special circumstances and are not recommended for the average dog. Collars that give electric shocks to a dog are sometimes used for training. These devices should only be used under the direct supervision of a veterinarian or a certified animal behaviorist. And don't forget, the aim here is to accomplish off-leash training for advanced agility/stunt work and television and film work.

Also, sometimes you'll hear that a harness should be used instead of a collar. This is nonsense. You cannot give a dog directions with a harness—it's useless as a training device.

Another "collar" that has gotten a lot of attention recently is the "halty," which looks like a harness/muzzle that fits around the dog's head, and is used much like a halter that leads a cow or horse. Many people gravitate to this device in search of a quick training fix. Unfortunately, there is no such thing as a quick fix. The dog won't really be trained. If you want your dog to be a StarPet, you'll have to give up this device, and use the proper training collar.

Whichever kind of collar you choose, it must fit securely. If it has too much slack, the dangling end can catch on things and be a hazard. Conversely, if it's too tight, there'll be no give to work with. To determine the right size, measure your dog's neck about halfway between his head and shoulders and add two to three inches (or the width of four fingers). Dog collars usually come in even-numbered sizes, so if you have to err, do so on the large size.

How to Put On a Training Collar

These collars are, in my opinion, the essential training tool. Used correctly, the tighten/release mechanism sends an immediate and clear message to the dog about his behavior. If he pulls, the collar will tighten; when he stops pulling and walks calmly, the collar loosens comfortably.

To a novice, figuring out the collar can be puzzling. It appears to be one long chain with two larger rings at either end.

1. The trick here is to hold one ring in each hand, one above the other.

2. Feed the top end of the chain down through the lower ring, as if you were threading a needle. This will form a loop.

3. Hold the collar in front of you with the dangling tail end of the chain and ring combining with the upper loop to form a P. As I like to say, the way to remember this is that the P stands for my three key training words, Patience, Persistence, and Praise.

4. Then, have the dog sit or stand, facing you. Hold the collar so it forms a P. The "tail" will dangle to the *left*. Place the "loop" of the collar over your dog's head, so the dangling "tail" will hang to the *right* side of your dog's neck. (This is important because, during training, your dog will work from your left side.)

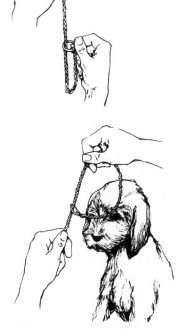

★ To use the control collar, thread the chain down through the ring to form a P. ★

The collar should slide easily up and down whenever you pull or release the leash. If it doesn't, but locks in place without releasing, you've probably put the collar on backward. You've made a Q instead of a P. With a Q, the collar will tighten when you make a correction, but stays locked and won't release. You can remember this by thinking Quit it. Start over. Remove the collar, turn it around to a P, and start again.

Remember, the secret of the training collar's success lies in the tighten/release motion.

THE LEASH

I always advise using a six-foot leash, whether you have a large dog or a small dog. The leash can be leather, nylon, or webbed cotton. All are durable. The six-foot length gives you the option of holding the dog close for on-leash control or giving the dog six feet of slack for more advanced training. Later on, as your dog progresses in his training, you'll need an even longer lead to use as a check-cord while you give your dog signals from farther and farther away in preparation for off-lead work.

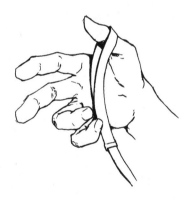

How to Hold a Training Leash

Just as there is a correct way to use a training collar, there is a correct way to use a training lead so that you can communicate well with your dog and achieve proper control.

★ The proper way to grasp the leash handle: Hook the loop over the thumb and clasp the leash. ★

People often ask me why the dog must always be on the trainer's left side. This is simply part of the standardized structure of training and communication, just as mounting a horse from the left-hand side is. I have a theory that this practice stems originally from hunting. When the first dogs hunted at the side of early man, the man held his spear in his right hand. When the game was spotted, the dog would circle around to the left side and drive the quarry toward the hunter's upraised spear. Later, when guns were developed, they were always held in a hunter's right hand while the bird dog walked on the left—same results when the dog flushed out game. So, when police and military canine work came along, the same way of handling dogs was adopted. Weapons are carried on the right-hand side, and dogs walk on their handlers' left. Seeing-eye dogs also work on the left, leaving their owners' right hands free.

By the way, this way of working can be easily adapted by a left-handed person. With the dog on his left side, and holding the leash in his right hand, the left-handed person can readily use his left hand for correction and his right hand to signal commands.

Basic Training

Training is a synchronization of words, sound, and body language. Each command, gesture, and sound must be simultaneous and clear. This is equally important for the tail end of the command—the praise—as it is for the command itself.

Therefore, when the performance is correctly completed, wait a beat—give your dog a chance to hold the pose and focus on the moment, as they say in acting—before praising your dog. This wait of the beat will give your dog the understanding that the job isn't over until the fat lady sings! Seriously, if you praise your dog too soon after he completes the command, he'll lose his focus, his control, his understanding of what is expected of him. You don't want to send mixed messages.

SIT

Since every exercise begins from a Sit position, naturally your first command will be Sit. The Sit command consists of an upward scoop of your right hand. Initially, a dog will probably need a little help from you in order to interpret this command. While you give the motion and say "Sit," pull upward sharply on the leash with your left hand. This causes your dog's head to go up and forces him to sit. Initially, you may have to reinforce the command by switching the leash to your right hand and using your left hand to push the dog's hindquarters into a sitting position, while simultaneously continuing

★ The Sit command, given with an upward gesture of the right hand. ★

to pull the leash upward to ease him into the sitting position.

When the exercise is complete, praise your dog lavishly for a job well done.

STAY

Now that your dog is sitting at your (left) side, it's important that he learn to stay until you tell him to move.

Dropping the leash from your left hand, lean slightly forward

and flash your open hand downward in front of the dog's face. This is a clear signal that says, "Don't move." Now, step forward with your *right* foot, making a half-turn to the left, so you are now facing your dog head-on. This places you directly in front of your dog. As you face him, repeat the command, "Stay," and step backward to half the length of the leash (approximately three feet from your dog: Later, you'll progress to the entire six feet). At this point, repeat the Stay command and pause in position. Here comes the hard

★ The Stay command, left hand flashed in front of the dog's face. ★

part. *Do not praise your dog yet!* Yes, I know he deserves it and I also know how proud you must be. But for a dog, praise signals the end of the training session and time to move on. *He must not move until the entire exercise is complete.* Now, walk back to your dog's right side (which places him correctly at your left), putting the two of you, in alignment, facing forward.

Congratulations! Now you've accomplished the two basic demands for print work: Sit and Stay!

HEEL

The Heel command tells your dog, "Walk by my side, at my pace." A well-trained dog should walk at your heel, whether the pace is quick or slow, whether you turn to left or right.

To begin, place your dog in the Sit position on your left side. Now, slapping your left thigh with your hand to get your dog's attention, step forward with your *left* foot, while giving a simultaneous verbal command, "Heel." Your dog, with his hypersensitive peripheral vision, sees your left leg moving, feels a tug on the leash, and hears the word Heel. It's a clear signal that it's time to follow the Alpha leader.

As you and your dog walk together, you should be in perfect sync. If you aren't, it's time to exercise your right of control. Continue to give short, almost imperceptible tugs on the leash to keep your dog in step with you. He must learn to walk at *your* pace, speeding up when you do, slowing down as your pace slows.

After you've walked a short distance, halt, and with a right-hand upward gesture, say, "Sit." Give your dog only three to five

★ The Heel command, given by slapping the thigh
and stepping out with the left foot. ★

seconds to respond. If he doesn't, give a short jerk of the leash, accompanied by a firm "No!" and repeat the gesture and verbal command for Sit. When the dog sits, praise him lavishly.

RIGHT-U-TURN (RIGHT ABOUT)

As your dog is heeling nicely by your side, take up the slack on the leash and make a "U-turn" toward your right. Lead into the turn with your *left* foot and slap your left thigh to get his attention to follow, while giving the verbal command, "Heel." Because your dog's path will follow the wider, *outside* turn, he may need a tug of the leash to encourage him to pick up his pace to remain at your side.

LEFT-U-TURN (LEFT ABOUT)

In a left U-turn, you will be turning *into* your dog. You will have the wider, *outside* path, he will have the shorter, *inner* turn. To do this, you must hold your dog's leash close at your left side with your left elbow slightly back to slow your dog's pace. Pivot your right foot over your left while verbally commanding, "Heel." This simultaneous combination of the pivoting right foot, the checking of the leash, and the verbal command tells your dog to make a left U-turn.

DOWN

The Down exercise is one of the most important in a dog's repertoire.

With your dog sitting at your left side, give the verbal command Down, while making an exaggerated downward motion with your left hand, palm facing the ground. At the same time, with your right hand, grasp the leash as close as possible to the collar, under your dog's chin. Gently pull the leash downward, guiding him to lie down.

To help your dog understand the command, continue to guide the

★ The Down command, gestured with the left hand. If the dog says "No!" a slight push on his shoulders does the job. ★

leash with your right hand and, with your left hand, apply gentle pressure on your dog's shoulder to urge him downward.

When your dog is in the correct Down position, pass your left hand in front of his eyes, and give the command to Stay. Pause for a moment, then praise him lavishly.

Congratulations! You just accomplished the second most important exercise for print work.

★ The Down/Stay command, given with the left hand. ★

But unless *you* plan on being in the picture yourself, it's important to train your dog to stay put as you walk out of camera range.

So, with your dog in the Down position, pass your left hand in front of his eyes *again,* then swivel on your right foot to face your dog, exactly as you did in the Sit/Stay exercise, repeat the verbal command, "Stay," and walk backward a few feet out of camera range.

Pause and return to your dog. Wait a moment—have him hold the Down/Stay—then praise him lavishly for his great accomplishment. What a good dog!

★ The Down/Stay command from a distance. ★

FROM DOWN TO SIT

Once you've trained your dog to hold the Down/Stay, you want to make your dog Sit from the Down position.

With your dog in the Down/Stay position, you slap your left thigh (the original signal for pay attention). As your dog looks up (thinking you're going somewhere—"Where are

★ To make your dog sit from a Down position, gesture upward with the right hand. ★

we going? Are we going somewhere?"), make an exaggerated upward gesture with your right hand, and simultaneously give the command to Sit and Stay.

If necessary, you might guide your dog with a gentle upward tug of the leash to ease him into a sitting position.

Pause for a moment to keep your dog focused, then praise him lavishly.

COME

"Come" is one of the most important commands you can teach your StarPet. It brings your dog to you when you call. The prompt response of your dog to the Come

★ Give the command to Sit. ★

command can be vital to his safety, whether he's at home, on location for a film, or on a soundstage.

To begin this exercise, place the dog in a Sit position and ask him to stay. Turn and walk backward till you've reached the end of the six-foot leash. Still holding the leash with your left hand, sweep your right arm toward your chest in an exaggerated beckoning gesture, slapping your chest. At the same time, using your dog's name, give the Come command. Lassie, Come! This command should be given with great excitement and enthusiasm. Coming to you should be a happy moment for your dog, not a fearful one, and will ensure the success of this command. With the verbal command, simultaneously pull the leash toward you to reinforce Come.

When your dog responds correctly by coming when called, .have him sit facing you. Pause, then praise your dog enthusiastically.

Eventually, your aim is to leave your dog with the Stay command and go to the length of a twenty-foot leash, so as to extend his threshold of distance for the Come command.

★ Finish with the Sit/Stay command. ★

★ For the Come command, sweep your arm in an exaggerated gesture toward your chest. ★

COME TO HEEL

As a finale to the previous Come exercise, you now will teach your dog to "Come to Heel." Historically, this command was used by shepherds with their herding dogs. The dog starts at his left side, he commands his dog to go out and bring the sheep in to the designated area, then to come back to his left side, the original starting position. This was the dog's cue, position, to be ready to begin again.

For sporting breeds, the retriever sits at the left side of the hunter, waiting for the command to retrieve game from the fields, retrieves the game, and, to the front of the hunter, places the game in his hand, and comes around to his left side, awaiting the next Retrieve command.

In obedience and police work, the dog is taught to Come, sit facing the handler, then Come about to the left side, to wait for the command to begin again.

Come to Heel tells your dog to come around your body to the traditional left-side starting position. Begin this exercise with your dog sitting, facing you.

★ Ask the dog to Come to Heel and bring him around to your right side . . . to the correct left-side starting position. ★

Holding the leash in your right hand, give a slight tug on the leash while simultaneously stepping back with your right foot. Stepping back with your right foot signals the dog to come toward you and follow, in close heel, to the right and around you. As the dog walks around behind you, smoothly switch the leash to your left hand. Continue, with your left hand holding the leash, to guide your dog around to your left side.

When your dog is standing in place, his shoulder in line with your leg, give the command to Sit, with the accompanying upward motion of your hand. Pause, then give your dog all the lavish praise he deserves for the great job he's done.

GO TO YOUR PLACE

This command is one of the most important for establishing a good working relationship with your dog, at home, in the office, or on the set. It lets you command your dog to go to his own place—his bed, his crate, any place in each room you've designated as his—and stay there, out from underfoot.

Select a special place your dog likes—his bed, a corner of the room, that warm spot next to the heater. Then, with the collar and leash in position, and your dog sitting or standing at your left side, command Go to Your Place while simultaneously pointing to that place and walking him to it at heel.

When you've arrived at the designated spot, give the Down/Stay command and walk away.

If your dog moves or breaks your command, catch him in the act, give him a quick, forceful No, and repeat the Go to Your Place command while leading him to his place. When he is back at his place, repeat Down/Stay. Once again, facing your dog, back away from him. After a moment, return to your dog, and give the Sit command. After a moment, praise him lavishly for doing exactly as you asked.

After your dog has mastered this exercise, and you are indoors, now is the time to practice this exercise off-leash. Once you have your dog in his place in the proper Down/Stay position, while you are facing him, drop the leash and slowly move backward. Pause for several beats and return to his side. Have him Sit. Pause again, and praise him lavishly.

If practice makes perfect, you can accomplish this without a leash in the safety of your home. Once your dog can do this off-leash, try leaving your dog at his place, while you go to another room out of his sight. Begin with thirty seconds, then progress in increments, ultimately leaving him alone for three to five minutes.

Again, when you return to your dog, give him extra praise and attention!

GO TO YOUR MARK

This exercise is designed for use at the advanced training level, but it's important to learn it now, so it becomes a basic part of your dog's repertoire.

On a soundstage, or theatrical stage, the "Mark" is the exact position given to an actor to ensure that he is in the proper light and camera angle. Marks are generally marked on the stage with tape or chalk.

In this case, we get a white cardboard, approximately eight by ten (roughly the size of a head shot and résumé!), take black duct tape or magic marker, and make a large X. Then, for wear and tear, have it laminated. Now you've created a mobile mark, which you can take or toss anywhere, for training your dog to Go to Your Mark.

To do this, place the mark on the floor approximately eight feet from your dog. Command your dog to Go to Your Mark! Then, on-leash, walk your dog to the mark.

When you've reached the mark, give your dog the Sit/Stay command. At that time, back away from your dog out of camera range. If you are indoors, and your dog is responding well, now would be a good time to drop the leash, in anticipation of future off-leash work. This is a good try-out. Either way, pause for a beat, and praise him lavishly for a job well done.

Eventually, your aim is to have your dog, off-leash, go to his mark on cue, then turn around and, facing you (out of camera range), Stand/Stay, Sit/Stay, or Lie Down/Stay, waiting for his next command.

Rin Tin Tin was a master at the fine art of meeting his mark—and more! Just as the director would block out the action for the human actors in the scene (they would follow their chalk marks like a road map), so would Rinty. Rinty's trainer, Lee Duncan, would draw chalk marks on the floor indicating his stunts, sometimes up to four or five separate moves or actions, and Rinty would follow them perfectly!

PLAYTIME

Larry Trimble always said that any dog that can play is a dog that can be taught. That is certainly true, and, for StarPets, I take that one step further, with the StarPet "credo": Always Keep the Play in Play-Acting.

In the beginning, with basic training, after each session or lesson you should add a period of playtime, which shouldn't last more than about fifteen minutes, because their threshold of attention is limited. As you progress, it can be better, but for now, fifteen minutes is a good guide. You want to always leave the session on a happy note, so you want to always follow up the lesson with a playtime, so the dog enjoys and looks forward to the lessons.

Postsession playtime lets both of you loosen up from the rigorous work of training. After all, learning a lesson and teaching one require equal concentration and are equally demanding. Relaxing and having a bit of fun will end the session happily for both of you. Being silly together, chasing and being chased, stalking each other, playing hide-and-seek—these are the games that are an integral part of your dogs' ancestry, the wolf games that wolves play with each other each and every single day. Since such play is a vital part of wolf society, it's natural that it's equally important to the wolf's descendant, your dog. Tossing a ball or a toy for your dog to retrieve is a great release of energies that have been under tight control during the training session. Now the focus is off, the fun is on. While you're at it, you have a perfect opportunity to teach your dog to fetch the ball or to drop it at your feet. This is training without the structure, a lesson your dog won't even realize he's learning.

Play sessions also can be used to promote agility. Catching a ball midfly, jumping over hurdles, going through tunnels, walking a seesaw, all develop the dog's reflexes, his muscles, and his agility. Equally important, exercises such as these depend to a great degree on the dog's trust in you. If you lead him safely from one end of a seesaw to another, he knows he can rely on you not to get him into dangerous situations. At the same time, he's learning to trust his own abilities. Play of this sort is obedience in action, a joyous release of spirit that tells your dog this doing-what-I'm-told stuff is fun! And *that* is the best way to learn.

In time, as you practice and become proficient in these exercises, you'll experience a unique synergy with your dog—the same kind of spiritual oneness I found with my wolf, Mariah. You will have created a foundation of perfect trust and love, communication that reaches beyond the words of human language, and a spiritual bond that links the human and animal worlds in telepathic harmony.

It's been said that the only way to get to Carnegie Hall is to practice, practice, practice! When you have done this, and you are beautifully in sync with your dog, then it is time to test your dog's ability to communicate his talents to those all-important people around him: casting directors, directors, producers, and—ultimately—his audience!

The StarPet Test is a level of evaluation I have developed and used throughout my career to assess the ability of an aspiring animal actor.

Dogs that may be trained for print work, commercials, television, and film have all met or exceeded this standard—whether they were my own StarPets, the pets of clients, or those chosen from my open casting calls and StarPet Workshops. In fact, it was this test that gave many of the wonderful dogs I later cast for *Dogue* and *Vanity Fur* their first chance to shine!

So think of this test as a kind of dress rehearsal—a sort of "first audition" or "out of town" tryout. If you can ace this test, you will know that your dog has what it takes to continue to the next chapter, Advanced StarDog Training—and may be well on his way to becoming a professional StarPet!

But before you take this test, I need you to review and practice everything you have learned. And if you should "fail," don't worry! The way to Carnegie Hall is to practice—and "practice makes perfect." Remember, even the greatest movie stars need more than one "take" to get it right!

StarPet Test for Dogs

A. Your dog must be up-to-date with his inoculations and have a current dog license.

1. Your dog must be checked by a certified veterinarian to determine that your dog is in good physical and mental health; is well mannered and not aggressive. A checkup that finds your dog healthy and physically sound will ensure that he does not harbor a condition that could become a problem in training (such as deafness or dysplasia).

2. Your dog must be properly groomed. Proper grooming helps a dog maintain a basic level of good health and contributes to a dog's sense of well-being. While your veterinarian can certify that your dog has no medical condition to impede his ability to perform, you or your groomer can make certain that your dog has no other condition that could impair his performance. Make sure your dog's nails are regularly clipped, as well as the fur around his pads. Overgrown nails and fur can make for sore, tender pads, and a dog unwilling or unable to participate in training. Make sure that your dog's ears are clean, and his eyes clear and free from overgrown hair, which may obstruct his vision and his ability to respond to commands.

B. Your dog must show his obedience skills on- and off-leash. You must teach him:

1. To Sit on command, by using voice and/or hand signal.

2. To Stay on command, by using voice and/or hand signal from a distance of six to ten feet away for a minute or more.

3. To Lie Down on command, by using voice and/or hand signal from a distance of six to ten feet away, and stay down for a minute or more.

4. To Come on command, by using voice and/or hand signal from a distance of six to ten feet away or more, and to Sit in front of you calmly until the exercise is finished.

5. To Remain, at your command, with a designated person, while you step out of his sight. Remain out of sight for a minute or two, then go back to your dog. Your dog should remain calm and well-mannered during the separation, as well as upon your return.

C. Your dog, with proper control, is to respond calmly and appropriately to all your commands, in an unpredictable environment. These commands may exceed—but must include—the commands in part B of this test. You must teach him:

1. To respond to your commands while in the company of a group of people.

2. To respond to your commands while in the company of one or more dogs.

3. To respond to your commands while large objects or equipment are being moved near and around him. (You have to be inventive here. A hand truck, a dolly, or even a child's wagon can help you simulate production equipment on a soundstage. Even a simple broom held high overhead can sub for a microphone boom.)

4. To respond to your commands despite distracting noises: bells, whistles, the clapping hands of an audience, or the sharp clap of the film's clapboard.

5. To respond to your commands during photo flashes or strobe lights. This is important during a photo shoot or a walk on the red carpet!

Congratulations!

Now that your dog has passed the StarPet test, he is qualified to receive the StarPet Certificate of Achievement, which is awarded to all my workshop graduates. (To learn more about the Certificate of Achievement, go to www.starpet.com.)

Think of this certificate as a StarPet "Actors' Equity" card, which recognizes that your dog has demonstrated that he has reached the level of ability of a basic, working professional. He could work in advertising with print work or television commercials—even be a spokesdog for a commercial product, or in representing a special event, group, charity, or business. Or, if your StarPet prefers more personal contact with his audience ("the smell of the greasepaint, the roar of the crowd!"), there is, of course, the theater, both community and professional.

And, if your pet prefers more intimate, one-on-one work, there is the important and satisfying world of pet therapy. When your dog passes the StarPet test, he demonstrates that his abilities have put him in the league of dogs qualified to participate in a pet therapy training program, making him eligible to be certified as a pet therapy dog.

I find, however, that StarPets, like so many of their *human* star counterparts, find a great deal of satisfaction working in *both* fields!

So, with stardom waiting in the wings, the following training, the advanced training, will take you and your StarPet a little closer to the stage door.

CHAPTER FIVE

Advanced StarDog Training

Now that you have mastered the StarPet test—your first "audition" really—you and your dog are ready for advanced, off-leash work. If you followed the steps of on-leash training outlined in the preceding pages, you will realize that your dog is doing so well, and responding to all your commands in such an eager and responsive way, that he is on the threshold of working off-leash, and off-leash training is a requirement for advanced theatrical work.

You've experienced working with a twenty-foot lead in some of the preceding exercises, and now it's time to advance to the next level. Here, you'll find that your dog listens to your voice commands, and his listening to you will, if effective, act as a kind of invisible, mental leash.

Basically, your voice substitutes for the control of the leash. And your body language, hand signals, cues, all supplement and reinforce your voice control.

In addition to using your voice, you will use a great deal of body language to signal your dog from a distance. I call this out-of-frame work, because the dog is performing on-camera, re-

sponding to cues from his handler, who is out of the frame, out of
camera range.

First, I must emphasize that you always work with your dog in
a safe location—in the house or in a fenced-in yard. Also, in the
beginning, you should work in a place with no distractions until
you're sure that your dog understands what's wanted. Later on
you'll need to introduce lots of distractions to test your dog.

STEP 1: THE NO-LEASH ILLUSION

As contrary as it sounds, the first step in preparing for off-leash
work is to attach the leash to your dog's collar. The trick here is

to convince the dog that you are not using the leash. The way to do this is to drape the leash around your neck like a scarf. Since your dog is on your left, the leash should drape from your left to right shoulder, with the handle dangling down in front of your right shoulder, so it's within easy reach of your hand, if necessary to use.

With the leash in this position, practice Heel/Sit/Stay, and walk with the dog in Heel position for a long time—several minutes to start.

Do not give any leash correction unless absolutely necessary.

All commands should be given by voice and body signals *only*. Work until your dog walks in perfect Heel position without any correction or reminder for at least five minutes at a time.

Again, let him know he's a very good dog and praise him lavishly.

STEP 2: THE THREAD TEST

Once your dog responds well while working without feeling the leash, you can begin to test it to find out if he really is reliable enough to begin to work without any leash at all. I'm a firm believer in making sure. Don't take any shortcuts in this respect.

For this test, attach a foot-long piece of lightweight, easily broken string to the clasp of your dog's leash and tie the other end of the string to his collar.

Then, go through all of the heeling and turning paces he's already learned, with this thread leash.

If your dog goes through the entire routine without snapping the string, you'll know he's so responsive that he could easily perform the entire routine off-leash.

STEP 3: THE LOOP LEASH

The next phase of off-leash training is a loop leash.

Do not attach the leash to the collar. Instead, slip one end of the leash under your dog's collar and pull it through, bringing it up so both ends of the leash are even and you can hold them in one hand (your left hand). You'll have both the handle and the clasp ends of the leash in your hand.

Have your dog at the Sit position (your left side) and give the command to Heel. As you begin walking, let one end of the looped leash slip through the collar, while you hold the other end, and let the rest of the leash dangle by your side in front of the dog's face.

The leash is now no longer attached to the collar. You may have to take up any slack in your hand, so it doesn't trail on the ground. Continue walking and let the leash hang next to you while the dog goes through his paces.

As you do this, your dog retains the illusion that he is still attached to the leash. In fact, however, you are testing your dog's responsiveness.

Again, praise him lavishly for doing such a good job.

STEP 4: THE LEASH HANDLE

If your dog has done well with the preceding steps, you can be pretty sure he's in good control when off-leash.

To be perfectly sure, however, I use what I call a leash handle for a while. Most pet supply stores carry some variation of this in stores or online. Or you can fashion one quite easily on your own. Simply take a short length of strong, lightweight rope (it could be nylon or canvas) and form it into a looped handle that you can slip

★ Jolie holds a one-hundred-dollar bill in her mouth. ★
COURTESY MERUET DIBRA

through your dog's collar. Tie the two ends together in a secure knot, and voilà!—you have a leash handle.

The beauty of this leash handle is that the dog cannot see or feel the loop hanging from his collar. In his mind, he's off-leash, and you have peace of mind knowing that you can gain control at any moment.

Put him through his paces, and praise him lavishly when he does a good job.

Basic Off-Leash Commands

There are two basic off-leash commands that must become second nature for the professional StarPet. These are Stand/Stay and Stand/Stay from Sit or Down position.

STAND/STAY

This is an important off-leash command for everyday use, but especially for theatrical work. It's designed for traditional show use (conformation), where the dog must stand calm and still while the judge examines him. This also works well for veterinarian exams, as well as for the groomer. Especially for theatrical work, we want a dog to stand at a specific place (meet his mark) for the camera, for the right lighting, for camera focus, and for blocking with another actor. Also, the Stand/Stay means not only that the dog is standing calm and still, but also that each paw is in the correct position. This is especially important for a print ad, where he must stand next to the company's product, or for a commercial, where he may have to walk to the product, meet his mark, with the feet positioned correctly.

To teach your dog to Stand/Stay, follow these steps.

The hand signal for Stand/Stay: As you command Stand, your hand (open palm) is positioned firmly and directly in front of his face. Then, as you command Stay, you slowly draw your hand (still in open-palm position) approximately a foot away from your dog's face, and pause.

The ideal way to begin the Stand/Stay command is to have your dog Heel (walking at your left side). After a few steps, come to a halt. With him still at your left side, place your right hand in front of his face, as close as possible without actually touching him, and command Stand. Then, almost immediately, keeping the palm of your hand facing him, draw your hand back from his face about a foot, commanding to Stay. And, simultaneously, put your left hand and arm underneath his chest/stomach, to support the Stand position, forcing him to maintain the Stand position. No sitting or lying down on the Stand/Stay command.

Once he has accomplished this, turn and face your dog. Then, slowly back away a short distance, and pause. After a few moments, return to your dog, and stand at his right side, keeping him at your left side, the traditional Heel position, where you started. Your dog should still be continuing to hold the Stand/Stay position. Then, command him to Heel.

After a few steps, command him to Sit and the exercise is finished!

Praise him lavishly for doing this new Stand/Stay exercise.

STAND/STAY FROM SIT OR DOWN POSITION

Now that your dog knows how to do the Stand/Stay, we want to have him do the Stand/Stay from a Sit or Down position. This is very important for a dog to do on a specific spot, his mark, in print work, TV, and film.

To begin the exercise, have your dog sit at your left side. Then, with the palm of your right hand close in front of your dog's face, command him to Stand, while simultaneously drawing your right hand away from his face about a foot. At the same time, your left foot should gently nudge underneath the belly area of your dog, to help bring him to a standing position. Once the dog is standing, finish the exercise with the command to Stay. Walk away from your dog, pause, return, and praise him for a job well done.

To perform the steps from a Down position, have the dog start in the Down position. Command him to Stand and Stay. At the same time, with your left foot, gently nudge underneath his chest area to encourage him into a standing position. Then pause for a moment, walk away, pause again, and then return to him with lots of praise for a job well done.

Practice Safely with Distractions

At this point, I must remind you of several very important safety measures. Once you've gone this far with your dog, and he has responded well and achieved so much, it is very easy to become over-confident. Don't ever lose sight of the fact that your dog, no matter how terrific, is still a dog, and doesn't have the judgment to know when he might be in danger.

No matter how well your dog does off-leash in the privacy of your home or backyard, that is an insulated practice area, and you should practice repeatedly amid all kinds of distractions in the real world.

For this interim stage, you may have to "stage" the distractions in a secure setting.

If you can find a safe, fenced-in place to practice where there are other dogs, children, and people walking around, this is ideal. Also, you can create your own distractions by having your friends or family engage in all kinds of activities in the area where you're working with your dog. Invite other people and their children over to the area—even ask friendly neighborhood dogs to come in for a while.

I often have my clients stage an off-leash obedience "show" to demonstrate their dogs' prowess. This is an excellent way for a dog to learn to deal with distractions, as well as preparatory work for the next level of advanced training for theatrical work.

Finally, use common sense about where you allow your dog to run free. And, most important, *no matter how well trained your dog is, never, never, allow him to be loose without proper supervision.*

Stunt Work Training/Agility

Now that you have mastered the off-leash control of your dog, and you're working in a safe, fenced-in area, this is where I recommend that you start incorporating the training you've done so far into more advanced control, making a dog learn to follow your cues, hand signals, voice (in the beginning you may need to use a leash, at times), using obstacles and other props to increase and create more advanced control and behavior in your dog.

Mastering the training and agility of this stunt work not only will increase your dog's StarPet repertoire for professional theatrical work, but will also provide a solid foundation of skills required for work as a service dog for the physically challenged.

To replicate the most advantageous rehearsal hall, I always recommend joining an agility club, or, as I did, with Canine

★ Jolie jumping through Bash's arms. ★
COURTESY MERUET DIBRA

Court, develop a "doggie playground" in the park, with obstacles and props for agility to practice these maneuvers.

Here, we take up where we left off, heeling off-leash, but we have the dog walk through a pipe tunnel or barrel, up and down a see-saw plank, jump over hurdles and through tire swings, and so on. All this is a way to increase the special communication and working bond that you and your dog have more for advanced work in theater, commercials, and film. Basically, this will make your dog like a stunt dog.

As with basic training, when introducing your dog to stunt/agility work, it's best to simplify the props and equipment, as well as what you're asking him to do.

For example, simplify each obstacle before approaching it with your dog. Don't expect your dog to master the highest hurdle on his first try. Start at the lowest rung, so he can master it with ease, gain confidence, and have fun. As with every other exercise, praise your stunt dog lavishly every step of the way.

If your dog runs around an obstacle instead of going through it, put him on his leash and guide him through it. This is positive reinforcement, and will give him confidence, so the next time he does it, he'll do it happily and with ease, eager for more.

As with out-of-frame work, use both verbal and hand signals when training your dog on the agility course. The aim is to have him respond to either method of communication you choose. This is important to accomplish if you want to progress to professional work. Remember that here, as with all training, signals must be clear and direct.

HURDLES

Since most dogs love to jump, I recommend introducing your dog to the agility course/playground with the hurdles. These hurdles have mobile bars that allow the user to place them at any height, based on the dog's ability.

Let's start with the bar jump. The single bar jump is good for the beginner. Place the bar at the lowest rung, nearest the ground. Then, walk your dog, on-leash (at your left, of course), and together step over the bar and give an enthusiastic command— "Hup!" or "Over!"—and a little tug of the leash as you step over the bar. After this first agility accomplishment, praise him lavishly.

Now, repeat this baby step a few more times, on-leash, with the bar at the same, low level. You should continue to step over the bar with him.

The next step is to have your dog approach and jump the hurdle by himself. To do this, have your dog Sit six feet (the length of his leash) from the hurdle. At this time, you are holding his leash, but instead of standing next to him, you are standing beside the hurdle. Now, give the enthusiastic command, "Hup!" and a tug of the leash. This signals your dog to approach the hurdle and jump over the bar. Praise his first "solo" flight lavishly!

As you practice, you will increase the height of the bar to an acceptable level, based on your dog's size and ability. When he does this well on-leash, you are ready to try it off-leash, and the fun begins!

TUNNELS

Tunnels generally come in two varieties, the barrel/pipe tunnel and the fabric/collapsible tunnel.

The barrel tunnel is a wide-open, barrel-like tunnel that allows your dog plenty of room, and he can easily see clear through to the end of it. The barrel tunnel is a good tunnel to introduce your dog to first, as it's less daunting than the narrower/longer pipe tunnel or the collapsible tunnel.

To teach your dog to go through the tunnel, have your dog, on-leash, Sit and Stay at the entrance to the barrel. Then, extend the handle of the leash through the barrel, as far to the end as it will extend. Placing it there, walk calmly around the barrel, till you reach the other side. At this point, you and your dog are at opposite sides of the barrel (he at the beginning, you at the end). While your dog remains in the Sit/Stay position, squat at the other end of the tunnel. In full view of your dog, pick up the end of the leash and give him the Come command. At this time, gently pull the leash toward you to gently guide him through the tunnel. When he successfully navigates his first tunnel walk, praise him lavishly.

Eventually, the aim is to walk him to the barrel, toss the leash through the barrel, and command your dog with an enthusiastic "Go!"—and have him go through as enthusiastically as your command. Again, praise him lavishly.

The fabric, or collapsible, tunnel is a malleable tube constructed of fabric that your dog must wriggle through. This is something he will really enjoy. Maneuvering his body through the collapsible tunnel is a lot like what children do playing under the bed covers, crawling from one end of the bed till they come out the other. They can't see where they're going, but they have fun finding their way. In fact, you've probably seen your own dog, especially if he's a small dog, "burrowing" under the bed covers.

To accomplish this stunt faster, you may want to have a friend hold the end of the fabric open, so your dog can literally "see the light at the end of the tunnel." This will encourage him to go through, and he will respond more confidently to your command when the tunnel is collapsed and the end is not in sight.

Again, praise your dog lavishly for being so good at having such a good time!

Remember, as with all advanced training, the aim here is to progress to the off-leash level.

DOG WALK PLANK

The Dog Walk Plank is for dogs what the balance beam is to gymnasts. Your dog won't be doing flips and somersaults, of course, but this will build his confidence and agility for stunt work.

The standard Walk Plank is usually waist-high, buttressed by ascending and descending ramps on either end.

Begin with your dog on-leash at your left side. With the command, "Let's Go!" approach the plank, tug the leash, and, with a taut leash and your body close to his (like a spotter for a gymnast), guide him firmly and confidently up the ramp and onto the plank. When he reaches the level plank, praise him, not too excitedly, with a proud, "Good dog!"

Then, for the Walk Plank, repeat the command, "Let's Go!" and walk the length of the plank. When you approach the end ramp, don't stop, but continue encouraging your dog downward. When he reaches the ground, praise him lavishly.

What your dog learns here will help him enormously in movie work. Just think of all the memorable Lassie and Benji stunts. You know the ones. A tree trunk falls over a swollen creek, and Lassie has to cross the creek via the tree trunk to rescue Timmy. Or Benji has to flee a raging fire by traversing a fire escape from the burning building to safety.

SEE-SAW

The See-Saw is just what it sounds like. It's just like in a children's playground, the rocking plank that two children sit on, one at either end, and as one end goes up, the other goes down. The See-Saw in Canine Court is just that.

But in a *dog* playground, the See-Saw is played with one dog at a time. The dog walks from one end of the see-saw to the other.

This will be a fun stunt for your dog, but remember, it *is* a stunt. He will be balancing in "midair" on the see-saw, so you'll want to be his spotter. Every stunt man has a spotter, and a stunt dog, too, should have a spotter! And you're it!

To do this, have your dog, on-leash, on your left. Command him to Heel, and approach the end of the See-Saw that is on the ground.

With the command, "Let's Go!" and a taut leash, keep your dog as close to you as possible. This is for support and encouragement. Have your dog step onto the See-Saw and gently guide him to continue walking to the center of the See-Saw and pause. This allows the See-Saw's center of gravity to shift and stabilize equally to a perfect balance in the air, at which point your dog is perched at the very center.

At this point it is very important to encourage him and praise him. Then, when you're ready to continue, repeat the starting command, "Let's Go," and continue to use your body as a "spotter" to guide him to walk down the plank to ground level on the opposite side of the See-Saw from which he started. Praise him lavishly, as this was a feat of superstardom!

PAUSE TABLE/PERFORMANCE PLATFORM

In agility trials, a dog will be called upon to jump onto a platform (usually four by four) in the middle of running an obstacle course, pause for a few moments, and then continue. In theatrical work, it's advantageous for a dog to be comfortable performing on a small stage or platform.

To teach your dog to jump onto the platform, begin with your dog, on-leash, at your left side. Command your dog to jump, with the verbal cue, "Hup!" Tug confidently on his leash to ensure he follows through with the command. Once your dog sees that the platform is as comfortable as the floor or ground he's already used to, give the command, "Down" (with the proper hand gesture, as well). Remember from basic training that, once he's in the Down position, you must *hold off on the praise.* This is especially important in agility trials, because the dog must stay in the Down position for seven to ten seconds.

Once this is accomplished, repeat the command, "Let's go!" and guide your dog down from the platform. Praise him lavishly.

Eventually, you'll want the dog to perform this maneuver off-leash, and with you directing him from progressively greater distances, even up to twenty feet, which is ideal for print and film work.

TIRE JUMP

This is pretty self-explanatory. The tire is secured to a grounded, stationary frame. Like the hurdles, the tire can be lowered or raised, depending on your dog's size and ability.

To begin, lower the tire as close to the ground as possible, so your dog can walk easily through it. With your dog on-leash at your left side, command your dog to Sit/Stay, approximately six feet (the length of the leash) away from the tire. With the end of the leash in hand, walk away from your dog and to the tire. Thread the leash through the opening of the tire, and stand on the *far* side of the tire with the leash in hand. With the verbal cue "Come!" encourage your dog to approach the tire. When he reaches the tire, give him an enthusiastic command, "Hup!" At this time, help him with an encouraging and confident tug of the leash. When he walks through the tire, praise him lavishly.

As with the hurdle bar, continue to raise the level of the tire, until he's actually jumping through the tire. Eventually, as with all agility, this will be done off-leash.

Here again, this stunt transfers beautifully for motion picture work when the script calls for your dog to jump through an open window.

WEAVE POLES

Weave poles are like the poles downhill skiers weave around. Unlike the ski slope, however, weave poles are placed strategically on an even playing field for your dog to navigate (weave) around.

To start, the aim is just to have your dog maneuver around a few poles, not the entire course. Three is a good number to start; then add more poles as your dog masters this skill.

This stunt requires real in-tandem training. With a taut leash, keep your dog as close to your body, on your left side, of course, as possible, while still allowing easy maneuverability. This will allow you to guide him through the continually changing directions, as he must weave, snakelike, in and out between the poles. The poles are placed in a straight line, with space for a dog to maneuver. As the two of you traverse the field, you will be walking a straight path, while your dog, at your side, is weaving in and out, in a zigzag path, around the poles. The two of you, however, always remain abreast, in perfect alignment. This is accomplished by skillful manipulation of the leash with the accompanying verbal commands, "In!" "Out!" "In!" "Out!" which guide your dog around the poles, while, at the same time, keeping him in alignment with you.

Make sure to praise your dog lavishly after this successful run.

The aim here, of course, is to accomplish this off-leash. This is a useful stunt for film and television.

After you've taught your dog to accomplish all this agility and stunt work, you may want to create your own contests where you choreograph the order and pace of the stunt work. For example, you might time yourself from the starting stunt to the end stunt. The aim is to have your dog, off-leash, perform each maneuver better and faster than the time before. He'll have fun running through his repertoire of tricks, and he'll be proud to "break his own record" and achieve his highest "personal best" possible. Don't forget, dogs love to show off! That's why we teach them and praise them so lavishly. Indeed, that's why our dogs are StarPets!

Congratulations. As much as they love showing off, StarPets also love to *serve.* And now you have reached the level where your dog could "understudy" for the role of the service dog.

A service dog is a dog that fits in the category of a seeing-eye dog or hearing-ear dog. It is to the physically challenged what the hearing-ear dog is to the hearing-impaired; the guide dog to the visually impaired.

This training puts your dog in the *league* of a service dog, and of what a service dog is *required* to do. This gives your StarPet the *foundation* for this highly specialized work. If you feel you want to go further in training for this wonderful work, and earn *certification,* check out the Appendix of this book.

Keeping the Play in Play-Acting

Continuing to keep the *play* in *play-acting,* the following skills of Frisbee and dancing seem, on the surface, more *play* than *acting*—but, in treading the theatrical boards, you'll find these skills will serve you well in action long shots and intricate ensemble work.

FRISBEE

This is a fun, interactive game with a dog and owner, where advanced training is used to a point where it becomes stunt training. In this game you toss a disk into flight and a dog chases, leaps into midair, grasps the disk, and lands, with that look that says, "Wow! Look at me! Aren't I great, I caught it in midair!" Then you command the dog to bring it back to you for another toss, and the game begins over and over again.

Take a Frisbee and engage your dog to chase it. Start by rolling it on the ground, so he chases it and brings it back to you. Then progress to holding it at eye level (for the dog) and turning in circles, and as he chases it, let him have it. With that reward, he connects that this is a game. Then you do another big circle turn while he chases the Frisbee, and then let go of the Frisbee and allow it to fly in the air (much like an Olympic discus thrower!). The dog chases it and makes the connection to grab it, and you applaud with enthusiasm, and he likes that he did something great. He grabs it, comes down with it, and the connection is made: "Ah hah! Now I got it!" and the game has begun.

★ Sally catching the Frisbee. ★
COURTESY BRUCE PLOTKIN

And if the dog becomes obsessed with the Frisbee, that's a good obsession, because he becomes a better Frisbee player—and this skill teaches him, through play, to catch and bring things back. This is good for stunt work in films and television, especially commercials. I find this to be very popular for pets in the industry, as it shows the dynamic relationship between owner and dog. The shot of a dog gripping the Frisbee in midair, for print or TV, has become a great point of reference for a commercial tagline of triumph.

A quick game of Frisbee between professionals has replaced the game of yesterday's generation—touch football. Yesterday, presidential candidates and Academy Award contenders alike would let off steam on the campaign trail or on the set with a little touch football—today, it's a little Frisbee!

My clients Matthew Broderick and his dog, Sally, are a perfect example! Matthew would take Sally on his movie sets with him, and, during breaks, he and the rest of the cast and crew—and Sally, the Border Collie—would engage in a boisterous Frisbee game. It was great fun for all, enhanced Matthew's and Sally's friendship, and everyone returned to work refreshed, proving, once again, that it always helps to "keep the play in play-acting!"

Dancing with Dogs

As with human actors, dog actors should have as many talents as possible. You never know when they will come in handy. Remember Fred Astaire's celebrated first audition, when the not-too-impressed casting director wrote on Fred's audition card: "Can't sing. Can't act. Balding slightly. Can dance a little"? Astaire's ability to dance not only saved his audition, but made his career!

Dancing with Dogs is a little bit theater, a little bit sport, all rolled into an engaging dance in which dog and owner move in tandem through a set of choreographed steps accompanied by the music of their choice. The dance moves in freestyle do not need to be elaborate, and aficionados advise that the music should be chosen by your dog (sounds and rhythms that your dog seems to like and that naturally get her moving). What at first blush seems like fun and games actually requires a great deal of skill. Again, think of Ginger Rogers's "backward and in heels" ability to keep up with Fred Astaire!

The choreography is based on a series of steps derived from standard obedience, such as Heel. But dancing is much more demanding, as you have to teach your dog how to Heel on *both* sides, not just on the handler's left side, as traditional obedience training demands. And, like Ginger Rogers, your dog will have to learn to walk backward in a straight line, and how to pivot in place and how to sidestep. (Later you will learn how to teach your dog to walk backward. Walking backward is an important theatrical skill for a StarPet.)

Still, dance in freestyle doesn't have to be elaborate, and you can be creative and playful, encouraging pivots, spins, leaps, and play bows. (All of which you will later learn to teach your dog.) The dance, like the music, should be based on what your dog lets you know she's enjoying. Musical freestyle, whether it's country, jazz, ballet, or ballroom, is a showcase that truly and artistically demonstrates the joy and fun of bonding with your pet.

Plus, dancing with your dog is a wonderful way for anyone, young or old, who wants to have fun with his dog. Any breed, any age, can do this. The only props you need are you, your dog, your favorite music, maybe a costume, and your imagination. The artistry, teamwork, costuming, and athleticism will work in your favor in the theatrical world, as well.

Starstruck

Now that you have mastered the StarPet communication between you and your StarPet—as Lee Strasberg brought the Marilyn Monroe out of Norma Jean—you are ready to bring out the best of your pet's abilities to play a role, to move the script's plot along, and to reach an audience. This is where Bash's Ark (finding the actor's arc within the *animal* actor) comes into full play.

You see, it is one thing to communicate privately, one on one— it is quite another thing, another talent, another skill altogether, to be able to communicate to an audience. You need to master the techniques that will allow your dog's talent to be communicated to an audience and captured on film.

To do this, you first need to develop trust.

Remember, for the agility and stunt work, you were your dog's spotter, which allowed him to explore, learn, and trust his own abilities, because he first trusted you.

Trust is very important here, because you will be choreographing his each and every movement—his muscles, his legs, the tilt of his head, the wag of his tail. There is no room for error here, because this is the work for the camera-ready StarPet, and he must follow a carefully scripted storyboard.

At first, you will be training him closely with his leash. Think of yourself as guiding his carefully choreographed action as a puppeteer—a kind of "puppyteer" for DogStars in training! Like a puppeteer's strings cleverly guide the puppet's movements, so the puppyteer's skillful use of the leash will surely and ably guide the dog's actions. This is very important, because the aim here is to eventually have your dog respond without the leash. If he is going to be a professional StarPet, he will have to be able to perform these cleverly choreographed actions and carefully blocked sequences from verbal cues and hand signals *only*.

Just as the kindly puppeteer Geppetto eventually saw his beloved puppet Pinocchio shed the directives of the puppeteer's strings and come to life, so your dog will be able to shed the leash, and, with your directives from offstage, out of camera range, your StarPet's performance will come to *life*!

Stage/Platform Work

The platform works as your own private in-house rehearsal hall. It provides the stage for you to direct your StarPet. Once your dog has mastered working on this small stage, he will be ready for the big screen!

This "small stage" is especially important if your StarPet is a small dog. This will allow your dog to assimilate to working on a platform that will keep him in camera range as well as sitting next to a product for an advertisement in a commercial shoot. (Remember, there are no small roles—just small dogs! And even the smallest dog can shine in the biggest role on the largest stage—it's all up to you!)

If you're teaching your dog to do theatrical work, this table duplicates the stage experience, and, if you're doing TV or film work, it acts as the marker for your dog, and he learns to perform from the specific spot asked of him.

Ideally, this platform should be a waist-high table with a non-skid rubber mat on top. A bathtub mat, shower mat, or rubber-backed doormat is best, because it will prevent your dog from slipping. Professional trainers often use special, carpet-covered tables. You may also consider investing in a portable grooming table (you can find these in professional pet industry catalogues). This is a good idea not just for the professional StarPet, but for the active, hard-working amateur in demonstrations, auditions, and community events.

But, whatever table you choose as your stage/platform, it must be sturdy.

The waist-high height of the table is important. It keeps your dog in a close and easy-to-handle position. It will be more comfortable for you (saving a great many backaches!)—and, if you are comfortable, you can proceed confidently. By the same token, your dog will pick up on your confidence and comfort level, and he, too, will work with more confidence and comfort.

This height, basically, facilitates better communication between you and your dog; the director and the StarPet. It brings you eye to eye, and you will be better able to determine when your dog is actually understanding his acting cue. This is where you really begin to become your dog's director. The enhanced eye contact is imperative in professional stage work, as it facilitates the all-important focus—and from that, along with motivation, allows the outward expression of your dog's inner drives to bring the script to life. And, when he masters that ability—when he can bring it out for the camera to capture and the audience to understand—he will be a professional StarPet.

And now, the strategy is to get your dog comfortable in working on the platform. To do this, first have him review—on the platform—his simple, past basic training. When he is comfortable performing basic training on the platform, he will have gained the confidence he needs to move on to the next level, which is the trick work. When this has been accomplished, not only will your dog respond, from the platform, effortlessly to your director's signals, but the platform will also signal to your StarPet that it is time to focus on the job at hand. He will become much more responsive to new learned tricks and to new learned behavior.

Just as the leash tells your dog it's time for a walk or on-leash training, so the platform will signal the StarPet that it's time to *perform*.

Thirty Ways to Make Your StarDog Shine

As much as I would love to have each and every one of you and your StarPets in my StarPet Workshops, it's simply not possible. What is possible, however, is that each and every one of your Star-Pets has, to some degree, that very special talent that, combined with the right techniques, can make your StarPet a professional StarPet.

Here, then, are some of the techniques I teach in my StarPet Workshops to showcase your StarPet's talent!

GIVE PAW/SHAKE HANDS

The script: To have your dog give first one paw, then the other, upon seeing your offered hand, or responding to your verbal command.

The action: Have your dog sit in front of you, and say, "Give me your paw!" or, "Shake hands!" Holding out your right hand to him, tap him under his right foreleg until he raises his right paw. Take hold of his paw and give him a treat and praise. Repeat this pattern again, until he extends his paw when he sees you extending your hand. Some dogs do better with praise, some do better with a treat. You figure out what's best for your dog, and that's the reward system you embrace for your dog.

After he has learned this, then command him to give his left paw. To do this, do as above, but simply tap under his *left* foreleg.

★ Give Paw. ★

When he raises his paw, take it immediately and reward him with a treat or praise. Eventually, when he hears your command or sees your extended hand, he will give you his paw *without* the encouraging tap.

The director's cue (handler's signal): The extending of your hand for the shake, after the signal for Sit, is the only gesture we need for this action. However, if you are out of the picture, and your dog has to shake hands with an actor, you give him the command, out of frame, from behind the actor whose hand your dog must shake, to sit, and give the silent cue, to give his paw up. At that moment, the actor's cue is to take your dog's paw and shake hands.

PUT PAW UP

The script: To place his paw up in a position ready to place, on cue, onto a prop, such as a table, chair, box, or person.

The action: The "Paw Up!" command is used for two different actions. The first action is complete and stands alone. It is simply what it says it is, which is to have your dog put his paw up in the air, as in a "high-five" position or a "give me your paw" position. The second way the "Paw Up!" command is used is to command your dog to put his paw up and onto a specific object (a table, chair, person's knee, and so on).

For the first command, have your dog come in front of the object, and command him to "Sit!" Now that he is in the Sit position, give him the command "Paw Up!" Simultaneously, tap your dog under his foreleg until he puts his paw up and in the air. The tapping of his foreleg not only teaches him the action but is the basis for the hand signal for this command. Then, make him hold his paw in position (in the air) with the command "Hold It!" This accomplishes the first, solitary action the command is used for. You can end this action simply by calling your dog to you. Praise him lavishly and give him a reward.

★ Copelia, Paws Up on an object. ★
COURTESY MARIAN HART

The second action the command is used for is to have your dog put his paw up and place it upon an object, such as a table, chair, or another person's knee. Here again, you have your dog in a sitting position in front of the object. Then, give the command "Paw Up!" while simultaneously pointing to the object you wish him to place his paw on. To reinforce the understanding of the

★ Put Paw Up. ★

command, cup your hand lightly over his paw and place it on the object, and, with the command "Hold It!" hold the position for a few seconds. When he has accomplished this, praise him lavishly and reward him with a treat. The aim is to have your dog perform the action with simply a verbal command and/or hand signal.

The director's cue (handler's signal): For the simple, singular "Paw Up!" command, make a quick short upward brushing motion with your hand, mimicking the tapping under his foreleg. This signals your dog to put his paw up. If you want him to hold this position, give the command "Hold It!" and point your forefinger upward in an expectant pause. This signals your dog to pause and hold his pose, as well as to wait for the next direction.

To command your dog to put his paw up and place it on an object, give the command "Paw Up" with the accompanying hand up gesture. Next, extending your hand sideways in a sweeping gesture, point toward the object he is to place his paw on.

THE WAVE

The script: To have your dog raise his paw high, "pawing in the air," as if he's waving at you in greeting.

The action: Have your dog go to his mark and sit. Give him the command "Paw Up!" as a preparatory command to "Wave!" When his paw is up, give the "Wave!" command. At the same time, extend your hand out and under his paw, stroking and pushing the underside of his pads up in the air and toward you like a wave. When he's done this a few times, keep him sitting at his mark but praise him lavishly and give him a treat. After he's become confident with the action, repeat the command as you walk away from him, mimicking the stroking of his paw, but in the air,

⭐ Wave. ⭐

from a distance. When he accomplishes this, praise him lavishly and give him a food reward.

The director's cue (handler's signal): Give the verbal command "Wave." From a distance, you need to exaggerate your hand signal into the just-learned wave you want him to mimic.

SIT UP

The script: To sit upright on his hindquarters.

The action: This is popular in all areas of entertainment, from print ads to commercials, TV shows, and movie work. There is nothing more appealing. Small dogs generally take to this more easily. To do this, start with your dog on-leash, in a Sit position, directly in front of you. Holding a treat above his head, and with a gently encouraging pull from the leash,

★ Sit Up. ★

command him to "Sit Up!" as you ease him onto his haunches. While he's balancing on his haunches, command him to "Stay!" for just a moment, give him treats to encourage him, and praise his newfound balancing talent. Then, have him return to the Sit position and praise him lavishly and offer an extra treat—certainly appropriate here. Eventually, Sit Up will be accomplished without a leash, without a treat, and for the entire designated time of the action. When this is accomplished, praise lavishly and give the treat he's waiting for!

★ Copelia, Sit Up command. ★
COURTESY MARIAN HART

For larger dogs, we need not only a leash, but also a special setting, because a larger dog needs extra physical support to understand what's required of him, and to build up his balance, muscles, and confidence. To do this, place him in the corner of a room, his back to the wall, facing out to you (after all, he's not a dunce—he's very smart to be in this workshop). Basically, imagine a corner china cabinet or bookshelf, an inverted V. The walls add support, like a brace.

Starting from a Sit position, command him to "Sit Up," with an accompanying tug of the leash upward. With your free hand, tap under his two front paws, until they're tucked under his chin, and command him to "Stay!" Praise him and give him a treat each time he attains the proper position. Have him hold a moment and praise him again and give him a treat for the proper action. After he masters the balance and position, move him away from the corner support and repeat the sequence of action, eventually without the leash. Praise him lavishly and offer treats.

Director's cue (handler's signal): Here you give a command with a treat hidden in your hand, gesturing in a scooping manner somewhat like an orchestra conductor, and then go into a freeze-frame pause or hold position, so the dog knows to Sit Up and Hold his position. Afterward, lavish praise and treats.

SAY YOUR PRAYERS

The script: To Say Your Prayers is a timeless, universally appealing pose for a dog actor.

The action: Place your dog in the Sit Stay position at the foot of a chair or bed. Now is the time to teach your dog Both Paws Up! To do this, command your dog *"Both* Paws Up!" and onto the bed. As he puts one paw up (as he learned before), reinforce the command to put the second paw up, as well, by taking your hand and gently flicking under his foreleg. Now, he has a new learned behavior where he'll put both paws up on command. Now that he has both paws up and on the bed, command him to "Say Your Prayers!" Simultaneously, hold a treat in front of your dog's face, at eye level, and slowly move the treat downward. Your dog will follow the treat, until his head comes to rest between his paws. If need be, place your other

★ Say Your Prayers. ★

hand on your dog's head and coax it downward into the prayer position. Have him hold this position for a moment, then praise him and reward him with the treat. Eventually, with just the one command of "Say Your Prayers," your dog will raise both paws up, place them on the edge of the bed, and rest his head between his paws in prayer. Don't forget to praise your dog and reward him with a treat after he has completed the action.

Director's cue (handler's signal): With the verbal command, "Say Your Prayers!" give the gesture for Both Paws Up, which is to hold both hands close together, palms up, with fingers flicking toward you. Immediately follow through with the command by pointing downward to the bed, where he is to lower his head in prayer.

HIDE YOUR EYES

The script: As with Say Your Prayers, Hide Your Eyes is a universally appealing pose that enables the dog actor to portray a myriad of storytelling possibilities. From hide-and-seek to Please Forgive Me!

The action: The best way to teach your dog this action is to set up a pressure gate (baby gate) in a doorway. Stand on one side of the gate and command your dog to "Sit," facing you, on the *other* side of the gate. With treat in hand, command your dog *"Both* Paws Up!" and onto the gate railing. When he has

★ Hide Your Eyes. ★

achieved this position, command him to "Hold It!" At that moment, take the treat and hold it in front of his face When he is focused on the treat, give the command "Hide Your Eyes!" and slowly draw the treat downward below his paws and the gate rail. This will cause him to lower his muzzle below the gate rail, and his eyes will be hidden by his paws. This gives the illusion that he is hiding his eyes, or embarrassed or begging forgiveness. Once this is accomplished, give him the treat and praise him lavishly. Eventually, you can do this from a standing position. This really adds dramatic appeal.

Director's cue (handler's signal): With the command "Both Paws Up!" give the accompanying gesture of hands together, palms up, fingers flicking toward you. Then immediately point to where to place his paws (in this case, the pressure gate). When he has accomplished this, command him to "Hide Your Eyes!" With this command, bring both your hands to your face, fingers clenched into a paw and, face angled downward, hide your own eyes.

TO GET ON HIS SIDE

The script: To have your dog lie down on his side, then straighten up, then lie down on his other side.

The action: To do this, first get your dog in a Down/Stay position. Then see which side he's lying on with his hind leg tucked under that side. Kneel in front of that side, with his belly facing you. Then, put your hand on his shoulder, gently pushing him *away* from you until he is lying on his side. Reinforce this by simultaneously pulling his front leg under him and toward you, with the command "On Your Side!" When he is fully on his side, with his head down, command "Stay." Praise your dog and give him a reward. (Praise should be conservative here, because the action isn't over yet, and he needs to hold that position, and continue to the next action.)

Then, give the command "Straighten Up!" with help of a food reward, so your dog goes to a classic ready position

★ Get on Your Side. ★

(Down position, but with his head and shoulder up, like a Sphinx). Then command him to "Down/Stay."

From Down/Stay it's time to redirect your dog with the command, "Other Side." To do this, repeat the earlier steps, but in the opposite direction, *counter*clockwise position. When the exercise is complete, give him a food reward and praise him lavishly.

Director's cue (handler's signal): The combination of body gestures and verbal commands should mimic your previous hands-on cues, but without touching the dog. When you give the first command, "On Your Side," your hand and arms are moving in an exaggerated clockwise gesture, as if you're steering the wheel of a car. The "Straighten Up" command is given with a rigid snap, your hands parallel as if holding an invisible box.

The "Other Side" command is given with your hands on the steering wheel in an exaggerated *counter*clockwise movement.

DEAD DOG

The script: To have your dog lie down on his side and remain still, to play dead dog.

The action: This is a simple variation of the lie down on your side. Give the command, "Dead Dog!" and follow the same procedures as you do when you have your dog lie down on his side. Here, we emphasize the command "Dead Dog" in a shaming, reprimanding voice, as if you were saying bad dog—like a faux scold. He's playing dead, remember; he cannot be happy and wag his tail. The point is to have him freeze and be totally still. After a period of time, praise him and give him a treat.

★ Dead Dog. ★

The Dead Dog action actually requires acting. Even though this looks simple, it's actually harder than it looks, for both the dog and you. Remember, this is play-acting. Your dog has to know that when you scold or reprimand him, it is part of the play-acting, part of the game to cue him to do his part. Therefore, when he's accomplished this feat, praise him lavishly and give him treats and a playtime. Then, from the start, he will know that he is play-acting, and next time you command "Dead Dog" he will look dead, but in his heart, he knows it's part of the game.

This action works very well from any position, from crawling to collapse and from standing to falling down dead. Even from a sitting or sitting up position: "Bang! You're dead!"

Director's cue (handler's signal): Give the steering-wheel signal to lie down on your side. Then follow immediately with the Dead Dog signal, which is an exaggerated, forceful thrust of the Stay signal, with your open hand, fingers widely splayed, pushing outward and downward toward your dog.

ROLL OVER

The script: To have your dog roll over, on his back, from one side to the other side.

The action: Give the command to "Lie Down on Your Side." Then, to teach him the roll-over action, kneel or stand in front of your dog and command him to "Roll

★ Roll Over. ★

Over!" Simultaneously with the command, brace his back into position with one hand, and with your other hand, grasp his two front legs and guide them up and over his exposed belly in the direction of the roll, until he's lying on his other side. So, basically, you've guided your dog through the complete roll-over. Praise him lavishly and give him a treat.

After he has learned the action with the verbal command and the physical guidance, use a treat to reinforce the hand signal, which will be the gesture to roll over. To do this, command your dog to "Lie Down on Your Side." When he's on his side, show him the treat. While he's focused on the treat, move the treat in an exaggerated arclike roll-over motion, until, following your hand, he completes the entire roll-over.

Director's cue (handler's signal): Once your dog has mastered this action, he must respond to the roll-over command from any position. This command is simply one sweep of the hand gesture, down, followed by a wide, sweeping arc in the direction you want him to roll over. These gestures should be quick and decisive, so your dog's action is clean and immediate.

THE BOW

The script: This is based on the wolf's play bow. Dogs love to play bow, it initiates any play-acting. The trick here is to get your dog to bow gracefully on command.

The action: To begin, have your dog stand at your left side. Then, turn and face him, so you're facing his profile, with his head to your right and his hindquarters to your left. With the command "Bow," take your right hand and slide his front legs forward in front of him, until his elbows touch the ground. His instinct will be to lie down. You then must encircle his belly with your left arm,

★ Bow. ★

to support his hindquarters in the standing position. Now, to keep his chest and elbows on the floor, quickly remove your hand from his paws and place it firmly on his neck/shoulder/upper back area. Now that you've manipulated your dog's body to conform to the position of the bow, continue to support him in the position, and

★ Copelia demonstrates the Bow command. ★
COURTESY MARIAN HART

reinforce the "Bow" command with the added "Stay" command. After a few moments, praise him lavishly and give him treats.

After a series of practices, you can now encourage your dog to bow with treats. So he'll bow faster and you can use your left hand to support his hindquarters, or use a scarf like a sling under his belly to help manipulate him into position. Or you might use a simple cardboard box that fits comfortably under your dog's belly. The proper size should support the hindquarters in a standing position, while allowing his front elbows and chest to bow down to the floor. Give treats and praise lavishly for every series of sessions.

Directors cue (handler's signal): Give the command "Bow," and follow through with an exaggerated version of the classic human bowing gesture, as if meeting royalty, bowing low from the waist, with your arm sweeping out and to the side.

CRAWL

The script: Have your dog take a Lie Down position and crawl slowly from one point to another, as if crawling under a low table or through a tunnel.

The action: On-leash, command your dog "Down" in a Sphinx position. Hold the leash in your left hand, under his neck, close to his collar. With your right hand in front of his face, point two fin-

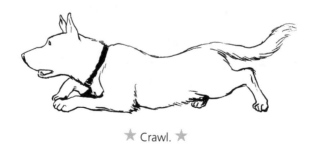

★ Crawl. ★

gers at the ground, and in a "creepy crawly" manner, wiggle your fingers enticingly, moving slowly away from his face. Give him the command to "Crawl," and simultaneously, gently pull his leash forward to encourage him to follow your "creepy crawly" fingers. To ensure that he follows in a crawl and doesn't stand, transfer the leash to your right hand. With the leash in your right hand, continue to wiggle your fingers while pulling your dog forward with the leash. This frees your left hand to apply gentle pressure on his shoulders to insure that he holds the belly-to-the-ground crawling position.

Once this action is taught, you will do this without a leash. Hold the treat in your right hand, allowing two fingers to continue to wiggle enticingly. Use your left hand when needed to ensure he stays down for the crawl. When he's accomplished this action, give him the treat and praise lavishly.

Director's cue (handler's signal): Give the commands "Down" and "Stay." Then, with the command "Crawl," bend over giving the same two-fingered enticing wiggle, about knee-high, drawing away from the dog, toward you.

TO SPEAK

The script: To have your dog bark on cue.

The action: To do this, have your dog on-leash, tied to a post, a doorknob, or any secure object. Having the dog leashed, but unable to be near you, will

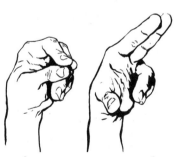

★ Hand signal for Speak. ★

excite the dog. Stand about four feet away from him with a favorite treat or toy. Make the treat or toy so enticing that he will make a sound or bark out of excitement to get the treat or join in the play. As soon as he barks, reward him by giving him the treat or toy, and praise him lavishly. At this time, you want to encourage him to speak on cue. To do this, have a treat in your hand to entice him. Then, still holding the treat, take your thumb, forefinger, and middle finger, and, in quick, staccato movements, mimic the barking motion, mouth open, mouth shut, mouth open, mouth shut. Simultaneously give the command, "Speak! Speak!" If need be, accompany with your own barking sounds, so he gets the idea and can mimic you. Once he does this, reward him with the treat and praise him lavishly. Eventually, your dog will respond off-leash and with just the hand signal. You can also teach your dog to speak more softly, to "whisper." To do this, give the initial Speak cue, followed by a finger-to-the-mouth ssshhhhing sound and gesture.

Director's cue (handler's signal): Here, the cue is to signal your dog silently from a distance. To do this, hold your hand near your head, and, with thumb, forefinger, and middle finger, mimic "chatting." This will give your dog the signal to speak. Doing this encourages your dog to focus and make the connection.

KISS

The script: To have your dog go to a stranger and "kiss" (lick).

The action: Here, you use food to motivate the action. Take some meat-flavored baby food to rub

★ Kiss. ★

onto the area of the person who is to receive the kiss. This is generally the face and cheek area. Baby food works well because it is flavorful, and the consistency is easy to work with. At this time, command your dog to "Go Kiss!" or "Give a kiss!" This is to encourage the dog to go to the person, put his face near the person's cheek, and lick the baby food. To direct the dog's focus, you may want to point directly to the smear of baby food to encourage him to go to the cheek and lick, which is the "kiss." After a while, this can be achieved with the direction from a distance. The aim here is to do this without the food motivator, and instead to give a food reward and praise *after* he's completed the action.

Director's cue (handler's signal): Here, the handler commands the dog to "Go Kiss!" with a sweeping gesture from the chest outward toward the direction of the action—a kind of universal Go gesture.

TURN TO YOUR RIGHT/TURN TO YOUR LEFT

The script: The aim is to have your dog make, on command, a complete 360-degree turn (circle) to the right, and then, on command, a complete 360-degree turn (circle) to the left.

⭐ Turn to Your Left. Turn to Your Right. ⭐

The action: To begin, have your dog on a leash, facing you head-on. Your dog should be standing, and you should be holding the leash in your left hand and a treat in your right hand. Then, with the command, "Turn to Your Right!" and keeping the leash taut, show him the treat in your right hand. When he is focused on the treat, lead with your right hand, in a sweeping, clockwise circular motion, guiding your dog in a complete right-turning circle, until he ends up in the starting position, facing you. Then, give him the treat, but don't praise too lavishly, as he is still in the middle of the action. Now, reverse the action. With your dog facing you, his leash still in your left hand, a second treat in your right hand, show him the second treat. When he is focused on the treat, command him to "Turn to Your Left!" And, with a sweeping *counter*clockwise motion (to your *left*), guide your dog, as he follows the treat in your right hand, in a complete *left*-turning circle, until he again ends up in the starting position, facing you. Give him the treat and praise lavishly for action well done!

Director's cue (handler's signal): The aim is for the dog to do this off-leash and without treats! The signal given is a complete sweeping, arclike motion, with the verbal commands "Turn to Your Right!" (clockwise) and "Turn to Your Left!" (counterclockwise). You may find your dog responds better if, when giving the right-turn command, you use your right arm for the signal, and when giving the left turn command, you use your *left* arm to gesture.

CIRCLE AROUND YOUR LEGS

The script: As you stand in a stationary position, with your legs placed approximately two feet apart, your dog will alternately circle each leg, in a figure-eight pattern.

★ Through the Legs. ★

The action: You should have a treat in *both* hands, which you will use *alternately*, to lure your dog to circle first one leg, then the other. To ensure that your dog follows the correct hand, make certain that the hand that is *not* in use is held close to your body, above your waist, so as not to distract your dog from the luring hand.

To begin, stand with your legs placed approximately two feet apart and command your dog to Sit directly behind you. Then, with the command "Through the Legs!" extend your right hand downward between your legs, at your dog's face level. Lure him to walk through your legs, and then circle the treat around your right leg, having your dog follow closely. As he gets behind you, where he started, quickly pull away the first hand you were using (the right hand) and replace it with your *left* hand, in the starting position, front and center between your legs. Then again command your dog, "Through the Legs!" and with treat in the left hand, circle around your left leg, luring him to follow around your left leg.

When he returns to the starting position, directly in back of you, he has completed one entire figure-eight pattern, but don't stop there. Continue luring your dog until he has completed three or four figure-eights in a row. When he has accomplished this, praise him and give him *both* treats! The aim here, however, is to eventually have your dog perform this feat *without* the lure, following only the guiding hand signal. Lavish praise and a food reward will come at the end of the completed action.

Director's cue (handler's signal): Here the command is "Through the Legs!" The gesture here emulates the figure-eight luring motion, but is not followed through. It's just a signal, a *suggestion* to each side to initiate the circle action.

ZIGZAG THROUGH THE LEGS

The script: While you are walking, your dog is weaving in and out, between and around your legs in a zigzag fashion.

The action: First, make certain that you have a treat in each hand to facilitate the luring action. As with the previous action, the luring hand is extended down low to your dog's level, while the nonworking hand is kept close to your body, above the waist, so as not to distract your dog.

To begin the action, extend your right leg forward, as if in midstride. Make sure your stride is long enough (approximately two feet) to allow your dog easy access to follow the lure through your legs. Have your dog sitting at your left side, facing you. Then, extend your right hand (with the treat) down *behind* your right leg and into your dog's line of vision between your legs, to encourage your dog to walk in between your legs. Give the command "In!"

As he moves in between your legs, toward the lure, draw your hand back and around to the front of your right leg in a half-circle, with the command "Out!" This will encourage him to follow the lure around the outside of your leg, so he ends up in front of you, facing you.

Now, step forward with your *left* leg, and, at the same time, also switch hands, bringing your right (nonworking) hand up to your waist, and extending your *left* (working) hand down low behind your *left* leg, to lure your dog through your leg (command "In!"), and around your left leg in a half-circle (command "Out!"), again ending up in front of you, facing you from your left side.

Repeat the walk—right, left, right, left, with your right and left hands alternating the lure for your dog's zigzag walk—for at least five or six paces to allow your dog to become comfortable with the action and familiar with the rhythm. In fact, once you and your dog get the hang of it, try to make the action as rhythmic as possi-

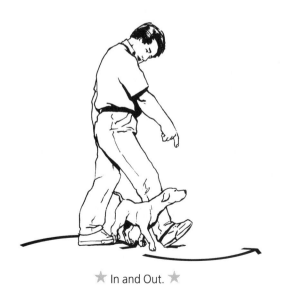

★ In and Out. ★

ble. When your dog has successfully completed this action, praise him lavishly, and reward him with *both* treats.

Director's cue (handler's signal): The verbal commands "In!" and "Out!" are accompanied by alternating hand gestures with a swinging, pointing motion to cue your dog's direction.

TO BACK UP

The script: To have your dog, from a standing position, back up; to walk backward as required.

The action: For this action, we need to set the stage. Whether you do this indoors or outdoors, the aim is to create a very narrow walkway, which does not allow room for your dog to turn around in. This can be a coffee table or sofa parallel to a wall, which

⭐ Back Up. ⭐

would create a pathway approximately eighteen inches wide and maybe six feet long. You could also open up an exercise pen until it becomes one long free-standing fence, which can be set up parallel to an existing fence or side of a house.

The aim, simply, is to have a walkway long enough for your dog to get used to walking backward and narrow enough to facilitate this learning experience, by making it physically impossible for him to turn around.

To facilitate this action, walk your dog forward through the pathway you created. When you reach the end, but while your dog is still within the confines of the enclosed pathway, command him to "Stand/Stay," and then turn and face him. This is a good way to begin the lesson, because it allows no room for error, as your dog is already in the enclosure and cannot turn around. You should hold his leash taut, with maximum six to eight inches give.

Then, command your dog to "Back Up!" and give an accompanying gentle but firm pull of the leash backward. This will give him the understanding of the command and the confidence to do it. In tandem with the "Back Up!" command, give the hand signal, which is a backhand gesture motioning backward. For further encouragement, take your knee and gently nudge him as he backs up and into the pathway. When he's accomplished this, praise him lavishly and give him a treat. Eventually, your dog will perform this action without the help of guiding pathways.

Director's cue (handler's signal): The verbal command here is "Back Up!" The accompanying signal is the back of your hand facing the dog, pushing backward into the air with short, sharp, wavelike shooing motions.

TAKE IT/HOLD IT/DROP IT

The script: Here your dog is to take any object and hold it in his mouth, for purposes of a commercial or ad shoot or a television or film role.

The action: Here, the action begins with your dog on-leash, sitting at your left side. The object you choose should be something your dog enjoys, like a favorite toy or stick. Begin by crouching at your dog's level. Hold the object in front of him, near his mouth; and give the command, "Take It!" At the same time, gently maneuver the object into his mouth. This can be done by applying gentle, firm pressure on either side of his jaw. This coaxing will open his mouth, allowing him to take the object. At this time, command him to "Hold It!" As he's holding the object, gently cir-

★ Copelia holding the flag. ★
COURTESY MARIAN HART

cle your hand around his muzzle, helping him to keep his mouth closed. Keep his mouth closed for a few moments and reinforce the action by continuing to say "Hold It!" "Stay!" "Hold It! "Stay!" After he's held the object for the desired period of time, extend your hand underneath his mouth and command him to "Drop It!" into your hand. Praise him lavishly and give him a treat for doing a good job. Eventually, your dog will take the object, hold it for any given period of time you ask, and drop it on command.

Director's cue (handler's signal): The verbal command is "Take It!" as you show the object in front of the dog. When your dog takes the object, you then command him to "Hold It!" Then, after a period of time, you put your hand under his mouth, and command him to "Drop It!"

PICK IT UP/CARRY IT/DROP IT

The script: To have your dog pick up an object, carry it, and drop it into your hands or at your feet.

The action: This action is a sequence of commands much like those in the previous lesson. In the previous lesson, you taught your dog to take an object from your hand. Here, you want to transfer the command from "Take It!" to "Pick It Up!" from the ground or a table. To do this, have your dog on-leash at your left side. With the object in your hand, command your dog to "Take It," but instead of giving the object to your dog, slowly lower the object to the table, encouraging him to follow it closely with his mouth. With your hand now resting on the table and still holding the object, change the command to "Pick It Up!" Now that he has the object in the mouth, command him to "Hold It!" After a moment, extend your hand under his muzzle and command him to "Drop It!" When he's completed this exercise, praise him lavishly. After a series of rehearsals, he will learn to pick up the object from the table or the ground, hold it for you, and drop it when you ask.

After he has mastered the "Pick It Up" and "Hold It!" exercise, you teach him a new command, which is to "Carry It!" To do this, as he is holding the object, command him to "Heel!" and move forward. As he's walking, put your hand underneath his muzzle and reinforce the command "Hold It!" as he's walking. This reinforces the message for your dog to hold the object and walk. Eventually the command is changed from "Hold It" and "Heel," to "Carry It!" After he has carried the object for several feet, halt and, extending your hand under his muzzle, give the command "Drop It!" Then, praise him lavishly and give him treats. The strategy here is to withhold the treats until the entire sequence of lessons is accomplished.

Director's cue (handler's signal): Here, the signals are a combination of pointing to the object and giving the command "Pick It Up!" then the command to "Hold It!" which is an open hand closing into a clenched fist. The accompanying gesture for the next command, "Carry It!" is to maintain the clenched fist, and, with a sweeping gesture, extend your arm, with fist clenched, in the direction you want your dog to carry the object (to the side, forward, away, and so on). For the final command, "Drop It!" there are two signals, depending upon what the script calls for. If the dog is to drop it into a person's hand, the gesture is simply the open hand under his muzzle. If the dog is to drop the object on the ground or a table, the signal is, with your fist still clenched, to extend your arm downward. As your arm becomes fully extended, and your fist is as close to the ground as possible, flick your hand open and downward, as if you're throwing something onto the ground.

LAME DOG/LIMP

The script: To walk holding one front paw up in the air; to dramatize a limp; to hobble.

The action: To learn this action, your dog will be using a prop: an Ace bandage, approximately four feet in length. To begin, have your dog stand in front of you, facing you, on-leash. Then, choose the leg that your dog will portray as the bum leg and loop the Ace bandage around it, with enough slack to allow you to hold your dog's leg up, like a sling.

For teaching purposes, the bum leg will

★ Lame Dog/Limp. ★

be your dog's left leg. So you should be holding the leash in your left hand and the sling in your right hand.

As you facilitate the action, imagine the movements of a puppeteer. Remember the puppyteer?

Puppyteerlike, you are guiding, directing your dog with the leash and the sling.

So, to initiate the action, to move your dog forward and toward you, command him to "Come!" with a slight tug of the leash. At the same time, hold the sling high (don't allow him to use his bum leg!). This will allow him to fulfill the command, to come to you, but on three legs.

As he is moving toward you, reinforce the action with a command he already knows: "Paw Up!" "Paw Up!" After he has taken five or six steps in this new manner, give him the command to Stay, and then praise him lavishly and give him a treat. As you rehearse this action, intersperse the "Paw Up!" commands with the proper command for this action, which is "Limp!" "Limp!" Now, your dog is ready to go to the next level, which is to limp for a longer distance, but without your help.

To do this, take the slack of the sling and wrap it around his neck and shoulders, so his leg is held up at his chest as if with an arm sling. Then, with him still on his leash, command him to Heel! and reinforce the command, "Limp!" "Limp!" Praise him lavishly and reward him with a treat. Eventually, he will master the Lame Dog role without a leash or a sling.

Director's cue: (handler's signal): Here, you give the command "Come!" with the appropriate signal. Bend down to the dog and give the command "Limp!" and point decisively to the paw. Quickly draw your hand back and up near your chest, as if it's in an arm sling, and, repeating the command "Limp!" mimic your dog's limping motion.

JUMP THROUGH THE HOOP

The script: To have your dog jump through a hoop.

The action: Since previously your dog learned to jump over hurdles and through tires in the stunt training on the agility course, we will now teach him to jump through a hoop, which will help him transpose this learned action to a specific required action with any prop in any studio setting, such as jumping through a window or making a flashy entrance through a paper hoop to promote a new product for an ad campaign.

★ Jump through a Hoop. ★

Here we need to set the stage to allow your dog to learn this action in a fun and effective way. Take a common hula hoop and wedge it or tape it to a doorway. This directs his path so that he must go *through* the hoop, not around the hoop. For the beginning exercise, start with the hoop affixed low to the floor (depending on your dog's size, approximately four to six inches from the floor). Also, it's important to block the empty space between the bottom of the hoop and the floor. This is important, so your dog can visualize the path he must take, which is through the hoop, and not under the hoop.

To start, have your dog sitting, on-leash, in front of the hoop. Give him the command to Stay and thread his leash through the hoop to the other side. This will put you and your dog at opposite ends of the hoop. Have a treat in your other hand, and to encour-

★ Copelia learning how to jump through a hoop. ★
COURTESY MARIAN HART

age the jump, show your dog the treat, and with a tug of the leash, command "Jump-Hup!" Immediately after he's cleared the hoop, praise him lavishly and give him the treat. When he has mastered this exercise, begin to raise the height of the hoop. Most dogs should be able to jump through the hoop at waist-high level. When your dog becomes comfortable jumping through the hoop at any height, it's time to take the hoop out of the doorway. He now knows to go *through* the hoop, and not around or under the hoop.

The aim here is for your dog to perform the action as high as he can, wherever you ask him, and without a leash. To do this, command your dog to "Stand/Stay" at your left side. Hold the hoop in your left hand, positioning it approximately midway between your knee and waist. Command him to "Jump-Hup!" When he clears the hoop, praise him and reward him with a treat.

Director's cue (handler's signal): With the command "Jump-Hup!" you simultaneously show him his course of action with a quick upward-and-over arclike motion, forefinger pointing and wrist snapping.

JUMP THROUGH YOUR ARMS

The script: To make a hooplike circle with your arms and have your dog jump through them.

The action: After your dog has mastered jumping through the hoop, you now want him to mimic this action as he jumps through your arms. To facilitate this action, return to the doorway with the hoop. This time, however, hold the hoop with your arms following the curve of the hoop as much as possible—your left arm draped up arcing over the top curve of the hoop, your right arm embracing the lower curve of the hoop. Your arms should be encircling the hoop almost as if they are a part of the hoop itself.

★ Jump through Your Arms. ★

Now that you're holding the hoop properly, kneel in front of the doorway. For the success of this action, where you kneel at the doorway is just as important as how you hold the hoop. Kneel at the *right* of the doorway, holding the hoop to your left in the doorway itself. Your dog should be to your left, in the doorway, in back of the hoop. This gives him a clear path to jump through the hoop. This position is important, because from your dog's point of view, your face is on the *other* side of the hoop, encouraging him to make the jump, with the command "Jump-Hup!" Praise him lavishly and reward him with a treat. When he has mastered this, the aim is to take away the hoop altogether. Then, once he's mastered jumping through your arms in the doorway, you can move this terrific action to any location.

Eventually, this action can be built upon for more dramatic effect. A longtime favorite movie ploy is to have the dog star leap into the arms of his human costar for a flashy finale!

Director's cue (handler's signal): If you are performing this feat with your dog, the verbal command "Jump-Hup!" will suffice. However, if you are cuing your dog for a commercial or movie scene, where your dog must work with others, the hand signal is the quick flick of the wrist, forefinger pointing the direction, in a short, arclike jumping motion. "Jump-Hup!"

JUMP INTO YOUR ARMS

The script: The action required here for your dog is the same action required for Jump Through Your Arms. The trick here, however, is to *catch* your dog in midair. For a more dramatic effect, a small or medium dog can jump from a platform, through the air and into your arms.

The action: For a large dog, position yourself as if he were going to jump through your arms, as previously learned. With the command "Hup!" hold your arms in a circle, which he will recognize as the Hoop Jump. With the command "Hup!" he will be eager to jump through your arms, as before. However, in midjump, as he enters your arms, grasp him and support him in your arms, with the command "Into My Arms!" Hold him for a moment, in a loving hug, praising him lavishly, and reward him with a treat.

For a small to medium dog, this jump can be dramatized by performing it from a slightly elevated platform, through midair and into your arms. To do this, position your dog on the platform and stand approximately two feet away, with your arms in the Hoop position that your dog will recognize as the signal to jump to.

With the command "Hup!" move your encircled arms closer to your dog, and then back toward you in a beckoning rocking motion that will encourage him to take the leap of faith! When he makes the jump, grasp him confidently and support him, with the command "Into My Arms!" Praise your dog lavishly and reward him with a treat. Eventually, your dog will perform this action with the single command "Into My Arms!"

Director's cue (handler's signal): With the command "Into My Arms," the handler's gesture is a two-armed, buoyant, bouncy lifting motion—a visual aid that will assure your dog that you are ready and able to catch him in midair!

HUP-UP INTO MY ARMS

The script: This performance works with small dogs. You and your dog will be standing close together (your dog directly in front of you), and, upon command, your dog is to jump straight up into your arms.

The action: To teach your dog this action, begin by sitting in a chair, with your dog directly at your feet, facing you. Encourage your dog to jump into your lap with the command "Hup-Up!" and tap your chest twice. You might want to reinforce the command by holding a treat with a guiding gesture, from your dog upward toward your chest, indicating the action.

When he has jumped into your lap, give him the treat, praise him, and begin again. This time, however, stand slightly up and out of your chair, making each jump up a little higher. It is important to remember to stand with your knees slightly bent. This will reassure your dog that he still has your lap to support him. Again, give him the command "Hup-Up!" tap your chest (with a ready treat still in your hand), and make sure to catch and hold him confidently and securely, with both your arms and the support of your lap.

Praise him lavishly and give him the treat. Continue practicing with your dog, each time moving closer and closer to a complete upright standing position. Eventually, your dog will do this on cue for you or for anyone else.

Director's cue (handler's signal): With the command "Hup-Up!" tap your chest twice and immediately hold your arms open in a catching position.

★ Hup-Up into Your Arms. ★

JUMP OVER BAR/LEG

The script: To have your dog jump over a bar and over your leg.

The action: The way to master this action is to follow the learning method we used with the hurdle and the hoop. To begin, have your dog in a Stand/Stay position. Hold the bar (this can be a yardstick, a cane, a broom, or any similar object) in your left hand a few inches off the floor in front of your dog. In your right hand, hold a treat, and motion from your dog to the other side of the bar. Simultaneously, give the command "Jump Over!" "Hup!" This will encourage him to jump over the bar. After he does what you ask, reward him with the treat and raise the bar.

When your dog has accomplished this action comfortably and at greater heights, he is ready to go to the next level, which is to jump over your leg. To do this, incorporate your leg into the action by raising your leg to the height of the bar and holding them together. Again, start low and work your way up. If you need to, support yourself against a wall or chair. You need to be steady for your dog to have the confidence to jump over you.

★ Jump Over Leg. ★

After he has mastered this stage, praise him lavishly, reward him with a treat, and remove the bar from the action. Now, the aim is to have your dog jump over your leg without the bar. The

★ StarPet dog Copelia: Jump through a Hoop. ★
COURTESY MARIAN HART

signal here is your raised leg, with the verbal command "Jump Over!" "Hup!" When he has mastered this, praise him lavishly and give him a reward.

Director's cue (handler's signal): As with the hoop action, with this action, sometimes you are required in the scene, working in tandem with your dog, other times your dog will be working alone or with costars. So, from a distance, the signal is a swift arclike gesture, with pointed forefinger and a flick of the wrist. The verbal command is "Jump Over!" "Hup!"

SNEEZE

The script: To make your dog sneeze.

The action: To do this, first command your dog, on-leash (so he can focus), to Sit in front of your or on a platform. At this time, massage his nose in a circular motion. This promotes the urge to sneeze. To reinforce the idea, mimic a sneeze yourself several times, alternating with the command "Sneeze!" To further encourage a sneeze, blow into your dog's nostrils with short, forceful, sneeze-like puffs. You can also try feathers and other means to tickle his nose and promote sneezing. Eventually, this action is done without a leash, and should be a fun, playful comedy routine you share. Still, don't forget to praise him lavishly and give him a food reward for every wonderful sneeze!

Director's cue (handler's signal): With the verbal command "Sneeze!" tweak your nose twice and mimic a sneeze, and your dog will follow your lead.

YAWN

The script: To have your dog yawn on command.

The action: To do this, the ideal time is after your dog has been rehearsing his repertoire of stunts, and it's almost finishing time, and he has earned a much-deserved rest. Your dog will naturally yawn, so you'll want to watch for this and catch him in the act. As you catch him in the act, this is a good opportunity to command "Yawn!" so he will associate the action with your command. Simultaneously, take this opportunity to reinforce the hand signal, which is simply a closed fist slowly opening into a mouthlike yawn. At the same time, mimic a yawn yourself!

To do this, place your hand under his muzzle, back toward his jaw. Then, with your thumb and middle finger on opposite sides of his jaw, gently press into the jaw from either side. This will encourage him to open his mouth. As he opens his mouth, repeat the "Yawn" command, as above. Eventually, your dog should emulate a yawn when signaled with the proper hand gesture and verbal command. And don't forget, always praise your dog and give him a food reward.

Director's cue (handler's signal): With the verbal command "Yawn!" emulate an exaggerated yawn accompanied, in tandem, by your closed fist opening slowly into a yawn.

SCRATCH

The script: To have your dog scratch on command.

The action: The best way to teach your dog this action is to catch him in the act naturally. When you see him scratching, give him the verbal command "Scratch!" At the same time, in an exaggerated fashion, lift your arm up and scratch around your armpit/

★ Scratch. ★

upper rib cage area, mimicking his scratch, so this gesture becomes his scratching cue.

Another easy way to accomplish this action is to vigorously scratch your dog on his chest, side, or tummy. That will feel so good to him that he will join in and continue to scratch. All the while, of course, you continue to give the verbal command "Scratch!" and emulate the scratching motion on your rib cage, as well.

You can also encourage scratching by attaching a child's hair-clip to a few strands of fur. This will stimulate him to scratch. Don't forget to give the verbal command and hand signal, as well as a treat—and follow up with lots of robust belly scratches!

Director's cue (handler's signal): The verbal command "Scratch!" with an exaggerated scratching motion up around your armpit/rib cage area.

OPEN THE DOOR

The script: To open the door, either by grabbing the door-knob and twisting it open, or by pulling a rope or fixed handle and pulling the door open.

The action: To start, have your dog on-leash, standing in front of the door. At that time, put a tennis ball over the door-knob. To do this, simply slit the tennis ball open on one side. It will fit snugly over the door-knob like a bonnet. Using a ten-

★ Open the Door. ★

nis ball will help your dog to get a grip on the doorknob. It's a familiar play object, and the texture makes for an easy grip.

At this time, command your dog "Open the Door!" and, with his leash, guide his head to the doorknob. Now, he should be focusing on the tennis ball. Command him to "Take It!" and "Hold It!" When he's got the tennis ball/doorknob in his mouth, command him to "Open the Door." As you do this, guide him backward with his leash, and simultaneously, grasp the door with your other hand and help move the door toward him, to reinforce the understanding of the action. Reward him with generous praise and treats!

With practice, your dog will be able to do this off-leash, without the tennis ball, and with just the one command "Open the Door!" This is one of the most-often-requested actions for a dog in TV and film work.

Director's cue (handler's signal): With the verbal command "Open the Door!" you make a sweeping sideways gesture pointing to the door.

DROP IT IN THE BOX

The script: To pick up an object, carry it to the box, and drop it in.

The action: Here, we use props to execute this action. Place an open box (about two feet by two feet square) approximately eight feet away from your dog. Take the object (a ball or favorite toy) about three feet away from your dog.

With your dog on-leash, walk your dog to the object, command him to "Pick It Up!" When he has the object in his mouth, walk him to the box, and command him to "Drop It in the Box!" Praise him lavishly and give him a treat. After a few rehearsals, have him execute the action off-leash. At this time, you will add hand signals to your verbal command. To begin, stand in one corner of the room, and give the command "Pick

★ Drop in Box. ★

It Up!" while simultaneously gesturing toward the object with a pointed finger. When he has the object in his mouth, give the command "Drop It in the Box!" and emphasize the action with a sweeping hand gesture pointing toward the box. He will then go to the box and drop it. When he has accomplished this action, praise him and give him a treat for doing such a good job.

A fun take on this action is to command your dog to "Clean up your room!" He will pick up and put away his toys in the toy box one by one! After all, a StarPet dog should keep his toys in order!

Director's cue (handler's signal): The verbal commands are the sequential "Pick It Up!" and "Drop It in the Box!" accompanied by directional hand gestures.

Adjust, Assimilate, Act

Now that your StarPet has adjusted to the set, theater, or sound stage and has assimilated into the ensemble effort of cast and crew working for a single production, he can now concentrate on the very best acting he is capable of.

I've often said that Bash's Ark is combining the knowledge of the actor's arc with the wisdom of Noah's Ark to discover the actor's arc within the animal actor.

This is what the Mariah Method is all about. Think of the famous acting technique, the Method, based on getting in touch with your primal self for motivation. The Mariah Method works with the wolf within the dog, your dog's inner feelings, for motivation.

Theater's famous Method acting immediately brings to mind its famous student, film legend Marlon Brando, and his now legendary primal cry, "Stelllllllllaaaaaaaaa!"

That famous film line is now such an intrinsic part of our lexicon that I even have a client—an actor, of course!—who named his beloved dog Stella just for the fun of practicing his Brando impersonation when he called for his dog at the playground!

Brando, and other Method acting aficionados, constantly ask, "What's my motivation?"

The Mariah Method will help your dog find his theatrical primal cry, so, that when the director cues him, he will be ready for a legendary performance! "Fidddddooooo!"

Here, then, is how to prepare your StarPet for his all-important close-up.

I'm Ready for My Close-Up!

In the school of Method acting, the acting coach will often work intimately with an actor to find the range of his arc to allow him to build a character, or to express an emotion. This often involves having the actor develop the skills to recall personal moments that elicited those emotions and transfer them to the character he is portraying.

This is called living in the moment. It is the actor's ability to bring up a past moment of emotion—happiness, sadness, pain—and apply it to his role.

Then, if the actor can capture and express that feeling, so pure and realistic, it is powerful enough to be captured on film and transmitted directly into the audience's hearts.

This ability is what made Strongheart such a powerful actor.

No one is better at living in the moment than a dog—or a child. They are pure and realistic, true to themselves, and never hold back. And that is a powerful, scene-stealing combination!

But the key to the success here is to remember to always keep the play in play-acting!

Your dog needs to understand that this acting is *play*, a *game*. This is especially important if the script calls for your dog to look sad or ashamed or frightened or angry. As your dog's director, you will have to elicit the called-for emotion by reminding your dog of a past incident, thus triggering the emotional response.

Still, just as young child actors learn that acting is make-believe, that it is all pretend, a game, so, too, can your professional StarPet, especially if you remember to keep the play in play-acting!

Being a soap opera veteran—where characters run the gamut of emotions from love to hate and everything in between one hundred times over (and that's just the first page of the script!)—Muffin was a real pro at Method acting! And he had a great deal of fun, too—because he loved all the attention, and knew it was just play-acting; just a game, just play.

So, when we would report to the set of *The Edge of Night* and pick up our script, I would immediately look for the action the character called for—and then search my memory for something, some action in Muffin's real life, that had triggered a similar emotional response. Then, I would use Muffin's real-life drama to trigger a matched response for his play-acting character.

And because, unlike a human actor, a dog cannot read the script and do this himself, you, as his personal director and acting coach, must bring up his personal experience to achieve the desired on-camera emotion.

For example, I might say, "Muffin! You're a bad dog! You didn't eat your cereal this morning!" Muffin would immediately think back to that time when he was bad—and I would have a very sad-looking dog. At the moment of that look, when it is perfect, and the camera captures it, and it's a "take" and the scene is a "wrap," I praise him lavishly, give him a treat, and wrap my arms tightly around him for a big hug! He knows he is *loved* and he knows it is a *game!*

In short, the StarPet, like the child star, knows he is play-acting!

And, sometimes, the director or the script calls for a more exaggerated, human emotion in a dog. This is often to help the audience understand the human drama behind it, or to move the plot along. So, basically, you are creating a somewhat symbolic, anthropomorphic language.

Getting this range from within just one emotion depends on you, your dog's director, having a good command of the commands you give your dog. You can create the desired effect in your dog with a skillful use of different inflections for the same word or command. This will emphasize the dramatic response you wish to elicit.

For example, a somewhat mild tone of questioning—"Muffin, what did you do?"—will elicit an equally mild response. A more teasing tone—"I know what you did!"—can elicit a sheepish or shameful response, depending, of course, on the script's anthropomorphic meddling with the audience's emotions, as well! And, finally, the same command given in a harsh, uncompromising tone will elicit the desired look of fright or anger.

As you rehearse, and are careful to always, after each take, praise and reward, your dog will catch on fast. Don't forget, as an "amateur," your dog has probably played this game many times with you *already!* What about the games where, to entice you to play with him, or to chase him, he will pick up one of his toys, and then, mischievously, if you don't respond, he will run to get something he knows he's not supposed to have (think of your favorite pair of shoes!) and shake it in front of your face! Your dog is teasing you! He knows he is being "bad," but he wants to play!

If you remember to always keep the play in play-acting, and follow every "take" with lavish praise and rewards, it won't take much rehearsing for your StarPet to understand—and love!—the fine art of play-acting!

I'm Ready for My Long Shot!

Even in an action scene in a long shot, the dog actor needs to express emotion and motivation that moves the plot along, just as in a close-up.

People think of the close-up as being more intense, but a dog has to draw on the *same* emotions and feelings to portray them in body language, from a distance, in a long shot. (You know it's been said, the actor's body is his instrument, and that's especially so for dog actors!)

This was achieved by Larry Trimble with Strongheart. He would use a rubber ball as a means to motivate Strongheart's actions.

Basically, for action long shots, in tandem with what the script is calling for, the rubber ball, and the intensity with which it is thrown, is employed like the inflections of a verbal command to get various intensities of emotional responses.

Just as the inflection in your verbal command was the stimulation to motivate your dog for his close-up, so, here, the ball is the stimulus to motivate for the long shot.

If the script calls for the dog to simply be seen trotting along the road, the ball is tossed in a simple, straightforward manner. (The audience, of course, due to camera angles, won't see the ball, just the dog.)

Also from a distance, the same look would work for a script that might call for a long shot of the dog jumping off the front porch to meet a school bus. "Joey just got off the bus! He's home from school!"

A dog responds differently to the different ways a ball is thrown out for him to fetch, and that is what you must marry with the script.

For example, if you kick the ball, rather than throwing it, the dog will run with far more zest and power. For a film script, this would perfectly illustrate a dog (think Lassie!) running back to the house to get help. (Will Timmy ever learn his lesson and stay out of that well?)

But you get the picture—and so, too, if everything is done right, will the audience!

After you praise your dog, you should engage your StarPet in a real playtime with a ball, for a job very well done!

This, truly, is play-acting in its purest form.

One Singular Sensation

One, singular sensation
Every little step she takes.
One, thrilling combination,
Every move that she makes.

This lyric from one of the most popular, longest-running Broadway shows ever—*A Chorus Line*—perfectly captures the moment you and your StarDog have finally arrived at.

You've learned the basics, the motivations, the nine inner drives, the techniques, and you've practiced and rehearsed. Your StarDog has learned to adjust to certain methods and to new surroundings, and to assimilate your craft within the surroundings of props and stage settings, other cast members, and production crews.

Now, you need to learn and practice the technique that will carry your StarDog's talent to the forefront. This is where the real acting comes in, and what separates the talented amateur from the polished professional.

When you can effortlessly marry your StarDog's talent and technique, he will truly be one singular sensation, ready for the spotlight to follow every little move that he makes!

From Pavlov's Dogs to Pavlova's Dogs!

The professional StarPet will be called upon, if he is cast in a commercial, for example, to follow the action of a storyboard (a rough picture book of a script, illustrating the action).

Or, if he should win a role in a film, the script may call for a similar sequence of events. For example, the script may call for your dog to enter the scene, walk to a front door, pick up a newspaper, take it to an actor sitting in a chair, place the newspaper in the actor's lap, then sit next to the actor, then give the actor his paw.

The action of this script calls for your dog to advance to the level where, instead of just performing one action at a time, or one trick at a time, he must instead perform several actions, in sequence, in one take!

Teddy the Great Dane was unsurpassed in his ability to perform a phenomenal series of action sequences. In fact, in one of his more memorable scenes—shot entirely in one take, and without missing a beat—Teddy opened a kitchen door, shut it behind him, then proceeded to the stove, where, match in teeth, he lit the burner. He then picked up a tea kettle, moved to the sink, filled the tea kettle, carried it back to the stove, and set it on the burner. He then picked up a broom and swept the floor while waiting for the water to boil!

To do this, we use a technique called "chaining"—chaining together several individual actions into one long sequence. You train for one behavior, it becomes a link, a second behavior, a second link, a third action, another link, and so on. But, the key, here, is that this must be accomplished all in one take, without a leash, and without stopping for praise or food reward.

So, to successfully accomplish this sequence of actions, think of it as each action as a link—like the link in the chain of your dog's training collar. Just as each link, in perfect sequence and tandem with the other chain links, allows the training collar to easily pull and release for direction, so the direction of your dog now becomes an "invisible" chain-link training collar.

On-camera, your dog is a working actor, playing a role, so you cannot be on the other end of the leash directing him. This is off-leash, and you are out of camera range. Your dog can no longer be directed by the pull and release of the traditional chain-link collar—the metal links that pull and release, facilitating good behavior—so we replace the collar with the invisible acting collar of chaining.

Equally important, you cannot run into camera range and reward your dog with praise or a treat!

This is where you marry talent and technique to the fine art of acting that will turn your StarPet into a singular sensation, winning raves from the audience as well as from the director, who will be thrilled when your StarPet can accomplish the sequence of actions all in the necessary one take!

To do this, you direct your dog with the clicker.

In the old days, the Old Masters didn't use the clicker. There was no such thing, and for those early pioneering dog stars, it really wasn't necessary. The great Strongheart and Rin Tin Tin both came from military war-dog backgrounds, with precision training. For those early dogs with a military background, basic training really was basic training! It was the foundation of precise, military behavior. The behavioral training links were executed in a series of staccato, precise, repetitive training sequences—directed by a series of appropriate hand signals from their trainers, who were out of camera range.

Still, although the clicker has its place in training, it is not the be-all and end-all. Indeed, it is most effective when used appropriately, sparingly, and in tandem with both traditional Golden Age methods and sophisticated modern techniques. And, as with any tool, it is only as good as the person who is using it. I could swing Tiger Woods's golf club, for example, but that wouldn't mean I had Tiger Woods's talent!

Mike, the Shaggy Dog, was the Tiger Woods of television commercials! He was talented, charismatic, and at the top of his very prolific game! He was a champion at chaining—he could have played an eighteen-hole golf course hitting holes in one every step of the way, and all in one take, to boot! In commercial after commercial, from Burger King to Cheerios, Mike performed effortlessly. He might have been working for Burger King, but it was the clicker that got his creative juices flowing!

For example, Mike would have to walk to Burger King, go to the table, get up on the chair, sit up on the chair, wave, and then bark and hold his position. To teach him the clicker method, he had to understand that the click signals a treat is coming, a reward is on the way, but only when the action is complete. Until then, keep on going, on to the next sequence.

So, first, I would give the command, Mike would execute the command, I would click the clicker and give him a treat. Then, on to the next command, Mike would execute the command, I would click and give him the treat. Then the third command, action, click, treat, and so on.

Then, I would run Mike through his paces, his sequence of events, but *without* the treat. Command, perform, click ("No treat now, but keep going, it's on the way!"), then on to the next action. Command, perform, click ("No treat now, but, I promise, keep going, it's on the way!"), then on to the next action. Command, perform, click ("Not quite yet time, but a promised treat soon!"), and on to the next action. Command, perform, click, and— "Cut!" "It's a wrap!"

The take was wonderful! Lavish praise! Good boy! And here, finally, is your promised treat! Job well done!

So the clicker can help your StarPet find his range, his Bash's Ark—how far his potential, talent, and technique can take him. Like an invisible chain-link collar, this invisible *"train* link" collar can help you, as your dog's director in controlling the scene, to draw him out more, or to hold back, and then release. When you can artfully execute the use of the clicker, you can help to bring out your StarPet's superbly executed performance, a seamless acting performance that will thrill the audience and the producer. (Remember, time is money!)

Your dog's ability to understand this concept (about the clicker, not the money!)—that several commands may follow the initial command, and that he should continue to pay attention until the director yells "cut!"—is what makes a true professional, a true StarPet!

The skillful use of the clicker marries technique and talent, science and artistry—the science of the groundbreaking Ivan Pavlov with the artistry of the gravity-defying prima ballerina, Anna Pavlova!

With the proper use of the clicker, you can motivate your dog with the certainty of Ivan Pavlov's science, to bring out the effortless artistry of Anna Pavlova.

The use of the clicker here is a promise that the food reward will come later. Just as the infamous bell signaled Pavlov's dogs that food was coming, so the clicker signals your dog that a reward is coming, but to continue acting. The difference is that Pavlov's bell triggered the dogs' gastric juices, while your clicker will trigger your dog's creative juices!

As a dancer creates intricate choreography from just five basic steps, and the dog creates beautiful action from just nine inner drives, the clicker, from the master choreographer or director, can signal the dancer, the dog actor, into each individual step, select each dog action, transforming them into an artfully choreographed sequence of dance or theater.

This skillful marriage of talent and technique turns Pavlov's Dogs into Pavlova's Dogs!

And when you have mastered your director's skills, and your dog reaches this pinnacle of understanding, your talented

StarPet will be transformed into a talented, savvy, and professional StarPet!

Make Your Own Storyboard

Now you and your dog are on the verge of becoming true StarPet professionals. As professionals, you and your dog will have to hone your craft, to bone up on all that you have learned. You need to practice all the methods, motivations, and techniques, and to emulate, dress rehearsal–style, a professional job.

As a professional, you now become not only your dog's director, but also his writer, so you will want to put together a dress rehearsal that can best showcase your dog's individual strengths and talents. Think of Larry Trimble as a mere kid busily writing all those tailor-made scripts to showcase his dog Jean's talents!

You can do it! And, more important, your dog can do it!

Still, you may want to start with something simple. Choose five to eight behaviors and actions your dog does best and combine these into a storytelling sequence, like the silent movies of the dog stars of yesteryear. Then, for the storyboard, break these behaviors and actions down into a sequence and put them together, like an illustrated story.

Why not try creating a storyboard from a favorite thirty-second commercial spot you may have seen before? You know, the one you saw a while ago, and you thought, Hey! My dog can do that!—and then you rushed out and bought this book? Yeah, that's the one!

Well, now that your dog has the training and technique to showcase his talents to their best advantage, he definitely can do it!

So, break down the action you see the dog performing in the

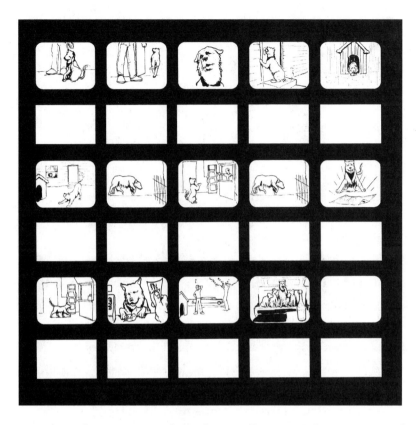

commercial into a series of simpler, smaller steps. This sequence of events becomes your storyboard and is what you want your dog to perform to re-create the commercial.

After you've practiced with your own Trimble-style, tailor-made storyboard, here's a sample of a commercial you may want to try.

As you read it, you will discover that it incorporates several of the actions your dog has mastered in this chapter, and they are the ones most frequently called upon for commercial work. It's entitled *Dreams Can Come True!*

The story starts and the action begins with the dog lying by the feet of his owner, scratching. The owner is a disagreeable fellow who should never have had a dog to begin with! Scowling, he yells at the dog, "Fleabag! Get out of here, you dumb fleabag of a dog!"

As the man continues his tirade—"Get out of the house, now!"—you can see the dog's face, as he dramatizes the sad look, as if to say, "Why are you yelling at me? I just want to be loved by you!" This is definitely a close-up!

As the dog sadly leaves, tail between his legs, the owner slams the door.

The dog then turns to look at the door, waits a moment, then tries to open the door, grasping the doorknob with his teeth, but to no avail.

Then, in the next sequence, the dog is outside in his doghouse, in the rain. He is still sad, but he gets up and stretches (play bow) and looks back to the house, then forward to the street, then back to the house. Finally, he walks off down the street, as the rain stops.

As he's walking, he sees a deli, stops, and sits up, looking in the window expectantly, but the store is closed. He continues walking.

As he's walking, head hung down in despair, he finds a dollar bill on the ground. He picks it up.

With the next shot, you see the dog walking into another store. He goes over to the counter, puts his paws up and onto the counter, and drops the dollar bill on the counter. The person behind the counter gives the dog a lottery ticket.

Then, the scene cuts back to the dog's owner, out in the yard, looking for the dog. "Where is that dumb fleabag of a dog?"

And, at that moment, from another angle, you see a stretch limo with the window down, and the dog sitting in the limo.

Then, another scene, from an angle inside the limo, widens to show the dog sitting happily with three beautiful poodles!

The dog begins barking happily (only on your command, of course!) and waving triumphantly—a good-bye to bad times, a hello to good times. If your dog could truly speak, his line would be, "Dreams really can come true!"

And that is what StarPet is all about—working to make your dreams come true!

So make your play-date for play-acting!

In fact, rehearsing this storyboard—or any others you may choose to create for your StarPet—is a wonderful way not only to train your dog, but to really have fun, not just with your dog, but with your family and friends. Get the neighbors involved. You don't need to have a real limo, of course. Just use the family car, or a wagon, and pretend. And don't forget the costumes! It's easy enough to fix up a bow tie for him, and a fun hat or skirt for his newfound poodle friend!

This is truly the spirit of "Hey gang! Let's put on a show!"— and a great dress rehearsal for your StarPet's professional audition, casting call, or job.

Because, as much as this is play, your dog is also learning. In fact, if you have a video camera, it's a good idea to tape your commercial. Just as, at the end of rehearsals and performances, directors and actors sit and critique their performances and learn from those critiques, your video will be a wonderful learning tool.

And, if you are really pleased with your video, you can send it out as a "demo tape" to advertising agencies, casting directors, and photographers, to give them a chance to see the caliber of your StarPet's work.

In fact, one pet owner's home movies made it all the way to the prestigious Cannes Film Festival!

But, at the very least, you will have a wonderful home movie of a wonderful dog and a wonderful time.

Because our StarPets will always be stars in our hearts and in our homes!

CHAPTER SIX

Training Your StarCat

*B*ack in 1979, the year that archeologists found evidence trumpeting the dog as mankind's "oldest friend," cat lovers everywhere were mourning the death of their "oldest friend"—Morris the Cat, America's favorite finicky feline. With legions of rabid fans (unparalleled and unheard-of even in the arena of dog food commercials!), Morris enjoyed rock star–like status as the popular barker for cat food!

As the legendary pitch cat for 9-Lives cat food, Morris's famous face and *purr*fect personality made millions for the company—and gave this nation of dog lovers a run for its money! In fact, so loved was Morris that his passing made the front pages of newspapers all across the country. The *New York Post* draped his picture in traditional black mourning, the headline lamenting that Morris had "Gone to His Heavenly Din-Din."

And, even in death, this iconic cat cast a long shadow, his stardom not only eclipsing that other news item touting proof that the dog is man's oldest friend, but also foreshadowing the phenomenal fanfare for felines that was waiting in the wings.

For, as I write this—with the new millennium barely into its kittenhood—cats have officially edged out dogs as the nation's favorite pet!

While a whopping 65 million Americans own dogs, astoundingly, another 75 million Americans own cats. For the first time in history, the cat has officially become America's "Top Dog"—infiltrating the heretofore exclusive dog domain, toppling the dog from his prime-time perch and sending him packing with his tail between his legs! Now, the cat has become the Alpha—the leader—of the great American pet pack!

And now, a quarter of a century since the front-page headlines of Morris's death and (for dog lovers, anyway) the hallmark headlines of anthropological and archeological importance, new headlines herald historic vindication of the reigning cat's newfound, dog-defying demographics!

While the dog still rules the roost as mankind's oldest friend and costar, reporters are now crowing that the cat is not far behind in man's cast of costars—only about four thousand years (give or take a millennium or two!).

You see, according to the Smithsonian National Museum of Natural History in Washington, D.C., and *Science* magazine, French scientists recently discovered an ancient tomb on the Mediterranean island of Cyprus, dating back to 7500 B.C.! The Stone Age grave in the Neolithic village of Khirokitia was filled with polished stone, axes, pigment, and flint tools. But what excited the scientists was the joint burial of a boy and a kitten cradled together; the kitten, about eight months old, curled in the crook of the boy's arm.

Researcher Jean-Denis Vigne reports that the remains nestled in such close proximity in a careful and loving joint burial implies "a strong association between two individuals, a human and a cat." Melinda Zeder of the Smithsonian National Museum of

Natural History was even more explicit. "In lieu of finding a bell around its neck, this is about as solid evidence as one can have that cats held a special place in the lives and afterlives of residents of this site."

Indeed, until this finding, it had generally been accepted that cats were first domesticated in ancient Egypt three thousand to four thousand years ago, but this recent finding certainly bolsters what those of us who love and live with cats have known all along: Our cats have costarred with us since time immemorial.

And so, just as Morris, as a professional StarPet pitching 9-Lives cat food to the public, lived far longer than the proverbial nine lives—more like nine thousand lives, given the astounding popularity that spawned a television life span encompassing a prolific commercial career in first runs and reruns—so it also turns out that all cats have been astonishingly popular far longer than we ever dreamed, having shared their lives with us, their oldest friends and costars, for over nine thousand years!

Until this phenomenal finding, the most well-documented co-existence of cats and people dated back to the Egyptians, circa 2000 B.C. As we know, the Egyptians not only cared for cats as pets, they also worshipped them for many reasons. Their attractiveness and grace were factors, of course, and their usefulness in controlling rodents and snakes was also much prized. Two of the distinctive feline qualities that amazed the Egyptians were their ability to see in the dark and the fact that their eyes can, in different lighting, noticeably change their appearance!

There are also many sculptures and bronzes of Egyptian cats, and cats that belonged to aristocratic families were mummified and given magnificent funerals and elaborate tombs. Another example of ancient reverence for cats and their place in man's life and afterlife is in the Norse culture. Vikings are said to have taken cats on board their ships to protect their storage from rats and mice, and their souls from evil spirits. And there is a Finnish saying that black cats carry the souls of the dead to heaven. Indeed, the Norse goddess of love, Freya, traveled in a celestial chariot guided and guarded by her two companion cats.

In the more sentient history of the species, however, scientists have grounded their theories of the ancestry of today's domestic cats on the small wild cats of Africa. Because cats interbreed easily, however, determining the exact ancestry of today's domestic cats is difficult, and European and North American wild cats may also have contributed to the gene pool. And, unlike dogs, it has only been in the very recent history, for barely more than a century, in fact, that cats have been bred to develop particular colors and body conformation.

Once our nomadic ancestors began to settle into farming as a way of life, cats became an important part of almost all households. For, although historically and statistically cats do not guard, herd, or hunt with humans (although I have heard some pretty amazing anecdotal evidence to the contrary!), cats *do* perform a very important and necessary service: They control the vermin population!

Early on in our shared, postnomadic history, cats protected grain stored in farms, and later, as we became a more urban creature and moved into towns and cities, our cats came along with us and kept the rodents away from our shops and homes. And in eighteenth-century Europe, when the plague (carried by rats) reared its ugly head, cats became particularly valuable for their rodent-hunting abilities.

Soon, though, with the cat's soft, affectionate nature, charming personality, and entertaining agility, this special creature, along with the dog, became a much-loved pet. Granted, cats' expertise in rodent control was ever important, but their newly recognized and appreciated quiet companionship endeared them to many.

Indeed, people soon discovered many qualities that make cats ideal roommates! They are decorative and scrupulously clean, washing themselves thoroughly at least once a day. They are quiet, neat, and rarely house-soil. And, because they are not pack-oriented, they don't require constant reassurance. (Now, that is a director's dream—no fussing over a diva that needs constant reassurance of her beauty and talent! On the other hand, though, not being pack-oriented might make for an aloof diva—one who doesn't work well with a show requiring ensemble acting!)

But that's typecasting—and I've been in this business long enough to know never to typecast an animal! Oh, there are certainly guidelines that can be followed in training and casting all types and breeds and mixed breeds of both cats and dogs, but those of us who know and love and work with our pets know enough to know what we don't know—and our pets, especially StarPets, are always surprising us!

And here I must add a cat and canine caveat to some of the following training analogies. Those of you who have both a dog and a cat will be reading both sections, and, along with their inherent differences, will find some intriguing similarities in the way dogs and cats are trained and the truisms that apply to both. And, for those of you who have dogs, but not cats, please keep reading. You'll discover many things about cats that may surprise you!

A case in point includes the Weatherwax dynasty of Lassie fame—and a couple of the stars in Lassie's stratospheric orbit!

Weatherwax himself always worked with dogs, until he began to notice (and be impressed by) the antics of some of the cats hanging around his ranch and kennels. He noticed that, far from being fearful of the dogs, some of the cats were intrigued by the dogs, even, seemingly, attempting to emulate their behavior. Eventually, Weatherwax took a few of the "stand-out" cats, and, along with his heralded hounds, turned them pro! Indeed, one Weatherwax cat, Whitey, even starred with the late great Katharine Hepburn, in the motion picture classic, *Stage Door!*

And the beloved actress June Lockhart—forever known as Lassie's mom—was actually a cat's *mom!* Oh, Miss Lockhart loved dogs—how could she not, being "Lassie's mom"? And she even served time as the celebrity spokesperson for the American Humane Association's Hearing Dog Program. But, at home, June Lockhart was a cat woman!

You see, when she wasn't toiling on the set of television's long-running hit series *Lassie,* Miss Lockhart loved to stay home, poolside, with her kids, basking in the sun and cooling off with long swims.

And, evidently, the family *cat* had the same idea!

You see, not only did the cat love to engage in "typical" cat activities, like the traditional basking in the warm sunlight, he also liked to swim! According to the actress, her cat loved interactive games and playtimes with her and her children, and like the children, was intrigued by the water. Eventually, the cat actually jumped into the pool to join the family fun and games!

At first, the actress was horrified and quickly rescued the cat, placing him firmly back on deck. However, the little water nymph jumped right back in! After more than a handful of times scooping the little surf-and-turf tabby out of the water, Miss Lockhart realized her rescue efforts were futile. The little guy didn't want to be left hanging out to dry. He wanted to ditch the turf, jump into the surf, and hang ten!

Finally, in a scene right out of the classic *Lassie* series, Miss Lockhart relented and allowed her eager children to give this extraordinary pet swimming and water-safety lessons. Soon, this unique cat was happily (and quite adeptly!) dog-paddling as if he had been doing it since *puppy*hood!

This is a wonderful story, and it beautifully illustrates the Star-Pet credo: "Always keep the *play* in play-acting!"

For, although June Lockhart's cat was not a professional StarPet and was not learning to swim for a professional job, Miss Lockhart had the right idea.

Whether you are training your personal StarPet for fun and games at home or training your professional StarPet for an acting job, always be keenly perceptive during your cat's off-times, her playtimes. When you are aware of the behavior and antics your cat exhibits and enjoys naturally, then you can base your training on those behaviors and antics that come naturally to your cat, and that your cat enjoys.

Here, however, I must add this cat caveat: I do not recommend or endorse attempting any sort of training involving cats in or around water. Miss Lockhart and her children were building on what their pet cat's antics had shown that he enjoyed. Don't forget, the cat kept diving into the pool of his own volition! As a rule, most cats don't like water, and you should not attempt this type of stunt. And, as a StarPet rule for you, although I encourage you to build your cat's trick repertoire based on what she enjoys doing naturally, that obviously does not apply if the behavior your cat exhibits, or the trick you would create, could possibly pose a threat to your cat's health and well-being!

Last, when it comes to stunts, although I warn against typecasting and encourage you to be creative in your StarPet sessions, you must learn to harness that creativity, mold that talent, and achieve a perfect marriage of talent and technique to create a successful professional StarPet.

And, to accomplish this, there are some immovable "givens."

As we saw in the last chapter, unlike a human actor, a StarPet not only has to attain a perfect marriage of talent and technique, she also has to first learn the language of the director, as well as to acquaint herself with the "foreign" land she finds herself working in: the theater, photographer's studio, or television or motion picture sound stage. Along with the traditional three P's in training I always tout (Patience, Persistence, and Praise), and the three C's, which those of you who read *Cat Speak* are familiar with (Care, Compassion, and Concern), the professional StarPet must also learn the three A's (Adjust, Assimilate, and Act). This is very important, because before your cat can begin to professionally act, she needs to adjust to the situation and assimilate into her surroundings—something human actors (thanks to the accident of birth into their species) already have a leg up on!

To help my clients understand the job ahead of them, I often use the analogy, as I do with dogs, of the famously successful dance duo, Fred Astaire and Ginger Rogers.

You see, a StarPet working with a human star or director is akin to Ginger Rogers dancing with Fred Astaire. Astaire, of course, was supremely talented, gifted—some dance aficionados even refer to his genius. Astaire was the star, and he received most of the accolades. But a tip of the (top) hat must also be given to Ginger Rogers, because, as the aforementioned dance aficionados are quick to point out, Ginger did everything Fred did—but backward and in heels!

So, as you learn to train your StarPet, you must pay deference to her difference. Just as our cats are familiar to us in many ways, so our cats—still loving, trusted members of our families—are unfamiliar to us; different in many (seemingly mysterious) ways.

Just as Ginger Rogers, backward and in heels, approached the dance from a different direction than did Fred Astaire, so our cats approach the art of "acting" from a different perspective. And, like a good director, as you are your cat's director, if you can plumb the depths of your cat's psyche, and understand her, you will be able to bring out the *best* in her, her best *performance*—and widen her (cat) actor's "arc," and soar into boundless horizons!

To do this, Bash's Ark incorporates what I call the Mariah Method. As we discussed in earlier chapters, the Mariah Method is a kind of Method acting for dogs.

Yes, I said *dogs*!

But the key here isn't to train your cat like a dog (although I have much anecdotal evidence from clients—and my own stable of StarPets—that suggests how doglike cats can be!). The aim and technique of the Mariah Method is equally applicable to all StarPets.

The Mariah Method for Cats

The key to The Mariah Method is gaining access to, and understanding of, the dog's nine inner drives, which are based on the wolf within the dog—the genetic code of behavior the dog has inherited from his ancestor, the wolf.

Obviously, your sweet tabby or cuddly calico is not descended from the wolf—so maybe we should call this the Muffy Method?—but the domestic cat is descended from eons-old wild cats!

And so, like the dog and the wolf, the cat also has a "prechoreographed" genetic code of behavior inherited from her ancestor, the wild cat. And, as any dance master (or Fred or Ginger!) will tell you, all the most complicated choreography of the most beautiful ballets is drawn, unbelievably, from only five basic dance positions. So, too, all the great symphonies incorporate the same eight notes of an octave. And so, too, in the art of animal acting, your StarPet, your cat, brings all her engaging, endearing, enigmatic talents from deep within her wild cat–based psyche of just seven basic wild cat-inherited inner drives.

And, just as all human actors are unique, with different strengths and weaknesses, so the same holds true for your cat star. Some of these traits may be breed- or type-specific, such as typecasting a Himalayan, who is naturally very calm and complacent, in the role of a homebody; or casting a Siamese, who tends to be very outgoing and vocal, in a role requiring great ensemble acting; or tapping a Maine Coon, who is a natural hunter and great in flight, for the long-shot Spiderman-style action adventure sequence!

But all cats—from the purebred to the random-bred type (mixed)—can bask in the spotlight of their own singular sensations!

So, in training your StarPet, try to imagine your cat's behavior as an incredible feline choreography, with the wild cat as the master choreographer—and you have just been handed the conductor's baton!

When you can identify and understand the seven inner drives from which all cat choreography flourishes, you and your StarPet—like Fred Astaire and Ginger Rogers—will be truly in sync. And when you can direct a perfect marriage of talent and technique within your StarPet to bring out her *best* performance, you will have a wonderful working relationship that would rival even that of Strasberg and Monroe!

And now, the stage is set for you and your StarPet.

Seven Instinctive Feline Behaviors

There are seven instinctive behaviors common to all members of the feline family. If you understand these behaviors, you will be well on your way to understanding how to make your cat a star.

1. FLIGHT BEHAVIOR

Cats have highly developed peripheral vision and an amazing sense of smell. If something or someone unknown—or with an unknown odor—nears, a cat will instinctively flee. Their sense of hearing is extremely acute; a strange or unaccustomed loud noise will also trigger flight behavior. Because they are able to jump amazingly high, their flight often leads them to high places. Cats are also able to compress their bodies, allowing them to squeeze into very small spaces.

Sometimes flight behavior will propel a cat into an impossibly small space. The best advice for an owner of a cat that has squeezed herself into a crevice or small hole is to go away and leave her alone. She will usually be able to get herself out once she calms down. Flight behavior stands many cats in good stead—when confronted with a pack of marauding dogs, for example.

2. CHASE BEHAVIOR

Cats are hunters by nature. Their keen senses impel them to chase down any small animal that moves fast and crosses their paths. Birds, lizards, bugs, mice, and rats are all fair game. Because they are able to pronate, or turn in, their front paws, they are extremely adept at grasping and playing with small prey—a practice some people find distasteful. But this is an instinctive act, not an act of cruelty.

Of course, chase behavior and the subsequent killing of rodents was one of the reasons that cats originally came to live with humans. Chase behavior may be turned into a game by cat owners who toss a small light ball (a Ping-Pong ball, for example) or a feathered object for a cat to bat at, chase, and retrieve.

3. HUNTING/STALKING BEHAVIOR

Closely related to chase behavior, hunting behavior is a very ingrained instinct in felines. Of course, wild cats hunt for survival. This instinct has carried over into the natures of many domestic cats, especially if they are allowed outdoors. Cat owners are often distressed when their beloved pets bring home small prey, presenting a dead songbird or field mouse seemingly as a present, very pleased with themselves and looking for praise. This is a difficult behavior to deal with if a cat is a determined hunter and is allowed outdoors.

4. TERRITORIAL BEHAVIOR

Territorial marking behavior is used by cats to delineate their "home turf" and is especially prevalent among un-neutered males, although neutered males and both spayed and unspayed females may engage in it. It is usually triggered by the presence of an unknown cat or cats, or an upsetting event such as a move to a new home or the arrival of a new person or animal in the house. Marking behavior consists of spraying urine against an upright surface, rather than squatting to urinate. Urinating in an inappropriate place, such as a person's bed, is another kind of territorial behavior.

Cats display territorial behavior when they scratch or claw surfaces other than designated scratching posts. Territorial behavior may also emerge as aggression toward the offender—a new cat, dog, or person.

5. AGGRESSIVE BEHAVIOR

Aggression is a form of defense and protection from harm. In general, when faced with an unfriendly or threatening person, cats prefer flight or avoidance. But cats can be aggressive to people and may bite or claw. A common type of aggression is chase, or predatory, aggression, in which a cat jumps out at a person as he walks by and sinks her teeth and claws into an ankle or leg.

Sometimes fear of something else (for example, an unknown cat outside) will cause a cat to strike out at a human. This is called redirected aggression. Some dominant cats will become aggressive and bite people who pet them even when seeming to have invited the petting. Cats can also be aggressive toward other cats or pets in a household.

6. VOCAL BEHAVIOR

Although cats regularly communicate with one another and their human companions through body language, they also use vocal sounds to communicate. From hissing to purring, cat vocalization can be subtle or demanding. Orientals, Siamese in particular, usually have loud, raucous voices, while other cats (typically longhairs) can have soft ones that are almost inaudible to humans.

A cat's meow to her owner may mean, "It's time to eat," "I need to go out" (or "my litter tray needs changing"), "Come here and look," or a number of different things. Her purr usually means contentment or pleasure, while a hiss can be a warning to "Stop it!" or "Go away and leave me alone."

Among cats, vocalization is often more strident, taking on a threatening quality, especially if there are strangers or an unknown cat wanders into another's territory.

An attentive owner will usually be able to discern the different sounds and qualities of his cat's vocalizations.

7. SOCIAL BEHAVIOR

Cats are not gregarious with their own kind. But domestic cats, perhaps out of necessity, or for other, more subtle reasons, are usually social with their human keepers and with other household pets, some more than others.

Those who don't admire felines often remark, "Oh, sure, your cat rubs against you and acts affectionate, because she wants to be fed." Perhaps this is so under certain conditions. But how to explain the purring cat that has just had dinner and lies by your side in bed or on the couch, nudging to be petted? Or the cat that greets her returning owner with happy chirps, even though she's been fed and cared for during the owner's absence? What about the pet cat that rubs affectionately against "her" dog when he's sleeping? Surely she doesn't expect the dog to feed her.

To be sure, cats do not *need* human companionship the way dogs do. They do not usually display separation anxiety or indulge in inappropriate behavior, even when left alone for long periods of time (although there are always exceptions). They seem to be quite content to be alone in familiar surroundings, especially if there is another pet in the household, ample food, water, and a clean litter tray.

However, they do seem to enjoy human companionship, and

some highly domesticated individuals and breeds (notably Siamese and other Orientals) often demand it.

Once you understand the seven instinctive drives of your cat, you have a further understanding of what cats are saying, what motivates them, what they respond to, and how they do these things, and this will help you have a better understanding of what they're capable of learning, expressing, or performing. Basically, you, as your cat's handler/trainer/director, will have a better understanding of *what* you can bring out of her and how you can bring that out. It's like the sculptor creating a fine statue. The sculptor will tell you he doesn't *create* the statue, but simply knows what's *inside,* within the block of unshaped marble, and chips away the excess to allow the beautiful form to come through.

I always say that you can command a dog to do something, but with a cat, you must ask her to do it!

Six Special Feline Abilities and Idiosyncrasies

Now that you understand the seven instinctive drives, you have to also learn that the six special feline abilities and idiosyncrasies your cat has are actually outward expressions of hidden talents.

An observant and learned owner/director/handler can recognize these "habits" as the glorious hidden talents that they are. When you can recognize this—along with their distinct instinctive seven inner drives—you, the handler, can work with these in molding, sculpting, and training the cat to express these drives and talents, to *act.* Thus, just as the human actor's abilities move the story line along by communicating what the script requires to the audience, so, too, can your StarPet!

Basically, as any theater purist will tell you, the actor's body is his instrument, and the same holds true—if not more so—for the cat actor!

1. COIL

First and perhaps most notable is the ability to *coil* their bodies like a spring, so that they can jump very high from a stationary position. This is a great help when they are in a situation demanding flight.

2. PRONATE

Then there is the ability to turn their paws inward, or *pronate* them, due to special muscles in their front legs. This ability is useful not only when grasping prey, but also in enabling a cat to climb extremely well and quickly, using the front paws to hold on. This, too, is very useful in assisting flight.

3. RETRACT THEIR CLAWS

Another physical trait that only domestic cats possess is the capacity to *retract their claws*. This enables them to walk on all types of surfaces without becoming stuck, and it also keeps their claws from wearing down, allowing them to continuously grow, and making them excellent hunting and climbing tools and defensive weapons.

4. SEE IN THE DARK

Cats' eyes have a great many more rods than those of other animals. This allows them to *see in the dark,* a very handy quality for hunting rodents and other small creatures.

5. SENSE OF SMELL

All cats also possess a highly developed *sense of smell.* I was made aware of this when we began photographing cats for *Catmopolitan.* The photographer used a roll of heavy paper as a backdrop and as a surface covering for the cat to sit or stand on. After the first cat model had had her pictures taken, I placed the second model on the paper. The cat went wild, fur standing on end, yowling and hissing! I quickly realized that she was reacting to the smell of a strange cat on the paper and from then on changed the paper after each model had finished. This ability to detect odors that humans can't is another very useful tool for ferreting out small prey. Also, most cats will refuse to use a litter tray that isn't clean, or one that has been used by a strange cat. A highly developed sense of smell can also lead to a finicky appetite.

6. SELF-GROOMING

Self-grooming is another typical feline behavior. With special, extremely rough tongues, cats groom themselves several times a day, usually after a meal, when they wake up from a nap, and after they have been petted. Each cat grooms herself in the same way, and in the same order, curling her front paws upward, licking them, and then using them to do a thorough job washing her ears, face, and the top of her head. Every other part of her body is then groomed in order. If a cat should stop grooming herself, it is a sure sign to her owner that she is not feeling well.

A StarCat Commercial

For a successful commercial you need to understand how to motivate your cat. The director's edge gives you, your cat's director, the edge, the insight, into understanding your StarPet's psyche. What motivates her?

Once you understand the seven instinctive feline behaviors and the six special feline abilities and idiosyncrasies, you will be able to look at your own cat in a different light—in the StarPet light.

With this book, you can understand that cats cannot be forced to act a certain way, but they can be motivated to act. Further, by using their natural instincts, you can teach them to act in the way the script calls for!

For example, I used a cat's natural instincts of flight and hunting to get the cat actor to follow the script for a Tender Vittles cat food commercial.

The storyboard called for the cat to be carried down a supermarket aisle, seemingly checking out and, ultimately, choosing, the very best cat food!

So, the script called for the cat to finally grab the Tender Vittles package off the supermarket shelf, as the food of choice. To make it appear that the cat wanted every single flavor, not just one, the action called for her to fling all the Tender Vittles packages into the shopping cart.

To do this, we used two instincts, flight and hunting.

In the beginning, we opened the backs of some of the boxes of food (out of camera range, of course) so the cat could smell all the products and focus on all the different boxes. Then, I would have the actor walk down the aisle holding the cat on his left side *under* his arm, gently but firmly keeping the cat's paws and legs tucked underneath—except, that is, for the cat's outer left front leg. This leg was allowed, indeed, needed, to be left out and draped over the actor's arm (like a summertime driver with his arm out the car window).

Then, the actor walks down the aisle, leaning, inclining toward the shelves, asking the cat, "Oh, you want this?" "You want this?" "You want that one, too?"

As the actor leans in toward the supermarket shelf, he is cuing the cat actor to act on his instincts of flight and hunting.

With the cat's sense of smell, the food cues in his instinct to hunt. And, by leaning the cat in toward the shelves, the actor is playing to the cat's instinct for flight. The cat wants to leap onto the supermarket shelf. But, since all of his legs but one are tucked safely and securely underneath the actor's arm, all the cat can do to act on the flight instinct is to reach out with just the one paw, pawing the air in attempted flight to the shelf.

The theatrical illusion is that the cat is choosing her favorite Tender Vittles! Based on instinctive flight and hunting, the cat reaches out to grab each box as she nears it. And, of course, cat food open and ready behind the boxes also feeds into that instinct (no pun intended!).

Motivating Your StarCat

Just as a director must give his actor motivation, so you must give your cat motivation, and help her find her motivation. As usual, the three P's, Patience, Persistence, and Praise, are always in use, but for the professional StarPet, *more* motivation and more inducements are sometimes needed.

Don't forget, with the dog, you can command; with the cat, you must *ask*—and sometimes bring *gifts!*

1. FOOD REWARD

Food rewards work well for most cats as a reinforcement for a verbal command you are teaching. When they respond to a verbal command, a food treat can be given in addition to praise. However, the whole idea is to give it in sparing amounts, so that the thrill of getting a food reward, a treat, gives you, as your cat's director, a greater window of opportunity for getting the job done, before your cat gets full!

This also works as a great stimulus for your cat to focus.

2. CHASE/PLAY REWARD

Here, by using a stick with string and feathers (this emulates a cat's natural prey and stimulates her to chase the prey, allowing you to direct what the action is), you can get your cat to focus and respond to a certain behavior/acting stunt by twitching and flicking the stick, manipulating the feather to cause your cat to focus, to chase, so that she follows the path and direction, sometimes by her head, or by any movement to any direction you want her to go.

The reward is to allow her to catch her "prey."

3. THE CLICKER

During training, I use a "clicker" as a sound motivator. The clicker is a simple child's toy, about the size of a car key. It can be plastic or metal and "clicks" when pressed between your thumb and forefinger. If the cat performs well, I give a click to confirm that she performed well, and then I follow up immediately with a treat. When it's not possible to give her a reward at the exact instant she performs the stunt, the sound of the clicker is a promise that she will get her treat as soon as possible.

Props (Training Equipment)

Still, although the cat actor's body is her instrument, as with any human actor, she still needs techniques, training, and props (training equipment) to support her performance.

The CatStar's props include:

THE PLATFORM

The training platform should be a waist-high table with a nonskid rubber mat on top. A bathtub mat, show mat, or rubber-backed doormat is best, because it will prevent your cat from slipping. Professional trainers often use special carpet-covered tables. Do not simply cover a table with a towel; it will slip and make the cat feel very insecure. This equipment is especially important if you want to progress to serious training.

It's important that the table be placed in a corner, so that it has two side walls for security and for preventing escape.

If possible, do not use the same table for training that you use for grooming. The training table should be a special place just for lessons. If it is impractical for you to have a special training table, a kitchen table or countertop covered with a nonskid mat can be a satisfactory substitute.

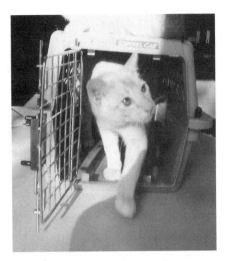

★ Cherubino comes out of the cage for a reward. ★
COURTESY MARION HART

While training the cat, you should stand close to your cat, approximately twelve to fifteen inches away from the edge of the table or counter. This distance allows you to work hands-on with your cat, as you will need to in the beginning stages of training, but also allows you to begin to introduce distance. This is because, eventually, if your cat is trained properly and you're working professionally, you will have to

★ Cherubino gets her reward. ★
COURTESY MARION HART

direct her from a distance outside camera range. So beginning training here with this distance begins to get your cat used to working with you from a distance.

This is important, because proper use of the platform is important for both on-leash and off-leash training, which we will go into later.

THE MAGIC WAND

This is simply a two-foot stick or dowel on which you can place a treat, a food reward for your cat. Any long-handled spoon or spoonlike utensil also works well. You can also make your own version of this by taking a small plastic spoon and simply taping it to the end of a stick or dowel.

The point is to have something long and slim and unobtrusive that you can put treats on the end of to motivate your cat for the action required.

THE CONDUCTOR'S BATON

You should also have a toy to help the cat focus. A stick with a feather "bird" on a string is particularly useful. It is important to be sure to always put this toy safely away so your cat cannot become tangled in the string when you're not around.

CARRYING CASE

Have your cat's carrying case on hand. It should be sturdy and comfortable. Part of her basic training will be to learn to go into the carrier on command. Also, your cat will feel safe and comfortable in her carrier. If your cat becomes a professional actor, her carrying case will become a haven on the set between "takes"—just like the thirty-five-thousand-dollar Winnebago trailer the human stars retire to between scenes!

The most commonly used type of cat-carrying case is made of rigid, waterproof material (airline-approved). There is wire on one side that provides air circulation and allows the cat to look around. Breathable carrier covers are available for cold-weather use. Plastic covers should not be used because they cause the interior of the carrier to become too hot in warm weather or in heated areas. I also prefer a carrying case that can be opened at the top as well as the end. Latches are better than zippers, which can snag the fur and skin.

There are soft-sided carrying cases (Sherpa bags), which are also approved by airlines. They are lightweight, and many cat owners prefer them to hard-sided cases.

SOFT COLLAR AND LEASH/HARNESS

A soft fabric or leather collar and leash are required. *Never* use a metal collar or harness on a cat. Ideally, the leash should be four to six feet long.

Basic Training

WALK ON A HARNESS (OR COLLAR) AND LEASH

To be a StarCat, your cat should be trained on-leash and willing to travel.

The leash is a training tool that provides security and control and promotes positive results. The choice of a collar or harness depends on what your cat feels comfortable in and what you feel brings the best results.

Whether you choose a collar or a harness, it should not be too tight, but should be comfortably snug, so your cat cannot slip out of it.

Put the harness or collar on your cat and let her walk around the house in short sessions with it on, for as long as it

★ A cat wearing a harness and leash. ★

takes until she seems comfortable. Then, attach a leash to the harness or collar and let the cat drag it around for a few minutes. Increase the time each day until she is at ease dragging the leash.

★ Cherubino, Walk on a Leash. ★
COURTESY MARION HART

Never, however, leave your cat alone and unattended with the leash on.

When she is able to walk around in a normal way when dragging the leash, pick up the leash and follow her around the house. Do this daily for five to ten minutes and your cat will soon become used to it. As you walk along with her, pick her up and walk a few steps holding her, then put her down again. Eventually your cat will learn that this is a comforting ritual and will feel secure when walking with you holding the leash. You can use a helper to hold a treat in front of the cat to encourage her to walk with you.

Once your cat has learned to walk on-leash, she is ready for basic obedience and StarPet training!

Your cat has to be willing to travel and adjust and assimilate to different environments, because much of the work will be in a studio or on location. She will be much safer, and you will have better control of her, if she is wearing a harness or collar and leash. Plus, she will begin to associate wearing her leash and collar/harness with sharing a new and positive adventure with you.

Your choice of a harness or collar will depends on what fits *both* your needs: Your cat must be comfortable with the collar or harness, and you must be able to control and train her with it. This is also important for security.

COME ON COMMAND

To begin, have your cat on the floor, on-leash. With a treat in one hand and a clicker in the other, call her name and entice her to come toward you: "Thomasina, Come!" You might also coax her with encouraging sounds, like kissing ("tch-tch"). You might also try shaking a box of favorite treats.

When she comes to you, click the clicker, give her the treat,

★ Teaching a cat to come when called. ★

praise her, and pet her. Show her how pleased you are by massaging her lovingly and lavishing more praise upon her. Make her coming to you a very positive experience. Once your cat has learned this action, repeat the lesson off-leash.

Once your cat has mastered this exercise, put her in her carrying case and take her to a different room in the house. Have a friend stay with your cat (still in the carrying case) while you move out of sight, into another room. Then, as you command your cat to come, have your friend open the case. When she finds you, give a "click," reward her with a treat, and make a very big fuss over her!

SIT ON COMMAND

Place your cat, on-leash, on the platform. Gently place one hand over her body and run your hand along her spine from head to tail. As you command her to sit, push down gently on her rump, while using the leash to help guide her into the Sit position. Once your cat sits, give a click and reward her with a treat. Eventually, she will sit with only the verbal command and a gentle tug of the leash.

Once she has mastered Sit with the verbal command, it is time to introduce the hand signal. The hand signal simply mimics the gesture of pushing her rump down. In the air, in front of her face (and without touching her), cup your hand up and over her head. When she sits, give a click and reward her with a treat. Eventually, she will sit on command without a leash, and with you standing at a distance from the platform.

STAY

Basically, this is a long Sit. Begin with your cat on-leash and give the Sit command. Once your cat is sitting, place your open hand in front of her face with your palm toward her face. Say "Stay," slowly remove your hand, and pause for a few moments. If she stays quietly, give a click and a treat and praise her. If she breaks out of the Stay, immediately put her back into a Sit and repeat the action. Step back farther and continue to say "Stay." Have her stay longer each time, then gradually back away from the plat-

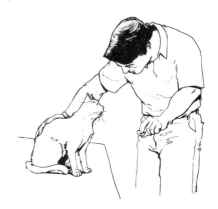

★ Training a cat to Sit/Stay. ★

form. Ideally, you will be able to have your cat stay when you are six feet away from her—or more—and without a leash.

LIE DOWN AND STAY

Review the Sit command. Begin with your cat sitting on the platform, on-leash. Then, put your left hand on your cat's shoulder and your right hand behind her front legs just above her ankles (you may change hands if it's more comfortable). Say "Down" and slide your cat's front legs forward while pushing down on her

★ Cherubino, Down command. ★
COURTESY MARION HART

shoulders. Keep the pressure light and continue saying "Down" or "Lie Down." Hold the position, pause, then give a click and a treat.

Now that you've taught her to lie down on command, you want to teach her to respond to the accompanying hand signal. To do this, again, begin in the Sit position. Then, with her leash in one hand and a treat in the other, in front of her face, at eye level, give the command "Down." As you say this, make sure she is focused on the hand with the treat, and follows it as you motion in a downward gesture to the platform. Simultaneously, gently tug her leash to guide her down. When she lies down, give a click, and give her the treat. Praise her lavishly. Eventually, with practice, she will lie down without a leash, with just the verbal command and/or hand signal.

Once she has learned this command to lie down, now you can add the "Stay" command.

To do this, once she is in the Down position, and you have given her a click and a treat, immediately put your hand in front of her face, palm facing her, and give the command "Stay." Then back slowly away from her, for a moment or two, then return to her, give a click, with an accompanying treat and much praise. Here the aim is to gradually increase the length of time your cat remains in the Stay position.

It's been said that the only way to get to Carnegie Hall is to practice, practice, practice! When you have done this, and you are beautifully in sync with your cat, then it is time to test your cat's ability to communicate her talents to those all-important people around her: casting directors, directors, producers, and—ultimately—her audience!

The StarPet Test is a level of evaluation I have developed and used throughout my career to assess the ability of an aspiring animal actor.

Cats that may be trained for print work, commercials, television, and film have all met or exceeded this standard—whether they were my own StarPets, the pets of clients, or those chosen from my open casting calls and StarPet Workshops. In fact, it was this test that gave many of the wonderful cats I later cast for *Catmopolitan* and *Vanity Fur* their first chance to shine!

So think of this test as a kind of dress rehearsal—a sort of first audition or out-of-town tryout. If you can ace this test, you will know that your cat has what it takes to continue to the next chapter, Advanced StarCat Training—and be well on her way to becoming a professional StarPet!

But, before you take this test, I need you to review and practice everything you have learned. And, if you should "fail," don't worry! The way to Carnegie Hall is to practice—and "practice makes perfect." Remember, even the greatest movie stars need more than one "take" to get it right!

StarPet Test for Cats

A. Your cat must be up-to-date with her inoculations and, if your community requires it, licensed.

1. Your cat must be checked by a veterinarian to determine that your cat is in good physical and mental health, is well mannered, and is not aggressive. A checkup that finds your cat healthy and physically sound will ensure that she does not harbor a condition that could become a problem in training (such as deafness or visual impairment).

2. Your cat must be properly groomed. Proper grooming helps a cat maintain a basic level of good health and contributes to a cat's sense of well-being. While your veterinarian can certify that your cat has no medical condition to impede her ability to perform, you or your groomer can make certain that your cat has no other condition that could impair her performance. First, make certain your cat's nails are regularly trimmed. This is of paramount importance for a StarCat. Short nails help to ensure a cat's manageability, which is all-important. If a cat is used to having her nails trimmed, she is used to being handled. Long nails—even on the most well-trained cat—can inadvertently impede training or stall production. Nails that are too long can inflict serious scratches on a model or actor who may be required to hold your cat during a photo shoot. And, more often than not, ad campaigns and commercials calling for cats invariably have them jumping onto or off a sofa, snuggling into a cushion, or walking or running across a carpet. Too-long nails can snag and fishhook into the sofa or carpet, trapping your cat and halting production. Second, regular brushing and massage also help to improve your cat's looks, manageability, and performance. Matted fur not only spoils your cat's camera-ready looks, but can cause discomfort and impede her performance. Further, shedding on the set is definitely looked down upon, and a StarCat with a hairball would be a major faux pas!

B. Your cat must demonstrate, on the training platform, that she is able to be handled and show her ability to work on-leash or with a harness. She must be able:

1. To demonstrate a willingness to come out of her pet carrier and into a new environment.

2. To come to you, walking across the platform, on-leash or with a harness.

3. To sit or lie down, on-leash or with a harness.

4. To allow a designated person—not you—to approach her.

5. To allow a designated person to pet her and pick her up.

6. To demonstrate a willingness to return to her pet carrier.

C. Your cat, on the training platform and with appropriate control, is to remain calm and manageable in an unpredictable environment. She must be able:

1. To remain calm despite distracting noises—bells, whistles, the clapping hands of an audience, or the sharp clap of the film's clapboard.

2. To remain calm during photo flashes or strobe lights. This is important during a photo shoot or a walk on the red carpet!

Congratulations!

Now that your cat has passed the StarPet Test, she is qualified to receive the StarPet Certificate of Achievement, which is awarded to all my workshop graduates. (To learn more about the Certificate of Achievement, go to www.starpet.com.)

Think of this certificate as a StarPet "Actors' Equity" card, which recognizes that your cat has demonstrated that she has reached the level of ability of a basic, working professional. She could work in advertising with print work or television commercials—even be a spokescat for a commercial product, or in representing a special event, group, charity, or business. Or, if your StarPet prefers more personal contact with her audience, there is, of course, the theater.

And, if your pet enjoys more intimate, one-on-one work, there is the important and satisfying world of pet therapy. When your cat passes the StarPet Test, she demonstrates that her abilities have put her in the league of cats qualified to participate in a pet therapy training program, making her eligible to be certified as a pet therapy cat.

I find, however, that StarPets, like so many of their *human* star counterparts, find a great deal of satisfaction working in *both* fields!

And so, with stardom waiting in the wings, the following training, the Advanced StarCat Training, will take you and your StarPet a little closer to the stage door.

CHAPTER SEVEN

Advanced StarCat Training

The StarPet Test is a wonderful test, similar to an audition. Once you acquire the certificate, it gives you more credibility as a professional who works with animals, and you can enjoy being a part of the StarPet family. Indeed, think of your certificate as a kind of StarPet Actors' Equity card. It signifies that your cat possesses the talents and skills necessary to work on a commercial shoot.

Ten Ways to Make Your StarCat Shine

The training techniques and acting skills that you will be learning here are what I put my StarPet cats through in my workshops in New York City and across the country.

Just to remind you, in cat training, we ask the cat to perform an action/stunt, whereas with a dog, we tell him to perform the action/stunt. To ensure optimum results as we ask our cats to perform, we use verbal commands and hand gestures, and we incorporate clicker training to motivate and fulfill the command by signaling the cat that the treat/reward will follow.

SHAKE HANDS

This is a behavior/stunt everyone will like—it makes a cat seem very smart, "just like a dog." It also encourages your cat to communicate with you. All cats use their front paws a great deal. For instance, when a cat wants attention or petting, she will often pull gently at her owner's hand or arm with a front paw. This behavior/stunt is a natural outgrowth of that action.

★ Shake Hands. ★

The script: To have your cat sit and extend her paw as if shaking hands.

★ Copelia and Cherubino both doing Paws Up. ★
COURTESY MARION HART

The action: Have your cat on the platform, on-leash. Then, give the commands "Sit!" and "Stay!" When she is sitting, extend your right hand as if you are going to shake hands, then nudge her right front leg behind her elbow, as you give the command "Shake!" Your cat may immediately raise her paw. When she does this, immediately click the clicker and take hold of her paw, gently. Praise her and quickly give her a reward. Practice this until you no longer have to touch her leg for her to respond to the command. The aim here is to get her to respond, off-leash, with just the verbal command and hand gesture.

Director's cue (handler's signal): Give the verbal command "Shake!" and the handler's signal is to extend your right hand, as if to shake hands.

Wave

Cats have a tendency to extend their paws in a waving gesture to get your attention, so this fun stunt builds on natural feline behavior.

The script: To have your cat give a waving gesture as if in greeting.

The action: To do this, have your cat on-leash, on the platform. Then, with the verbal command "Wave!" extend your free hand with a treat between your thumb and forefinger. Hold the treat close to her in front of her face, wiggling your

★ Wave. ★

★ Cherubino, Wave command. ★
COURTESY MARION HART

★ Cherubino (cat) waves as Copelia (dog) looks on. ★
COURTESY MARION HART

fingers in a teasing motion. At that moment, her reaction will be to extend her paw to try to get the treat. At this time, pull your hand away, as her paw continues pawing (waving) in the air as she tries to get the treat. At that moment, click the clicker and give her

the treat and lavish praise. The aim here is to accomplish this be-
havior/stunt without a leash and at a distance.

To do this, you'll want to put the treat reward on the magic
wand (the two-foot dowel with the plastic spoon attached to the
end). Facing your cat and holding the magic wand in front of her
face, slowly move back and away from your cat, while waving the
magic wand in front of her. This allows you to achieve the Wave
from a distance.

Director's cue (handler's signal): Here, the cues are a hand
gesture (enticing wiggle of your fingers, mimicking a wave) and a
verbal command "Wave!" At this point, the wand is optional.

SIT UP AND BEG

This is another action that is associated with dogs, and many cat
owners enjoy proving to their friends that *cats* can do it, *too!* And,
for the *professional* StarPet, this is a much-requested stunt.

The script: To have your cat sit upright, both paws up in the air,
and beg.

The action: Have your cat
on-leash, on the platform, in a Sit
position, facing you.

With a treat in your hand or
using the magic wand, hold the
treat a few inches above your cat's
head. Give the command "Sit
Up!" or "Beg!" and raise the food
reward a few inches above your
cat's head. Your cat will focus on
the treat and reach up with her
front paws to get the treat. The

★ Sit Up. ★

★ Cherubino, Sit Up and Beg. ★
COURTESY MARION HART

★ Cherubino demonstrates "Sit Up"
as Copelia looks on. ★
COURTESY MARION HART

trick here is to keep it tantalizing her just out of reach. When she attains the Sit Up and Beg position, give a click of the clicker, give her the treat, and praise her lavishly. If your cat needs some coaxing to attain the Sit Up and Beg stance, gently guide her with her leash. After she has mastered this, the aim is to have her perform this without a leash, and at a distance.

To do this, simply have her stay in the begging position a little longer each time, and, in tandem with that, move away from her a foot or two at a time.

Director's cue (hand signal): The verbal cue is "Sit Up!" or "Beg!" The gesture here is to use both hands in an upward scooping gesture to encourage both paws up to beg.

ROLL OVER

As a rule, cats have a natural tendency to roll on their side in a happy position. When they greet you, they roll on their sides back and forth, happily. Now we need to transpose this action into performance on cue.

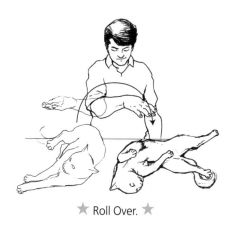

★ Roll Over. ★

The script: To have your cat perform, from a Lie Down position, a complete roll-over.

The action: On-leash, on the platform, command your cat to "Lie Down!" This action requires real hands-on teaching. With the leash and clicker in your left hand, and the treat in your right hand, give the command "Roll Over!" and slip your right hand under her chest with the treat near her nose. When she turns her head to focus on the treat, that will naturally initiate the roll-over. At that moment, help to follow through by gently pushing her body further into the roll-over. Simultaneously, help her to complete the roll-over by gently pulling the leash around and under her to the other side. At that time, click the clicker, give her a treat, and praise her lavishly. As you rehearse this exercise, she will be more willing to respond by following the motion of the treat, rolling over her body in an arc (half-circle). Eventually, she will be able to do this without a leash.

Director's cue (handler's signal): The verbal command is "Roll Over!" and the hand gesture is a sweeping arc.

SPEAKING

Some cats are natural talkers, like the Siamese, and others barely make any sounds at all. But they all have the ability to vocalize when it comes to feeding time. They're always happy to see you and love to talk to you. So, like an actor, you need to encourage them to project!

The script: To have your cat speak (meow) on command.

The action: The best way to teach a cat to speak is to pay attention to the times when she meows naturally. When she meows, give the command "Speak!" emulate the facial mouth movement, and softly mimic the meowing sound. The best time to create a "meow frenzy" is when you open a can of food, and your cat's meowing and you're meowing and you're commanding and she's speaking, and then you reward her with the food she's asking for. Eventually, you want to formalize the training, using the platform. At this time, the magic wand will be helpful to signal your cat to meow when you give the command "Speak!" At the moment she meows, click the clicker and give her a treat.

Director's cue (handler's signal): The verbal command is "Speak" and the handler's signal is a facial mouthing—mimicking a silent meow.

RETRIEVING

Some cats are very good retrievers; others never seem to get the hang of it. If you start when your kitten is young, she will learn this trick more quickly.

The script: To have your cat chase a tossed toy, retrieve it, and bring it back to you.

The action: Tie a favorite toy, feather, or piece of rolled-up cloth or yarn to the end of a

★ Cat retrieving ball. ★

long (approximately eight to twelve feet), lightweight piece of string. Smear a tiny bit of wet cat food on it to make it delectable to your cat's senses—just enough for your cat to smell it and lick it, not a whole meal. Show this to your cat, close enough that she can smell it and focus on it. When you have your cat's attention, toss the toy away from her, to encourage her to go for it. When she pounces on it and takes it in her mouth, give the command "Fetch!" and click the clicker. Then, gently pull the string, to guide your cat back to you. To further encourage her to return to you, slap your thigh in a beckoning fashion. When she comes close to you, click the clicker again and give her a treat. This is important, because this will cause her to drop the toy to take the treat, completing the classic retrieve behavior. Praise her lavishly and practice again later. The key to success here is to keep the excitement in the action. Eventually, your cat star will fetch and retrieve as well as any dog star!

Director's cue (handler's signal): The hand gesture to go for the ball is the toss. The verbal command "Fetch!" is given in tandem with the handler's signal, which is a beckoning slap of the thigh.

JUMP TO THE SHOULDER

Jump to the Shoulder is a behavior/stunt that is very popular in movies where a cat jumps from a cabinet onto a person's shoulder. It's one of those classic *thriller* moments, when the door opens and the cat leaps onto the person's shoulder, startling him or her. Cats are natural jumpers—you've probably experienced your cat jumping from a dresser to a bed or one bookshelf to another. The trick here is to have your cat do this on command!

★ Jump to the Shoulder. ★

The script: To have your cat jump from a high shelf or cabinet onto your shoulder.

The action: To do this, have your cat on the platform, either sitting or standing. Kneel next to the platform, not more than a foot away. Your back should be to the cat. Holding a treat in your right hand, cross your hand in front of you, till you are holding the treat over your left shoulder. At that time, lean backward toward your cat, pivoting your left shoulder slightly toward her so he can see and smell the treat. As you do this, give the command "Jump!" or

"Hup!" This should encourage her to step onto your shoulder. When she has stepped onto your shoulder, click the clicker and give her the treat. Praise her and pet her. As you are petting her, support her so she is comfortable on your shoulder and carefully and calmly stand up and walk around with her on your shoulder. As you are doing this, continue to pet her, praise her, and give her treats.

The aim is to have her actually jump onto your shoulder from a greater height. To do this, slowly graduate her to higher pieces of furniture she feels comfortable with.

Director's cue (handler's signal): The verbal command is "Jump!" or "Hup!" and the hand gesture is to cross your arm over your chest and tap your shoulder to encourage the jump.

THE BIG LEAP

The Big Leap is the natural behavior of cats when they are happy playing with other cats. They leap happily around each other, as well as objects. You might have seen your cat leaping from the bed

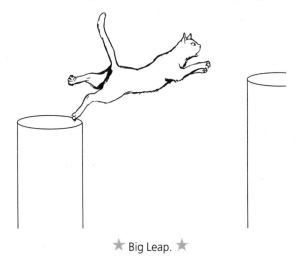

★ Big Leap. ★

to the chair then to the dresser, and so on. Here again, the trick is to make your cat do this on command.

The script: To have your cat leap as great a distance as possible, like a broad jump.

The action: The action here is a continuation of the previous stunt, Jump to the Shoulder. The important difference here is the *distance.* And because of the greater distance, you'll want to wear a more rugged jacket that will support your cat's leap and make her feel secure upon landing!

To begin, have your cat sitting or standing on the platform. Stand approximately three feet from the platform, with your back to the cat. With a treat in your hand, tap your shoulder and give the command "Hup!" When your cat lands on your shoulder, give a click and reward her with the treat. The aim here is to push the limit of your cat's Big Leap!

Director's cue (handler's signal): The verbal command is "Hup!" and the hand gesture is the tap of your shoulder.

THE FLYING LEAP

This is a popular stunt for film work that is based on the Big Leap. Here, however, the cat must leap from one platform to another, or from one object or location to another.

The script: To have your cat jump from one platform to another in a flying leap.

The action: To do this, place your platform a distance of two or three feet from a similar piece of furniture, such as a table, coffee table, or counter.

With your cat standing or sitting on the platform, give the command "Jump!" or "Hup!" To motivate your cat, shake a box of her favorite treats and tap the *opposite* platform (the one you want her to jump to). This will stimulate him to make an enthusiastic flying leap to the opposite platform. When he lands, click the clicker and reward him with a treat. Don't forget to praise him lavishly!

Director's cue (handler's signal): The verbal command is "Jump" or "Hup" given simultaneously with a sweeping arclike gesture, following the path of the leap from where your cat begins to where she lands.

★ Cat jumping through a hoop. ★

★ Cherubino, Walk on a Leash through a hoop. ★
COURTESY MARION HART

JUMP THROUGH THE HOOP

Since you have taught your cat how to jump onto your shoulders and from one height to another, this is a stunt that adds showmanship and style.

The script: To have the cat jump from one platform, soar through the hoop, and make a clean landing on the opposite platform!

The action: To do this, first place your platform close to a second platform (or table or counter) no more than a foot away. Have your cat sit or stand on the platform to your left. With your left hand, hold the hoop (a hula hoop is ideal) between the two platforms. Holding the clicker and a treat, position your right hand in midair in the center of the hoop, but closer to your cat. At this time, give the verbal command "Hup!" and draw your hand (with the treat) back through the hoop to the other platform. When

★ Cherubino jumps through a hoop. ★
COURTESY MARION HART

your cat jumps through the hoop, click the clicker and reward her with a treat.

Eventually, you will increase the distance between the platforms and raise the height of the hoop.

Director's cue (handler's signal): The verbal command is "Hup!" The gesture is a sweeping arclike motion indicating the path of the action.

Adjust, Assimilate, Act

Now that your StarPet has adjusted to the set, theater, or sound stage, and has assimilated into the ensemble effort of cast and crew working for a single production, she can now concentrate on the very best acting she is capable of.

Can a cat act? Can a feline feign emotion?

Of course she can! Just look at Pepper and all her wonderful films with Teddy the Great Dane!

And, in my experiences over the years—training cats in hundreds of commercials and print ads, not to mention *Catmopolitan,* when I directed many different breeds and types of cats from diverse and varied backgrounds—I have found that cats can indeed act, but they can also act up!

And, although I often caution against typecasting, I find that an amazing number of cats are *wonderful* at portraying divas!

So, now that you are poised—catlike, I assume!—on the brink of stardom with your StarPet (excuse me, StarDiva!), it is time to prepare for your StarCat's premiere.

Everyone works better when they enjoy what they do, and the StarPet is certainly no exception, which is why I can never repeat enough times to my clients: "Always keep the play in play-acting!"

If you do, not only will you and your StarPet (and the cast and crew around you, as well!) have fun and fond memories, but you can also be proud of your work—*and* your StarPet!

For your StarCat to have a successful shoot, it's important for you to understand how to bring out the very best in your StarCat and marry that need with the needs of the production. You will not only be your StarCat's director, but a liaison between your cat and the director, to advise the director of what your cat is capable of, and the best way to elicit that performance. This must be done skillfully, keeping in mind both the needs of the production and the needs, abilities, and (sometimes) shortcomings of your StarPet.

I find that most cats, even the professional StarPets, work best when they are fresh and in the moment. Too many rehearsals or too many takes can leave the cat utterly bored and looking for fresh material! Like divas, I find that StarCats love to make an entrance, show off, and then—"Okay, I'm bored, where's the next show? I'm out of here!"

With this in mind, I try to alert the director to the cat's nature, and how that affects the nature of working with the cat!

All cats are individuals, of course, and your StarCat may be an absolute workhorse, a real trouper, doggedly giving her all until the last technical check. But, if your cat, like most StarCats, has a divalike work ethic, I suggest that, to achieve a performance *worthy* of a diva, you don't put your StarCat through too many rehearsals or takes.

So, when your StarCat, beautiful, bewitching, and bedazzling, breezes onto the set—"I'm here, darlings! Aren't I beautiful! Look what I can do! Aren't I just too, too much?"—you advise the director to have the cameras ready and rolling!

I'm Ready for My Close-Up! Are You?

The close-up shot is very important for any actor, human or animal, because it shows off her beauty and ability.

The close-up shot is equally important for the director, because it conveys a feeling or information that moves the plot of the film along. And, as it so often happens with the role of the animal actor, the look will later be anthropomorphized to facilitate and express emotions, character development, or relationships between the characters.

Because of this, as well as the nature of how films are shot—often out of sequence or minus the presence of the costar, who will be added later—actors oftentimes find themselves working in a vacuum, playing only to the director and the production crew!

This, however, is fine for your StarCat, because, as her director, you will be bringing along her costars from home to elicit those looks and emotions—the wand and the conductor's baton!

On the set, your knowledge of your cat's interests and play-times—combined with the skillful use of the feather string teasers!—will ensure the success of those all-important close-ups!

The intensity of the enticement of the feathers will increase the intensity of her "look" (her gaze, the turn of her head, the cock of an ear, the twitch of a whisker), and vice versa.

And here, again, expect your StarCat to be a diva. She will sweep onto the set and hold a few fabulous poses; twirl a few star turns. Was the director cued to this? Was the camera operator ready? Along with your conductor's baton, it will be up to you to synchronize a symphony that will have everyone singing the praises of your StarCat!

So, when your StarPet throws that look that says, divalike, "I'm ready for my close-up—are you?" her star-making performance will be captured for posterity!

I'm Ready for My Long Shot! Are You?

Unless your StarDiva wants a stunt double—and, if it's a lazy, sunny day, she might just want to leave the work to a stand-in while she basks in the sun!—the same premise holds true for the long shot as works for the close-up.

With her costarring props of feathers, strings, teasers, fishing poles, wands, batons, balls, and creepy crawlies, you can elicit all manner of action shots and varying degrees of speed and intensity.

And, again, when your StarCat tosses her head with a look that says, "I'm ready for my long shot—are you?" the camera operator will be ready for the director's cue: Action!

One Singular Sensation

One, singular sensation
Every little step she takes.
One, thrilling combination,
Every move that she makes.

These lyrics from one of Broadway's most popular shows—*A Chorus Line*—perfectly captures the moment you and your StarPet have finally arrived at.

You've learned the basics, the motivations, the seven instinctive drives, the techniques, and you've practiced and rehearsed. Your StarPet has learned to adjust to certain methods and to new surroundings, and to assimilate your craft within the surroundings of props and stage settings, other cast members, and production crews.

Now, you need to learn and practice the technique that will carry your StarPet's talent to the forefront. This is where the real acting comes in, and what separates the talented amateur from the polished professional.

When you can effortlessly marry your StarPet's talent and technique, she will truly be one singular sensation, ready for the spotlight to follow every little move she makes.

In fact, your StarCat just might be ready to headline a blockbuster revival of Broadway's record-breaking, longest-running show ever—*Cats*!

From Pavlov's Dogs to Pavlova's Pussycats

The professional StarPet will be called upon, if she is cast in a commercial, for example, to follow the action of a storyboard (a rough picture book of a script, illustrating the action).

Or, if she should win a role in a film, the script may call for a similar sequence of events.

For example, the script may call for your kitty to enter the scene, walk to a chair, jump up on the chair, and lie down.

The action of this script calls for your cat to advance to the level where, instead of just performing one action at a time, she might be asked to perform two, maybe even three.

On-camera, your cat is a working StarPet, playing a role, so you cannot be up close with your conductor's baton or wand, or giving her treats. This, now, is where you, as your StarPet's director, must direct her from out of camera range.

To accomplish this, we now apply the clicker training, which we learned earlier. You signal your cat to begin the first action, click when she accomplishes it. This promises her that she will have a nice treat, but not just yet; go on to the second action. When she has accomplished the second action, you click again, again the promise of a treat to come, but to now continue. And, as she does, and accomplishes her third (and final!) stunt, you praise and pet her. A job well done!

Again, the clicker signal is to respond and repeat; respond and repeat—and finally, at the end of the sequence, there is the reward for a job well done.

When my cat Bebe starred on *Sesame Street,* she was required to perform multisequential clicker work, as her character explored New York City's vast and mysterious Metropolitan Museum of Art. Bebe did an outstanding job, but she was a very special cat, with a great deal of experience.

Most cat actors, however, will never be asked to do more than one or two stunts in sequence, all in one take. In fact, you will find that with camera angles and editing, you will more than likely never be asked to have your cat perform more than *one* stunt at a time. This is good news, given that the first precept of StarCat training is that we must never command our cats to perform; we may only ask our cats to perform!

Seriously, though, it's important not to push your cat, if you want her to be free to act.

To capture her all-important freshness and naturalness—being all that she can be—it's important not to over-rehearse your Star-Cat. You will only have a limited moment to capture the script's directive, whereas dogs generally have the ability to repeat eight to ten or even fifteen peak-performance takes. With cats, the window of opportunity to capture your cat's best performance is much smaller, certainly not more than three takes, and I'm a firm believer in just rolling the camera and getting it on the first take!

This is where you marry talent and technique to the fine art of acting that will turn your StarPet into a singular sensation, winning raves from the audience—as well as from the director, who will be thrilled when your StarPet can accomplish the sequential action all in the first take!

The skillful use of the clicker marries technique and talent, science and artistry—the science of the groundbreaking Ivan Pavlov with the artistry of the gravity-defying prima ballerina Anna Pavlova!

With the proper use of the clicker, you can motivate your kitty with the certainty of Ivan Pavlov's science, to bring out the effortless artistry of Anna Pavlova.

The clicker promises that the food reward will come later. Just as the infamous bell signaled Pavlov's dogs that food was coming, so the clicker signals your cat that a reward is coming, but to continue acting. The difference here, of course (aside from the obvious, that Pavlov had pooches, not pussycats!), is that Pavlov's bell triggered his dogs' gastric juices, while your clicker will trigger your pussycat's creative juices!

As a dancer creates intricate choreography from just five basic steps, and the cat creates beautiful action from just seven instinctive traits, the clicker, from the master choreographer or director, can signal the dancer, the cat actor, into each individual step, select each cat action, transforming them into an artfully choreographed sequence of dance or theater.

This skillful marriage of talent and technique turns Pavlov's Pussycats into Pavlova's Pussycats!

And when you have mastered your director's skills, and your cat reaches this pinnacle of understanding, your talented Star-Pet will be transformed into a talented, savvy, and professional StarPet!

Make Your Own Storyboard

Now you and your cat are on the verge of becoming true StarPet professionals. You need to practice all the methods, motivations, and techniques, and to emulate, dress rehearsal–style, a professional job.

As a professional, you now become not only your cat's director, but also her writer, so you will want to put together a dress rehearsal that can best showcase your cat's individual strengths and talents.

You may want to start with something simple. Choose just two behaviors or actions your cat enjoys most, and combine these into a storytelling sequence. Then, for the storyboard, break these behaviors and actions down into a sequence, and put them together, like an illustrated story.

Or, you may want to try creating a storyboard from a favorite advertisement or commercial spot you may have seen before. You know, the one you saw a while ago, and you thought, "Hey! My cat can do that!"—and then you rushed out and bought this book? Yeah, that's the one!

Well, now that your cat has the training and technique to showcase her talents to their best advantage, she definitely can do it!

So, break down the action you see the cat performing in the commercial into a series of simpler, smaller steps. This sequence of events you want your cat to perform to re-create the commercial becomes your storyboard.

After you and your kitty have warmed up with your very own, tailor-made storyboard, I've come up with a storyboard myself that you may want to try.

As you read it, you will discover that it incorporates several of the actions your cat has mastered in this chapter, and they are also the ones that are most frequently called upon for commercial work.

Our storyboard is a takeoff on the classic Norman Rockwell painting depicting people and their pets in the veterinarian's waiting room and is entitled, "Misty Meets the Vet!"

We begin with a classic shot of all the people and their pets in the waiting room.

Misty is sitting on the lap of her person, Kayla.

A door opens, and "Dr. Jane" peers into the waiting room. "We're ready for Misty. Which one of you is Misty?"

Hearing her name, Misty sits up, and, as if to say, "Here I am!" performs the wave.

Kayla puts Misty down, on-leash, and says, "Come, Misty, time to see the doctor."

Misty, on-leash, walks into the examining room.

Doctor sits in her chair. "Okay, Misty, let's see you."

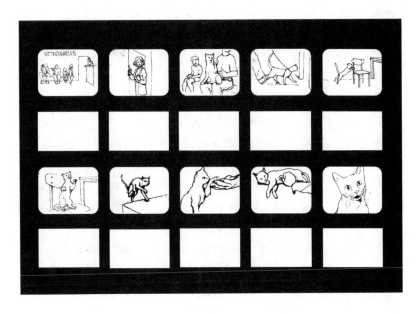

Misty jumps up onto the chair meant for the client.

The doctor says, "No, Misty, I need to be able to see you."

Misty then sits up, paws in the air!

The doctor then says, "No, Misty, on the table."

Misty jumps up onto the examining table.

The doctor then says, "Pleased to meet you. I'm Dr. Jane."

Misty gives paw shakes in greeting her veterinarian.

With stethoscope in hand, Dr. Jane says, "Misty, let's check out the old ticker!"

Misty lies on her side, and the vet examines her.

Misty then completes her roll-over and up.

Dr. Jane says, "Okay, see you same time next year! What do you think about that?"

Misty: "Meow!"

As you can tell, all the behaviors and stunts and actions that you have learned previously have been totally incorporated into this storyboard to emphasize your cat's abilities and to showcase her talents.

This is an ideal way to practice and perfect your StarCat's techniques—and your own directorial skills! In fact, I recommend making these practice times a real event—truly a Showtime! Why not get your family and friends involved to play the various roles? And don't forget the costumes! Many of my clients' cats love to dress up—in fact, in *Catmopolitan,* cats were clamoring to get involved with the costumes as much as the wardrobe director!

This is a great way to spend a Saturday afternoon or an evening after dinner. With family, friends, and pets all contributing, this truly captures the spirit of "Hey, gang! Let's put on a show!" as well as providing a terrific dress rehearsal, out-of-town tryout for your StarPet's professional audition, casting call, or job.

Because, as much as this is play, your cat is also learning, as are you! In fact, if you have a video camera, it's a good idea to tape your commercial. For, just as at the end of rehearsals and performances, directors and actors sit and critique their performances and learn from those critiques, your video will be a wonderful learning tool.

And, if you are really pleased with your video, you can send it out as a "demo tape" to advertising agencies, casting directors, and photographers, to give them a chance to see the caliber of your StarPet's work.

In fact, one pet owner's home movies made it all the way to the prestigious Cannes Film Festival!

But, at the very least, you will have a wonderful home movie of a wonderful cat and a wonderful time.

Because our StarPets will always be stars in our hearts and in our homes!

CHAPTER EIGHT

Managing and Marketing Your StarPet

When the director cries out, "Lights! Camera! Action!" and you give the command to your StarPet to act out his role, your pet, at that moment, has become a star, but his meteoric ascent to the spotlight, his stairway to the stars, was built on every little bit of moonglow, every little piece of stardust you could collect and fashion into one big bright shining star!

All those sessions where you were training your pet to become an animal actor paid off, and now your personal StarPet is becoming a professional StarPet, and you are becoming his professional handler.

To take your pet from a talented, well-trained amateur animal actor to a talented, well-trained professional animal actor depends on *you*. Just as you trained your pet to be a StarPet by teaching him movie stunts and theatrical tricks, now *you* have to learn the tricks of the trade—the entertainment industry—to allow your pet to shine.

As with human actors, the only difference between equally talented professionals and amateurs is that one is getting the work, one is being seen, one is out there—and that is your job.

In the professional world—whatever level you take it to—you will be your pet's handler, agent, publicist, casting director, manager, lawyer, trainer, tutor, baby-sitter, and on-set nurse. Indeed, you will be your pet's stage mother or stage father in the very nicest sense of the term. No one knows your pet better than you, or cares for him or loves him more than you do. So your love and loyalty—combined with professional show business savvy—is a winning combination for a fun and successful StarPet career.

Just as your StarPet had to learn the three A's (Adjust, Assimilate, and Act) to reach the level of a professional StarPet, so you have to master the two M's (Managing and Marketing) to guide your pet through this exciting new adventure.

I would like to share with you the steps and stages of managing and marketing a successful StarPet.

First, you need to "brand" your pet. This means establishing your pet's professional identity. You need to create an identity that is unmistakably all his own, one that sets him apart from the pack and makes those all-important people (casting directors and producers) sit up and take notice!

Just as you learned to make your StarPet the very best actor he can be, with a succinct merger of his talent and technique, so you can make your StarPet a recognized *star* with a savvy merger of talent and *style*. This is a tried and true formula, pioneered by the StarPets of yesteryear and used by successful StarPets today.

To do this, you need to assess your pet's looks, personality, and talent. It's a good idea to enlist the help of family, friends, and neighbors. They may see your pet in a different light, or pick up on something you hadn't thought of. Ask yourselves these questions: What do his looks resemble or remind you of? Do you want to play up those looks or go against type? What is his personality? Does his behavior seem to "match" his looks or is it surprisingly "different"? And, most important, what does he do best? What are his trademark tricks and performance skills? The key to successful branding is in finding the best of your pet's looks, personality, and talent and combining them into a persona or trademark that is uniquely his own—one that will make people sit up and take notice.

One of the best—and certainly one of the most dramatic—examples of successful branding is Rin Tin Tin.

A handsome German Shepherd, Rin Tin Tin was hale, hearty, and heroic, and he played that persona to the hilt with unbelievable movie stunts that showed off his brawny bravery. He scaled thirty-foot walls, climbed ladders, and jumped from rooftop to rooftop to save damsels in distress or to collar the bad guys. Yes, Rin Tin Tin had mastered many breathtaking stunts, but Lee Duncan—Rinty's owner and trainer, who had rescued the remarkable dog from the trenches of World War I Germany—still felt that the camera had yet to effectively capture the soul-stirring courage that was at the very heart of Rin Tin Tin.

But then Duncan, building on both Rinty's courageous character and his astounding athleticism, and taking into account what Rinty loved doing most, which was jumping, came up with the perfect brand: spectacular rescues that featured the amazing dog, at full speed, crashing through windows just in the nick of time!

Duncan, of course, wouldn't *really* let Rinty crash through glass, so he worked with Warner Brothers' technical staff to devise windowpanes made not of glass, but of finely spun translucent sugar candy, allowing Rinty to sail effortlessly through them!

The visual effects of Rinty "crashing" through the window—his entire being framed in showering shards of sugar candy "glass"—were nearly as powerful as the dog himself.

★ Here I am with some stars of StarPet. ★
COURTESY BRUCE PLOTKIN

Known as the "Rinty Rescue," this became the classic climax to nearly every Rin Tin Tin film, and really made the dog's career. By devising the "Rinty Rescue," Lee Duncan provided a classic example of successful branding. He built on the best of his dog's looks, personality, and talent, and found a hook to make it uniquely his, and a way to make it work.

And when the cameras stopped rolling, the "Rinty Rescue" became the "Rinty Reward"—and a classic example of "Always keep the play in play-acting!" As a reward for an outstanding job, the kindhearted Lee, ever the old "softy" when it came to his beloved Rinty, would give in and allow Rinty to have a few pieces of the tasty candy he had crashed through!

Another pioneer of the fine art of branding was Props. To the untrained eye, it may have seemed that Props was the furthest thing from movie star material. He came to the Fine Art Studio as an injured stray, when Bill Buskirk, the kindhearted head of the Property Department, rescued him. Props became the mascot of the Property Department (hence, his name) and had never made a film. Props had a pathetic "little dog lost" look about him, but his personality was plucky and upbeat. He enjoyed playing with the child actors at the studio, even allowing them to play "dress up" with him. He was also very agile. In caring for the endearing little dog, Buskirk soon realized that Props's pathos could be his strength. The nimble little dog soon learned to limp along on three legs, developing what would become his trademark "limp." Adding a sling and bandages molded Props's signature statement into a poignant and powerful picture, and the little dog "limped" into motion picture history when he starred opposite Dorothy Gish in the classic Civil War epic *The Little Yank*!

But dogs didn't corner the market in successful branding, and more than a few cats more than ably found their niche. In fact, Hollywood's most famous cat actor, Orangey, literally strong-armed his way to the top!

Orangey had a sour look about him, and a sour personality to match. His owner and trainer was Frank Inn, who, today, is renowned for his famous dog star, Benji. Before Benji, however, Inn was the most revered and prolific cat trainer in the industry. But Orangey—by Inn's own admission—was a grumpy, "I'll work if and when I want to" kind of cat. Consequently—and not surprisingly!—Orangey never found work. And he certainly didn't seem a candidate for stardom! But when Frank gave in to the nature of his ill-tempered cat, and branded him for what he was—a cat curmudgeon—he promptly landed the role of a lifetime! Orangey portrayed the title role in the film *Rhubarb,* about a cat who became the owner of the Brooklyn Dodgers. The script called for a "foul-tempered, scar-faced sourpuss," and Orangey fit the bill perfectly! Starring opposite Ray Milland, Orangey became the world's best-known, highest-paid cat. Given his demeanor, he wasn't always easy to work with (Orangey disliked Milland, and Inn had to cement their onscreen friendship with discreetly placed liverwurst), but that didn't stop Orangey's rise to stardom. He worked with Jackie Gleason in *Gigot* and won a Patsy Award for his costarring role opposite Audrey Hepburn in *Breakfast at Tiffany's*.

Not all StarPets can be superstars, of course, but the stories of Rin Tin Tin, Props, and Orangey are illustrative of what a powerful tool branding can be—on any level—in marketing and managing your StarPet.

Plus, discovering and molding your pet's distinctive brand helps to further the bond you and your pet already share. Branding, like training, is done in tandem. And, like training, branding is a shared, continuing adventure. In the same way that training together strengthens the bond between you and your pet, by fostering communication, trust, and understanding, branding also focuses on your pet's strengths and weaknesses, what he enjoys doing, and what the two of you are capable of accomplishing together.

Still, most of my clients and their StarPets just know that they're having a good time—and that is the most important criterion of all for a successful StarPet at any level!

Pets in costumes, for example, are a great way to play up the versatility of your StarPet's appeal and "look." Colorful costumes can accent your StarPet's photogenic strengths, as well as play to your StarPet's ability to "emote" for a picture or scene—to play up the theme of the costume.

I found this to be quite true when I cast and directed all the cats and dogs for *Catmopolitan, Dogue,* and *Vanity Fur.* Not only did the StarPets enjoy being fussed over and given the attention they received when dressed in wardrobe, but they really seemed to play into the characters suggested by their costumes!

But don't wait to have your StarPet cast for a role before you think about branding. Branding allows you to "cast" your pet in a role tailor-made (by you) for his looks and talents, a role sure to win him notice in that first all-important audition or casting call.

One of my workshop students took my advice literally, and actually tailor-made individual costumes that portrayed the many moods of her dog's very versatile repertoire! Her dog is a real "people" person—a plus in this business—and he loves dressing in costumes and all the attention it brings him. Now, my student has created her own niche in the business, by creating fashion shows—complete with custom-made costumes—for people and pets. My student has created a "win-win" situation with her Star-Pet. They have fun putting on their own shows, and their performances also double as auditions, as ways to be seen. Plus, with all the practices and dress rehearsals that go into launching a fashion show, she and her StarPet are more than prepared when a call comes in from a casting agent!

Sometimes, though, in trying to zero in on your StarPet's one-of-a-kind unique brand, you need to think outside the box.

One of my students from the StarPet Workshops is having a very good time pursuing her dog's career, and forging his own distinctive, personal branding. But it almost didn't happen. Her dog was very photogenic, and had a calm and steady demeanor. He was perfect for print work, but he never seemed to stand out, to get noticed, to get the job. My student (now client) was about to give up when we hit on the perfect brand for her dog. Her dog's distinction was his ability to be indistinct—to be a chameleon—to be Woody Allen's Zelig or Chevy Chase's Fletch; to be Every

Dog. Put him anywhere with anybody or anything and he blended right in, became one of them, and made them come alive. Sitting on a leather sofa in a book-lined study, you'd think he was the erudite dog of a college professor. But next to a chain-link fence at a gas station, he looked like a junkyard dog. And beside a swing in a patch of grass, he most definitely had to be some little boy's best friend!

So, I suppose it could be said that, in this business—even with StarPets—when it comes to branding, sometimes product placement is everything!

In fact, you may just find your pet's brand by taking a good look not just at your pet, but at who he's sitting next to; who his friends are.

One of the greatest cat stars ever was Pepper the cat. Pepper was one of Mack Sennett's biggest stars (and that's saying a great deal, seeing how the great Charlie Chaplin was one of them!), but she commanded the stage not when she stood alone, but when she shared it. You see, Pepper's unique brand was her ability to forge friendships with the unlikeliest of candidates, and to bring those friendships to life on the silver screen. She shared star billing in film after film with Teddy, the Great Dane, but won even greater accolades for her stand-out performances with her buddy, Frederick Wilhelm—a talented white mouse!

Several years ago, a client of mine rescued a wonderful Shepherd/Lab-mix, "Lizzie," and ended up with an entire menagerie. You see, like Pepper, Lizzie had an uncanny knack for finding friends in unlikely places—and then bringing them home! Between cats and rabbits, mice and birds, even a rooster, I was often called in to make sure that Lizzie's newfound friends assimilated well together. Things generally went pretty smoothly, but there were times I felt like a Keystone Kop in a Mack Sennett film! But

Lizzie's greatest friend was a wonderful Belgian hare. They got along famously, and were very entertaining. Lizzie's talent for forming special friendships made her ideal for the business—as well as for pet therapy and humane education, which Lizzie, together with her rabbit friend, reveled in.

But when you're thinking outside the box, don't forget to think outside, period. After costarring with Charlie Chaplin in *A Dog's Life*, little Brownie rode to even greater success in a series of adventure films with her great friend and equine costar, Queenie. Together, the little dog and magnificent horse rescued children from burning buildings, saved damsels in distress, and dragged wounded heroes to safety—whew!

When you've had a chance to catch your breath, take a deep one, because, now that you've "branded" your StarPet, you have to become your pet's "barker."

"Barker" is an old show business term that refers to the energetic guy who was always outside the theater drumming up business for a show by snapping tickets in the air and shouting, in sharp, staccato shouts—barks, actually, hence the word.

You, too, need to be your dog's special barker. You need to be out there drumming up business for him, tooting his horn, telling everybody out there how wonderful he is! Don't forget, that's what got the great Larry Trimble his start in the business—not just his great dogs, Jean and Strongheart, but his own determination.

To be out there barking for your dog—or cat—means you are looking for every opportunity for him to be seen, to further his career, and you do that by initiating and following through in all areas of managing and marketing, publicizing and promoting. Remember, Larry Trimble was Strongheart's owner, trainer, manager, writer, director, and publicist. In fact, most of the pioneers of the business, Rudd Weatherwax and Lassie, Lee Duncan and Rin Tin Tin—and all who made up the old guard, the old masters—did the same. That's not to say, of course, that these great StarPets didn't have the backing of their studios' powerful publicity departments, but it is true that, when it comes to our pets, most of us—including the legendary owners and handlers—like to keep an intimate, hands-on control when it concerns the well-being of our pets.

A perfect example of the rare breed that we are is "The Hollywood Motion Picture Dog Preview." This was a rock star–style bus-and-truck tour to promote the films of the dog stars of Hollywood's Golden Era. It was the brainchild of noted dog trainer Carl Spitz, whose dogs included Terry, the tenacious Cairn Terrier who played Toto in *The Wizard of Oz,* and Buck, the lovable St. Bernard who costarred with Clark Gable and Loretta Young in *The Call of the Wild.* These dogs were major stars, and the studios could certainly have handled a major publicity trek such as this, but Spitz *himself* drove the busload of bowsers across country, chaperoning not only his own dogs, but a contingent of a half-dozen diverse dog stars, as well!

Even today, the world of StarPets allows for far more individuality, creativity, and control in our pet's career than the industry allows the human actors. This may be because animal actors—despite their incredible contribution to the entertainment industry—are still thought to be part of the property department, the department that oversees the inanimate objects that grace the set, such as books, furniture, art, or pots and pans! So perhaps it is because animal actors, their enormous popularity notwithstanding, are still the "underdogs" of the business that we are left to our own devices. This may be daunting to some, but if, like the old guard, you have a sense of adventure and really want to guide your

StarPet's career, just think of Props's incredible journey from stray to mascot to star. You may find that being the underdog is just the ticket to launch a successful StarPet career—so get out there and "bark!"

And don't wait for the business to come to *you*. You go out and *find* the business, or you create your *own* business. Once you've branded your StarPet it's time to rustle up the business.

Believe it or not, a little hometown in the heartland of America can have all the panache of New York or Hollywood, once the film crew comes to town—and they're always working to farm out as much work as possible to the local community. It saves on their budget and adds flavor to the film.

Local people can enjoy work as film extras—and so can Star-Pets! The key here is to let your local film commission, municipalities, chambers of commerce, and mayors' offices know in advance that you're available, so they can contact you, or the film company can contact you directly. Or you can get a head start and contact the film company directly yourself.

Whether you remain working solely within your local community or want to reach for the stars and really go all professional, the first and most important step is to contact your local mayor's office—or municipal office of film commission (if they have one for your town). They will let you know what films are being filmed in town, coming from New York or Hollywood to get film permits— basically who's in town and what movies are being made.

Then you can contact these people and find out if they are interested in using a dog or cat for the film! That's a good opportunity to be there first, to be the first in the limelight. Because usually, the film companies send their scouts ahead of production, during preproduction, to scout out the locations and meet with local film commissions, mayors' offices, and municipalities to find out just who and what can be made available to ensure the best possible production.

You want to be there first to make sure they know what your pet can do, and that you are available.

Local Bookings

Although local bookings may be the beginning of your StarPet's journey, the way to manage and market your StarPet in the early, baby steps, puppy steps of your journey applies equally to the later, giant steps.

As with human actors, or just about anything in life where one is just starting out, the bigwigs won't necessarily know you or know where to find you. In fact, they may not even know that they need you!

So you need to get out there and tell them, and find the opportunities and create the opportunities for your StarPet.

And the best way to do this is to use the old reporter's method of how to report a terrific story: who, what, when, where, and why.

You need to let it be known *who* your StarPet is, *what* your StarPet can do, *when* your StarPet is available, *where* your StarPet can work, and *why* your StarPet would be so terrific for any production!

And, when you've finished, you need to bring out the second rule of telling a good story.

Tell them what you are going to tell them; then tell them the story; then tell them what you told them!

In other words, tell them what you are going to tell them about your StarPet (a nice teaser!), tell them more completely about how terrific your StarPet is, and then, for an encore, reprise the story, and tell them again just how terrific your StarPet is!

COMMUNITY EVENTS

Part of marketing your StarPet is to develop your home base, just as you developed your talent. Let everybody know who your pet is, what he can do, and what he's available for. To do that, get involved in community events, a local Rotary Club, a Lions Club— they are businessmen who are very strong in the community, and they hold special events, fund-raisers, and so on.

Anything that is a civic-minded community event can offer your StarPet a chance to shine, and you should offer your StarPet as part of the attraction for these events, from picnics and bake sales to fundraisers. And if you do a good job, it won't go unnoticed!

Before you know it, these businessmen and women now will consider using your pet to attract business to their business, so your pet now becomes a commodity in the business community, where you could create a special kind of "meet the celebrity pet at this location" kind of event to promote the business. If you are successful, and the business grows, the owner of the business will recognize and appreciate that your StarPet is a great attraction, and facilitating the pull of the business. He may just decide to include you in a business marketing plan!

MERCHANTS AND STORES

Take advantage of your local community affairs' tie-in with the Rotary Club and the Lions Club, and so on. Contact local merchants or stores or other businesses to create and develop some form of special event tie-ins and store promotions. Sometimes if you do an event where all the businesses get together—it doesn't have to be a pet store or a pet-related business, it could be a stationery store, hardware store, bank, or grocery—you will have a golden opportunity for lead-ins to professional advertising jobs for these businesses.

CHARITIES

Local charities are wonderful opportunities to be a part of good cause-marketing, and a positive way for your StarPet to be the voice for that charity, or the theme, the face that represents the philanthropic effort. This is a wonderful opportunity to tie in my twin endeavors of film and philanthropy. It gives you a chance to make a difference in this world, as well as the opportunity to have your StarPet build a circuit for himself in entertaining at various charity events.

SENIOR CENTERS

Senior citizen centers are a great place to practice your StarPet's showmanship. These centers book all sorts of recreational activities and shows for senior citizens to enjoy and/or participate in. Local theater groups regularly bring abridged versions of their musicals to these recreation centers, as do school and church choirs, and so on. They'd probably love to book a StarPet performance!

PET THERAPY

StarPets are the perfect pet therapy team. They are the ideal make-you-feel-better prescription for good health. The whole concept of pet therapy is to create a therapeutic means for the pets to be involved in an interactive way with the patients in nursing homes or hospitals, helping them to feel better.

A wonderful way to entertain patients is to show your StarPet's ability as a showman—as an actor and performer. You may also find that these showmanship abilities make your StarPet a very good candidate to become a well-trained, certified pet therapist! This would create a win-win situation: You're having fun, your pet's having a good time, and the people are having a good time.

And that's what it's all about. Pets give you unconditional love as they entertain you. They make you feel better, so, for that moment, you're absolved of any sadness, any pain you might have; all that is put aside for that moment. It is also a good opportunity to rehearse all the behaviors and stunts you've learned that make a StarPet and a therapy dog. This is nice to add to your life—and to your résumé!

CHILDREN'S PARTIES

Here you have the opportunity to have your StarPet hired for a kid's party. If you have a stunt or an act that's really dynamic or hot, you can put it together into a whole entertainment package, and this is a wonderful thing, because kids are always looking for an excuse to have a party! And what better way to party than to have *real* party animals?

You may need to dress up and get in the act, as well. So, get dressed up, entertain, do a fashion show, agility demonstrations, and so on. You can also orchestrate interactive tricks, games, and skits.

SCHOOLS

This provides a great opportunity to get a fan club going! Children of all ages have pets, and they can't wait to go home and practice tricks with their pets! Plus, even children who don't have pets, but want a pet, can benefit from your StarPet.

This is a chance to give these kids a great learning experience, a positive and inspiring way of giving back the message of StarPet!

Your StarPet can also be the mascot for sporting teams, or for a classroom, or school groups, such as the drama club, as well as the school newspaper. And, of course, the 4-H Club is a wonderful organization to get in touch with.

Be part of a wonderful movement like National Pet Week, and you can actually go to the schools and educate and explain to both children and teachers what it is to own a pet—the commitment and the care, as well as the joy. Promoting responsible pet ownership is the hallmark of the StarPet message.

Humane education is another commitment I am passionate about. And, as humane education is part of the national pet week, it is a perfect time to promote humane education as a continuation of the historic requirement of all schools to educate and promote this curriculum of responsible pet ownership and kindness to animals. Eleanor Roosevelt initiated the concept of humane education and promoted it diligently until it became law.

But education can be entertaining, as well—certainly with StarPets around!—and this is a winning and powerful combination. As you work within the education system and on the school grounds, you can also put on shows with other pets—I've found that the school bands and 4-H Club marching bands love to accompany our performances!—as well as agility demonstrations or demonstrations by precision horse and dog troops!

Along these lines, there is also generally an abundance of fairs, school plays, and so on.

And never underestimate the power of the parade! Muffin did some of his best work when he took his show on the parade route!

READING PAWS

Reading Paws is a project with libraries to promote literacy for young and old alike. Here, your StarPet can be an aid in facilitating and motivating people in being comfortable to read. And what helps them, literacy experts have found, is to read to a dog! Much as in what has now become traditional pet therapy, your dog is the therapy in reading, because his presence makes the person relax. He is nonjudgmental, and that allows a person to focus on the reading.

Reading Paws dogs offer therapeutic effect and real results. The program is a true learning experience for young and old. Used as a catalyst to facilitate reading, by providing a comfort zone, dogs help the people by taking away the anxiety, and thereby allowing the learning to flow. With StarPet Training and Reading Paws, before you know it, your StarDog will be reading all his own scripts and storyboards!

COMMUNITY THEATER/LITTLE THEATER

Community theater groups, summer theaters, little theater—all of these groups perform all the wonderful old classic shows and musicals, and very often, there are plenty of roles for pets! So, just visit these groups and explain to them you have a dog or cat that fits into their particular production. For example, if you have a Cairn Terrier, he would be perfect to play Toto in *The Wizard of Oz*. And, of course, there is Sandy in *Annie*.

Plus, many of the actors in these community groups, these theaters' stars, are stars in real life, in their real jobs. They are businessmen and women and leaders in the community, who might want to offer your pet a job to represent their business or organization. Perhaps they may work at a radio station, or own a store, or a business that prints out local advertising fliers. This is a perfect chance to create opportunities for you and your StarPet.

PLACES OF WORSHIP

Local churches, synagogues, and other places of worship should not be overlooked in your quest for stardom (with a spiritual edge!). Oftentimes, these places offer their facilities for local theater groups who are in need of space, looking for space, or actually have their own resident theater groups, dance troupes, art centers, and so forth, which are open to the public.

This is a perfect opportunity to mix art and theater, as well as the many altruistic and community-minded events these places of worship generally play host to.

And don't forget the most basic—and the most fun! Check to see if your local places of worship conduct a blessing of the animals, either during Be Kind to Animals Week or National Pet Month, along with of course, the birthday of the patron saint of animals, St. Francis of Assisi! The blessing of the animals is often very colorful, theatrical, and full of pageantry!

FILM SCHOOLS AND PHOTOGRAPHY CLUBS

Film schools are a wonderful opportunity for you to explore. Photography clubs abound—there are lots of photography buffs, enthusiasts, and talented amateurs looking to master their craft, and maybe break into the professional world as well; just as you are hoping to do. This could benefit both of you. The photographer could use your pet as a model, and your pet would have the experience—and the exposure—to perfect his camera-ready skills. A bonus, of course, is that the photographer would probably give you copies of your pet's photos in exchange for your pet's modeling services. This is a terrific way to build a professional-quality portfolio.

In each community there are different kinds of film schools— and colleges that give film courses are wonderful to contact. Talk to the professors of film studies or filmmaking, and let them know your pet's available to be part of students' film projects! Each student is required to do an actual semiprofessional movie, commercial, or video production. And what better way to have both students—the human and the pet—develop their talents, skills, and technique, than for the student filmmaker and the StarPet to work and learn and succeed together?

You're always hearing in interviews about big stars nowadays that roomed together in college, worked on school film projects together, and stayed in touch over the years and worked together and then hit it big. Indeed, Matt Damon and Ben Affleck are a perfect example, triumphing in their shared, Oscar-winning work, *Good Will Hunting*!

And, one day, you might find that the student you worked with turned out to be the famous director or filmmaker who has hired you again at a more professional level! His new professional career could help your new career! These kinds of stories always happen, so be a part of it, enjoy the journey, from the beginning to the end, and one day you'll find that this filmmaker may be as happy to see you as you are to see him!

RADIO STATIONS/TV/CABLE TV

You could become a guest on your local radio station or a local TV show and talk about yourself and your dog or cat and his life and career as an animal actor. These shows also offer boundless opportunities to promote events you might be doing for a local community or charity. This demonstrates that your dog or cat is available for professional work, so when businesses think of advertising, they think of using you, because you've been marketing yourself for just that purpose. No pun intended, but working the TV/radio circuit provides a good opportunity to network! Also, don't overlook the opportunity of doing promotionals for the stations themselves, or the special events they're sponsoring or promoting.

NEWSPAPERS, MAGAZINES, AND FLYERS

This is a good opportunity for your pet to be featured in a story about you and your pet, what you do, or a special event you're promoting. The key here is to approach the publication with a prepared story idea, and be prepared to tie it into something currently noteworthy, like National Pet Month or Be Kind to Animals Week. Or, conversely, create an appropriately current and newsworthy story idea that just happens to have an opening to feature your pet!

Also, let them know that you are available to promote them—to promote their upcoming business and social events. Be prepared to toss out plenty of good, workable ideas.

This is the old Larry Trimble mode of operation, believing that nothing is impossible, if you give it your all with as much enthusiasm, creativity, and hard work as your StarPet enthusiastically gives his all for his work! Make the can-do spirit the canine-do spirit, and there will be nothing that you can't do!

Getting Your Paw in the Door

After you've aced the local bookings and achieved stardom there, it's time to reach for the stars in the professional arena of advertising, TV, and the film industry.

To play in the big leagues, you have to be part of the team. You will have to present yourself and your StarPet in the customary, professional way, adhering to certain standards. You'll need a portfolio of photographs of your pet, a résumé/credits, and achievement video clips of your dog's performance, stunts, and acting ability. Also, if your dog or cat has received notice in any of the reviews of the plays he has been in, highlight those as well. The guys in the big leagues will not have the time or inclination to read through entire columns or pages of newspaper clippings just to find your one or two lines, so spotlight those all-important lines if you want your StarPet to get noticed and have a chance in the spotlight! It doesn't have to be a body of professional work that you are showing, but you should display what you have done in a professional, traditional portfolio. Be sure to include everything, from the film school work, to community theater, special events, and newspaper clippings, and, if you have any work on video or CD, be sure to include it!

There is no better barker for your dog than your dog himself! Actions always speak louder than words, especially if they are the accomplished stunts and actions of a StarPet! When you have put everything together, piece by piece, bit by bit, into a standard, professional form, you now have the tools to be a true manager and agent for your StarPet. Here you have the means of selling your ideas, your creative way of convincing the players of the industry that you're a member of that community.

Again, think of Larry Trimble, just a young kid, successfully convincing Vitagraph's head honcho to cast his pet Collie in a major film!

Résumé/Portfolio

First impressions stick. You may not always meet the powers that be right away, so your dog's résumé/portfolio is your calling card. Therefore, it is very important that, for the casting director, you captured the right stunt, the right picture, the right expression— as well as having done the best job possible of writing about his skills and talents. Unlike your local work, when you're in the big leagues, direct access to the players, the movers, and shakers may not be easy. In fact, as with human actors, your only connection, at times, may be your pet's résumé/photo/portfolio, video, and so forth.

Think of the résumé/portfolio not just as your pet's calling card, but as your pet's stand-in as well! So it's important that your pet's résumé reflects just how wonderful he really is and why this targeted production cannot possibly be a success without him!

PHOTO

They say a picture is worth a thousand words. As with your local work, you may want to take your pet's photos, have a friend take the photos, or use photos you already have. Unless they're really professional quality or show your pet to his best possible advantage, it may be wise to consult a professional photographer.

A plus to using a professional photographer is that he may already be "in the loop," working for many of the ad agencies and businesses you're looking to work with, and if he's impressed with you, he may be able to give you a head's up for other jobs, or may remember your pet and how well you work and recommend you for a specific job.

It is important to have both a color photo and a black and white photo, because some ads are made in black and white, either because of budget (standard black and white is cheaper), or because of the venue (if the ad is in a low-cost flyer or brochure), or for artistic design.

WHAT'S NEEDED

One head shot (close-up) and one full-body shot: Ideally, this should be with some prop that helps to indicate the size of your pet. For example, a telephone or a book. (I highly recommend *Dog Speak* or *Cat Speak*!) Props such as these, unlike a yardstick, add entertainment value, making the entire photo, your pet included, more appealing!

Vital statistics: Fact sheet, including height, weight, age, breed, distinctive markings.

Talents: What tricks, stunts, actions, and so forth your pet has to offer.

Credits: Anything and everything that shows not just his talents, but his versatility and marketability. And this is where your talents and versatility come into play. Don't be too quick to dismiss what may seem unimportant or ordinary. Sometimes, the trick is in the packaging and in simply looking at your wonderful pet with new eyes. It may be helpful (and fun!) to do this with a friend.

Contact information: Include your email, cell phone, mailing address, home phone—any means that is a sure way to contact you. (Really adventuresome, ambitious StarPet people may want to create their pet's own website. If you want some ideas on this, please visit my website, www.starpet.com.)

Also, think outside the box. It doesn't have to be just a résumé, or even a résumé at all. It could simply be a postcard with your pet's photo and some catchy copy that alerts the media, and that you could mail to the people you're seeking work from within the industry.

Portfolio: This is a big, black, slim, oversized artist's portfolio, and can be obtained in art shops, office-supply stores, photography shops, and so on. In your portfolio, you should include your pet's résumé, standard head shot and long shot, press clips, and a variety of photographs that show your pet off to his best advantage. If you're a computer whiz, you might want to put all this onto a CD or MP3, to personally deliver, mail, or e-mail.

Basically, whatever way you feel comfortable, just to do it, make it work. Remember, producers, directors, casting directors, and casting agents cannot choose your pet or hire your pet unless they know your pet exists!

From the Classroom to the Green Room

Now that your training is complete and you've made a splash in your local community, and you're armed with your talent and your portfolio, there are many arenas for your StarPet to strut his stuff.

You've left the classroom and now you're in the world of profes-

sional show business. After I had paid my dues, working in print ads, commercials, television shows, and motion pictures, and making my dogs the celebrity dogs they were—as yours will be!—I remember being asked to hit the TV talk show circuit (Jay Leno, David Letterman).

Before actually walking onto the stage for your appearance on national TV, the producers ask you to wait in the Green Room.

The Green Room is like a hospitality room you share with the other celebrities also appearing on the show. The Green Room is where you're made as comfortable as possible. There are TV monitors to keep track of the show, as well as catered refreshments and comfortable seating, and you're treated like a star. As the human actors and celebrities say, when you've made it to the Green Room you know you've made it!

Here's a rundown on some of the professional steppingstones to forge your path to the coveted Green Room.

Print Work

This is the first line of work. It's still photography. It's a starting point, simple, basic, and easy, because it's print, it's frozen. You have time to position your pet, work with him, make sure he does it right, and time to take a break and to accomplish those desired poses and positions. Print work helps to get your professional career going for TV and film work. It's part of the advertising industry, where pets are used a lot to promote products in magazines, newspapers, and catalogues. Here the StarPets are creating their portfolios of professional credits. Another advantage of print work is that it is easy to have the print ads to show. Print work is available for pets for everything from the obvious (dog products and dog food) to children's toys, swimming pools, lawn products, furniture, and fashion (this includes catalogue work, as well).

Modeling/Fashion Shows

Here the pet is actually working with high-fashion models working the runway (catwalk—pun intended!). StarPets are sought after to accompany a model when she or he walks the runway and shows the designer's works. The dog or cat at the side of the model lends added drama and flair and movement, depending on the breed, and makes a statement about the designer's creations.

Sporting breeds might show a sport coat (think a Pointer or a Jack Russell Terrier), and something elegant, evening wear, might have a sleek, sophisticated Afghan or an Italian Greyhound.

Television Industry

TV work is both advertising and entertainment; it combines both worlds.

In commercials, the advertising community focuses on the right way of promoting a product using pets, and they're very creative and appealing to the mass audience. In fact, they are so appealing, they've really created a homogenous American culture and family with manufactured, shared memories and points of reference.

For example, just give a tag-line or sing a jingle from a popular, instantly recognizable commercial and a person knows he's got a friend or like-minded thinker. So the StarPet becomes the pet of American culture. In fact, the advertising agencies are proud of their creative commercials with their pets, and they have won numerous Cleo Awards (the Oscars, the Academy Award of commercials/advertising)—and those with pets seem to win more!

So, pets are good for advertising, good for the client, and good for the consumer to be entertained. Everybody has a good time with these animal-oriented campaigns. In fact, there are TV specials/documentaries built solely around popular (and not so well-known) commercials, both here and abroad—and the majority of them feature animals!

But in TV entertainment, shows are broken down into situation comedies, dramas, daytime dramas (the soap operas), movies, miniseries, and documentaries. And with the popularity of the

★ Bash with Bloodhounds during the filming of a
Burlington socks commercial. ★
Courtesy Meruet Dibra

newest genre, the newest rage—the reality shows—who knows,
StarPet: How to Make Your Pet a Star could become the next big
reality show!

Film Industry

The film industry is what every human actor and animal actor
wants to work in.

The film industry has a history of working with animal actors.
It's been proven in the past that they were a big draw for the studios, and that still holds true today. Every major film that has
starred a dog or cat has catapulted that cat or dog into status as an
iconic part of our American culture, our society, and the tradition
shows no sign of abating.

StarPets are the ideal candidates for this industry because they have been trained and taught the proper acting skills and proper techniques that attract the filmmakers and also appeal to the mass audience that enjoys seeing animals in films.

A lot of times a book is made into a movie, and I also see that this book, *StarPet,* is a potential movie in the making! And don't worry, all of you have a job in it—none of you will end up on the cutting room floor!

Theater

Even big movie stars confide to talk show hosts their longing to get back to their roots, to tread the boards once again on the great stage. The stage, the theater, is traditionally where actors begin— and oftentimes return—triumphantly!

Returning to the theater, however, generally requires a paycut (and quite a substantial one), and sometimes, actors will waive their fee simply for the experience of returning to Broadway. Everyone knows Sandy in the Broadway (and film) production of *Annie,* but you have to think about all the Broadway and other shows that don't star animal actors, but do use them in the ensemble, as part of the production—and the same holds true for community theater, regional theater, and summer stock throughout the country.

CAST OF BEHIND-THE-SCENES CHARACTERS

Every time you see a commercial, TV show, or movie, there is a behind-the-scenes cast of characters making that movie magic happen. Actually, I take that back. Your StarPet is making the magic—the cast of behind-the-scenes characters is providing the skilled mechanics that make the magic work!

Just as for every one minute of film that the moviegoers enjoy, there may have been two hours of work/film they don't see, so for every one actor/animal actor, there are ten production people making that moment of movie magic happen. And knowing who these people are and how their work directly relates to your work, and what's asked of your pet, will help you to market and manage your pet better, allowing him to shine in the best possible light.

These people are experts, professionals in their field, in their world, the entertainment industry, which you are now a part of. But you have to remember that they are not experts or professionals in *your* field—that's why they hired you! So you have to be prepared to work with them, to advise, to consult, to be part of the cooperative effort, to make the end result—the movie, the product, the commercial, or whatever—be the best that it can be. And have fun doing it!

THE PRODUCER

There are many different types of producers. One producer, the kind most people think of when they think of a producer, is the financier, the one who puts up the money to produce the project, to make it happen. This project could be a motion picture, a television show, or a Broadway play. He is responsible for everything, from the idea to the completion of the project. And in film work, he is also responsible for the release, distribution, promotion, and residual sales.

Traditionally, the producer would approach the studio with a package he had put together and the studio would come up with the money. But in independent films, the producer either puts up his own money or seeks out investors.

Television producers, unlike their motion picture counterparts, generally don't put up the money to produce a film. They're not required to be financiers. Their responsibilities are more hands-on, handling and overseeing the production of a TV program. They're not the financiers, but they are responsible for how the money is spent to create and complete the production from beginning to end, and for overseeing the work of the production and the quality of the finished product.

THE CLIENT

In TV commercials, the client (the product) is technically the producer. The client is financing the production, the commercial (and the money goes into hiring the ad agency), but the advertising agency is the creative, driving force. It hires the production company, but the production company takes on the role of the hands-on producer, attending to the mechanics, the logistics, that turn the ad agency's vision into marketable reality—the final stage shot. The production company that the ad agency hires (which includes directors, cameramen, lighting, sound, props, wardrobe) brings the ad agency's storyboard to life.

THE ADVERTISING AGENCY

The advertising agency is hired by companies or individuals that spend millions and millions of dollars to promote their product and brand name in all media (television, radio, newspapers, magazines). The agency then comes up with an overall ad campaign for the client. At the same time, the ad agency hires the production company that is responsible for making the commercial.

THE DIRECTOR

The director is the person who takes the script or storyboard and brings it to life, whether it is a TV show, commercial, film, or play. The director motivates the actor (in this case the animal actor) to bring out the emotional feeling, or what he has to do for that scene, which later will be part of the finished product. The director explains to the StarPet how to portray himself with other actors or (in commercials) the product. He is the dramatic coach on set and brings out the best in the actor, as well as the animal actor, so the script or storyboard comes to life, to reality, to the finished product. He makes the intangible tangible.

The director directs the interplay, combining the functions of other support members of the production into one cohesive creative effort—camera, lighting, sound, and so on. Simply, the director is pretty much the one you should keep your eye on to look for direction. I always enjoy the opportunity to talk to the director, so that I can be helpful in making his vision come through on film by consulting with him to show what a StarPet is capable of achieving.

THE ART DIRECTOR

The art director is the creative force who ensures that the product is visually appealing. The art director is the one who creates and lays out the storyboard, and is the person who is responsible for the appearance of the product in the ad, how it visually comes across, and how it appeals to the consumer. Because of this, the art director oftentimes decides or has the last word on what type of animal or breed of dog or cat may be used in the ad. In the advertising community, the art director is looked upon as the person in charge of the project.

SCRIPTWRITER/COPYWRITER

The scriptwriter for films and the copywriter for commercials are responsible for the message that comes across in the TV show, film, or commercial. The producer relays his thoughts/ideas, as does the director, to the scriptwriter or copywriter, and they combine their thoughts on how the copy should be written for the movie or commercial to make it work. It's a cooperative effort, deciding what is creatively possible and realistically feasible. For the StarPet, you may have to consult with the scriptwriter or copywriter, explaining what the StarPet is capable of doing within the parameters of what's being asked for. I always take the opportunity, when possible, to be a part of this team. It makes a better end product.

THE PRODUCTION COMPANY

The production company takes the ad agency's vision or idea and produces the finished product. The production company is hired by the ad agency to take its creative vision or idea, its script or storyboard, and bring it to life. The production company brings the idea to fruition by providing the nuts and bolts, the logistics, the mechanics. Oftentimes the production company, in putting together the finished product, may be the entity that hires you. The production company hires all the members of the production staff and the experts (you, for example), and it supplies the animal, the StarPet.

THE CASTING DIRECTOR

The casting director works for the film company. The film company subcontracts a casting director to get the best talent at the best price for the film company. If a major motion picture calls for an animal, the casting director will either audition animals for the role himself or work through an animal talent agency. As with human actors, these casting directors can be very helpful in your career, and once you know them you should keep in touch with them, not just wait, hoping for a movie to be produced.

With a casting director, be proactive. Let him know your pet is available and what your pet can do. If you send casting directors your StarPet's photo/résumé, they may keep your StarPet on file and remember you and call you for an audition when a movie is casting for an animal. They may also send your StarPet's information along to the props and wardrobe people at major studios (remember, animals still come under the auspices of the properties department in film), or the art directors of production companies. And this can get you work and set you on your way.

THE ANIMAL AGENCY

Animal agencies supply and coordinate the booking of animals and pets for print work, commercials, television, movies, promotional events, public relation tie-ins, and so forth.

Just as the production company delivers the package to the client, the animal agency delivers the complete pet package, which includes, first and foremost, the pet who can do the job, as well as everything that goes into making that StarPet—all expenses and fees include the training, grooming, transportation, and insurance—so that when the StarPet and his handler show up on the set, business has already been taken care of, and they are there to deliver the talent, to act.

Some animal agencies may want exclusivity, meaning you can only work with that agency, and you cannot work with another agency, or book work yourself. Other animal agencies, however, may sign you on, but still allow you to be a free agent, working with other agencies as well, or even getting your own bookings. There are advantages to both arrangements—seek out the one that best fits you and your StarPet. Your desire to work on a full-time basis, or a freelance or part-time basis, will also be a factor in your decision.

The third choice is that you and your StarPet work alone. You are your own agent, manager, and publicist. Sometimes this is the best arrangement, because nobody knows your pet, or your personal and professional life and commitments, and how much you want or are willing to commit to this new adventure, better than you. Remember, you want this to be a fun adventure for you and your StarPet.

Taking Your StarPet on the Road

Now that you know where the work is and who the players are, it's time to let them know who you are and what you can do. This might take you to a casting call, a call-back, or a more intense one-on-one audition. But remember, whatever it is, you and your StarPet are on the road, so make sure you have everything your StarPet needs to look and act his best!

The most important factors for success (you've got the talent and training, obviously) are to be properly prepared (for both expected and unexpected challenges) and for your pet to be comfortable, just as any actor is kept comfortable on the set with his own trailer, catered food, a comfortable bed, and whatever else he may request or need.

It's a good idea to enlist the help of a friend or family member who knows your pet, for two reasons. First, it helps facilitate your pet's comfort and ability to work and allows you to concentrate on working with the professionals on the set, and so forth. Second, this person will be recognized as your assistant. This gives a professional look to your StarPet presentation. It sends the message that you are part of the professional team—the StarPet professional team.

For your StarPet's needs, it is a good idea to have a duffel bag or tote bag to carry all that he'll need. The bag should be large enough to carry all that will be needed, but still small enough for you to carry easily and still control your dog or carry your cat's carrying case.

FOR YOUR DOG STAR

Make sure you have:

1. a variety of extra collars and leashes.
2. bowls for food and water.
3. food and treats for reward.
4. your clicker.
5. focus toys—squeaky toys to get his attention and that favorite look or pose.
6. a rubber mat for traction.
7. his favorite bed or mat to rest on.
8. his crate for traveling and to rest in.
9. brushes and combs.
10. a small first-aid kit.

FOR YOUR CAT STAR

Make sure you have:

1. her carrying case and her favorite mat.
2. a variety of leashes, collars, and harnesses.
3. dishes for food and water.
4. her food and reward treats.
5. her magic wand and conductor's baton.
6. focus toys and catnip.
7. the clicker.
8. her litterbox.
9. her combs and brushes.
10. a small first-aid kit.

TWO REMINDERS

1. Do not overfeed your dog or cat before the job or audition. Remember that you will be using treats as rewards, so it is important to keep your dog focused on the task—and reward—at hand. If you overfeed your pet beforehand, he will become lethargic and lose his focus. Remember, you want your pet to be alert and energized for the action or job at hand. Once the job is over, you can feed your pet more as a reward for doing such a good job.

2. It is important to keep your pet hydrated, but don't keep his water dish filled to the brim. Instead, fill his dish with ice cubes. As prescribed by veterinarians, ice cubes will keep your pet from drinking too much water too quickly, which can cause bloat or regurgitation. Ice cubes or frequent, small amounts of water keep your pet happily hydrated and ready to shine.

Show Me the Money!

Your StarPet gets his reward for his performance, and it's time for you to get your reward for your marketing and managing skills.

My rule of thumb in negotiating the proper fee structure is to follow what the going rate is for human actors (the extra, not the star). These actors are called day players, and generally make about $100 to $200 a day. Keep in mind that our animal actors at this time do not get residuals. They get one flat fee. Understanding this helps me create a proper fee structure. It could be three times the fee the day player receives, or it could be less. You can figure this by what your StarPet is asked to do.

You have to see the importance, in the beginning of your pet's career, of getting the job, and now is the time to negotiate a price that is acceptable to both you and the agency or production company that is hiring you. The point I'm trying to make is just get the job (whatever fee you may have to agree to), which will lead to many jobs, and build up your credits, and then you will have the opportunity to get the best fee for your StarPet.

Eventually, once you have earned credits and the respect of the show business community, you will be in the circle of high performers who make anywhere from $500 to $1,500 a day. For the super StarPet, the Lassies, the Benjis of our time, they can make from $5,000 to $10,000 a day. For your first job, it might just seem like they're throwing you a bone—but if your have a Super StarPet, you could end up with the entire meat market!

On-Set Stage Presence

Now that your StarPet's training and charisma—stage presence!—have gotten his paw in the door, *your* stage presence matters. Your presence on the set, your behavior, is a reflection of your professionalism, and it is important that you follow a certain protocol (etiquette) that all the professionals working on the set—from the director, to the stagehands, wardrobe, lighting, and so on—adhere to. You will be expected to be a part of this, and it is to your advantage to show both your StarPet's and your own professional manner and presence. Remember, it's not just how you handle your StarPet, but how you handle *yourself* that will make a lasting impression.

STARPET CHECKLIST

1. Give yourself plenty of time to report to the set. You don't just want to be on time, you want to be early. This gives you a chance to get your pet adjusted to the set, to assimilate with the new situation, and to be better prepared to act.

2. Check in with the assistant director or production manager to let him know that you've arrived and you're ready. Also ask for a copy of the script or storyboard, so you will have time to rehearse and review, if needed.

3. Both the pet and the handler (that's you) should be well-groomed, well-rested, well-rehearsed, and ready to work.

4. Wear clothes and shoes that are comfortable and will facilitate any kind of action required. Don't wear dangling necklaces or bracelets. These can be distracting noisemakers and would be the ultimate faux pas in TV and film work: Remember, "Quiet on the set!"

In my personal work, I always wear a photographer's vest, with all the pockets and pouches for my clicker, treats, squeaky toys, anything I might need at a moment's notice. That keeps my hands free for work. This photographer's vest (some handlers might use fishing vests or safari jackets) provides both function and form, providing you with an immediate identity on the set: "Oh yeah!—The dog trainer's here!"

5. Do not discuss your fees or financial arrangements. Whether you have been booked through an agency, or you've booked yourself, all business arrangements and contractual agreements have already been formalized.

6. If you have brought along a friend or family member to assist you, remember that person is an assistant—not an entourage! Just one assistant is all you need, and that person should follow your lead in on-set protocol. By all means, have fun, but remember this is not a party.

7. You may find your StarPet working with a celebrity. It is natural that you would want a picture with the celebrity and your pet to capture the moment. This is okay, but the right time and place and approach is important. Wait till a break—a lunch break or the end of the shoot. And, most important, ask permission first. The same protocol holds true if you're seeking an autograph.

8. Coordinate your pet's comfort needs with the needs of the production. The well-being of your StarPet is paramount, but it is up to you, as the professional handler, to manage and coordinate your pet's needs with the schedules and framework of the production. One golden rule: Make sure your StarPet has had a chance to relieve himself before he is required to perform.

9. When the opportunity arises, and you know that your Star-Pet is capable of doing one more take, at that moment, you tell the director or photographer, "He can do one more take—he's okay. If you need it, he can do it!" This just shows you're supporting the production and making every effort to be part of the winning team to make the production (and you and your StarPet's contribution to it!) the best it can be!

10. When you finish with the day's work, always leave a positive ending to your performance. They were pleased with your performance, so always say goodbye by shaking hands with the people you've worked most closely with on the set—the director, the actors, and the key production people—telling them you enjoyed working with them. This tells them that you are a gentleman or a lady, that you're professional, and leaves a lasting impression. This also confirms that you have finished your day's work. This is important because you must never just leave without proper confirmation that all the spots were done right, the tape is finished, there are no more takes—you've been given clearance to leave for the day.

It is also a good idea, if possible, to check the call sheet for the next day, just in case your StarPet's name has been posted for further work.

And, again, always leave with a final handshake.

The handshake is a traditional, universal sign of goodwill. Its historical origin was to show, with the open palm, that no weapon was held, and, later, to demonstrate that there was no ill will. As time went on, a handshake became a gentleman's way of sealing a deal in trust and honor.

So it is appropriate that this age-old symbol offering partnership and friendship between people has become one of the most endearing and popular action for StarPets!

CHAPTER NINE

From StarPet to Pet Laureate

*N*ow that you have learned how to navigate the wonderful adventure that awaits you and your StarPet, I hope you will chart a course for yourself and your StarPet that is uniquely yours to share. For, whether you choose to stick close to home in a personal Star-Pet adventure or go out into the world in a professional StarPet adventure, always remember to keep the "play" in play-acting!

That is just what the Old Guard, the Old Masters, did at the turn of the last century, when *they* were young and the *industry* was young. They were scrappy, imaginative youngsters who carried their dreams in their hearts and their love for their pets on their sleeves, and when they rolled up those sleeves to *work,* they made sure that the work was fun—an adventure!

But all kids grow up, and so did the legends and so did the business. In fact, the business grew into very big business! So much so, in fact, that breaking into the business now as a youngster can, at first glance, seem a little daunting, an insurmountable, uphill battle.

You see, since Hollywood's Golden Age, some fifty-odd years ago, the industry has become something of an exclusive club. You have to understand that, when moviemaking was in its infancy—in the early 1900s, when Strongheart made his dashing debut and Lassie had yet to be born!—the animal trainers and suppliers were also in the infancy of their careers. It was a whole new business—a whole new world, actually—and the trainers were the pioneers, creating careers and paving paths in the training and supplying of animals for the entertainment industry. Eventually, these trainers—the handlers, the wranglers, the suppliers—became a close-knit, professional family, with a tradition of apprenticeship within the family. And, naturally, the individual trainers who composed this family themselves started families, and the industry work became a family business—also with the tradition of apprenticeship within the family. So, from generation to generation, the business stayed within these families, with apprenticeship passed on from fathers to sons and daughters.

But now, with the advent of the new century, the entertainment industry has the opportunity to become new again, to become young again! Oh, the patriarchs will always be in charge, of course—as well they should be, with their talent, wisdom, and experience. But this new age has also fostered opportunities for the new kids (and their pets!) on the block to forge new paths, explore new possibilities, and pioneer a new Golden Age for StarPets.

Because now, in the infancy of the twenty-first century, you aren't just the new kids on the block. You and your StarPet are the pioneers of the new era of show business—and there is a new furry frontier!

Just as the rudimentary technology at the advent of the last century gave birth to the motion picture industry, allowing it to grow and flourish, from the silent films to the talkies, and from black-and-white to color, so today's technology, when married with your pet's innate talent and rehearsed techniques, and your own newly acquired theatrical training skills and in-house industry knowledge, can give birth to a new Golden Age for StarPets.

With today's digital technology, we have gone from Shakespeare's Globe Theater to the Hollywood Theater to the Global Theater! But as grand as this sounds, its real strength, its real magic, is that it makes the industry not just young again, but small again, accessible again!

Just as the Hubbell telescope allows scientists to discover (and the public, also, to see) heretofore unknown, unseen stars, so, with today's cutting-edge technology, your heretofore unknown, unseen StarPet can be seen and enjoyed, discovered, by all the right people: producers, directors, agents, casting directors, and photographers.

Indeed, with a newcomer's knack for mixing talent and technology, marketing and managing—and an old-timer's instinct for mixing mutts and moxie, hounds and hubris, cats and chutzpah—Rin Tin Tin wannabes can crash the glass ceiling of the old dogs' club as effortlessly as Rin Tin Tin sailed through his special glass windowpanes of translucent candy!

Just as desktop publishing changed the face of publishing, making it accessible to all would-be authors and publishers, so digital technology can change the face of the motion picture industry.

In fact, motion picture history would not have been robbed of the face and talent of one very special little dog—history's very first StarPet, to be exact—if today's technology had been available when the industry was just a young scruff of a pup.

History considers Larry Trimble's Collie, Jean, to be the very first dog star—but Trimble himself always credited a nameless little stray as the first shining dog star, whose light cast a spotlight on Trimble's talent, allowing Jean, and later Strongheart, to find their way to stardom.

The year was 1912, and the legendary Larry Trimble—barely more than a pup himself—was a young kid hanging out at the Vitagraph Studio in Brooklyn, New York, hoping to make his mark as a cub reporter in writing about the exciting new world of the "moving pictures." Indeed, the only thing Larry loved more than the moving pictures was his beloved Collie, Jean—and the time spent with her in training sessions and playtimes.

Larry left Jean at home when he went to the studio, but dogs and Larry always seemed to find each other. A bright and intrepid little stray dog eventually found her way to Larry, and before long, he had the little dog running through her training paces nearly as deftly as the remarkable Jean.

One day, Larry came upon the legendary Alfred E. Smith, head of the Vitagraph Studio, lamenting that a cute story with a dog as the lead character would have to be shelved, because no dog could possibly act the demanding role that the script required.

Hearing those words, Larry knew that fate had tossed him a bone, and if he didn't grab it and run with it, it would be lost forever. Somehow, the small boy persuaded the big studio boss that he had a dog who fit the bill perfectly. Larry, of course, was thinking about his beloved Jean. But Smith was skeptical, and growing impatient. There was no time to get Jean.

Still, Larry had faith that his newfound friend could handle the script, and that she did. Indeed, the hardest part of the impromptu audition was cajoling the frightened little dog to come out from hiding and into the cavernous studio!

But when the little dog stepped onto the stage, she aced every trick!

Alas, this was not to be a "straydom to stardom" story. The year was 1912, and in those fledgling film days, technology was also in its infancy, and the shortcomings of the rudimentary movie camera dictated that all the important acting had to be blocked out exactly ten feet—no more, no less—from the camera, or the actors would not be captured on film. So an actor of average height standing at the all-important ten-foot mark would always be cut off from the knee down.

Larry's little mutt, unfortunately, was barely knee-high to the actors, and totally out of camera range. The lovely, intelligent little dog with the ten-foot-tall talent was just too small in stature to be seen at the stage's ten-foot mark.

So this remarkable little dog who captured the hearts of the producers with his engaging personality and performance would never be seen on screen, but Trimble credits the dog's winning performance with enabling the fledgling trainer to win the attention and respect of the great Alfred E. Smith. For when the studio heads were ready to admit defeat in their search for a dog with just the right talent—along with just the right size—they sat up and paid attention when young Larry (thinking of his Collie, Jean, at home) piped up with the brazen announcement, "I've got a dog that can do this, and more!"

And the rest, as they say, is history.

However ephemeral that little stray's fame was fated to be, her influence was rock-solid in launching the careers of Larry, Jean, and Strongheart.

We'll never know how many faces of famous felines and talented tailwaggers may have been lost to posterity by archaic camera angles—but our future posterity will never have to worry, thanks to today's technology that can unleash StarPets and give wings to their dreams, and careers!

In fact, one StarPet did just that!

As you know from the training chapters, I always encourage my StarPet Workshop students to videotape their work with their

StarPets, whether it's a training session or acting out a script or storyboard. This works not only as a good, foolproof way to critique your pet's performance, but as a way to critique *your* performance, as well! Such a video can also be used as a demo tape to send out to advertising agencies and casting directors. And, at the very least, such videos make wonderful home movies of StarPet memories.

But one pet owner actually ended up creating her very own independent film based on her dog and her life. It started out as a simple straightforward story of her every(dog)day life, chronicling her day-to-day routines with her dog and their quest for happiness. She was a single woman looking for a husband, and he was a puppy looking for a daddy!

This charming, poignant little pup of a film was simply titled *A Dogumentary,* and was shown at film festivals all around the world—and even feted at the internationally renowned Cannes Film Festival.

This just shows that, with today's technology, we can have not just the world, but the world of show business, at our fingertips. If you don't want to pack up your StarPet and literally take your show on the road (like Steinbeck and Charlie, or Carl Spitz and his Hollywood Dog Motion Picture Preview), you can take your show on the information highway, and from New York to Hollywood, from London to Rome, your pet can still be a StarPet!

So it is my hope that this book, along with the StarPet Agency and Workshops, will help to widen the camera apertures of the entertainment industry to welcome today's StarPets. Because now, Hollywood is everywhere, and so, too, are the stars.

When I left Hollywood nearly twenty-five years ago to return to New York, I didn't leave the dreams or the business. I simply anchored my dreams to, and based my business in, the Big Apple. Of course, New York, like Hollywood, has always been an entertainment capital of the world, so I still had the necessary proximity to the industry of my business. Still, today's technology provides an accessibility to the business that I—and I'm sure many of my colleagues, also—wish had been available years ago. Today, no matter where an actor hangs his hat or a StarPet drops his leash, Hollywood or New York can still be anybody's hometown.

Indeed, our love for our StarPets makes us family, and our love for the industry makes us neighbors in an intimate, yet universal, community. And as cat and canine compatriots, we need to raise our collective voice for the welfare of our pets, both onscreen and offscreen. Comte Georges-Louis de Buffon, as France's "Naturalist Laureate," championed greater understanding and appreciation of all the animals—especially the dog—with whom we share this planet. Now we, today—as surely as we instinctively draw our pets close to us—must don that noble mantle, but draw it even closer to protect our pets.

We must don the mantle of "Pet Laureate."

In fact, as I was putting the finishing touches on this book, friends and colleagues alerted me that the media's prestigious *Yearbook of Experts* had just published its in-house industry guide, dubbing me "the 'Pet Laureate' of our times."

I was bemused by their well-intentioned piece of flattery, but impatient that they had missed the greater message I try to impart to all my StarPet clients: that we—each and every one of us—must don the mantle of Pet Laureate.

As Pet Laureates, we must educate and celebrate, publicize and eulogize, the roles of the dog and cat, and all pets, in our lives today. Pets have the ability to help us transcend our human frailties and uplift our souls. For our benefit, as well as theirs, we need to remember and resurrect the soulful symbiosis we share with our animal companions.

The Poet Laureate is the original celebrity. A public figure of talent—who has the rare ability to discern the collective soul of a people and to reflect that uniquely nuanced group identity—the role of the Poet Laureate is to foster understanding and support of his country and compatriots and give that consciousness a public, proud, and productive voice. And perhaps it is no coincidence that two of the world's most celebrated Poet Laureates were also devoted to pets.

Appointed by President John F. Kennedy, the twentieth century's greatest Poet Laureate, Robert Frost, was seldom seen without his loyal Border Collie, Gillie, at his side. And back in the nineteenth century, the visionary Alfred Lord Tennyson put pen to paper and words to action by establishing the passage of the Cruelty to Animals Act in 1876. This revolutionary act, which, among other criteria, made law the licensing of researchers, as well as the adequate inspection of laboratory premises, also had the foresight to include the far-reaching Pain Rule clause, which set a limit to the amount of suffering inflicted upon any animal in any circumstances.

Because of this joyful, generous, and noble task, the post of Poet Laureate is an honor conferred by a nation's leader, and one that is taken very seriously. And now, with the advent of the twenty-first century, the post of Pet Laureate is an equally honorable job, but, like the dog himself—joyful, generous, and noble— we do not need to be appointed to take on this task. Rather, like the dog, we embrace our role and give generously of our time and talent because it is the right thing to do.

Therefore, to be a Pet Laureate is to take responsible pet ownership to the highest level possible. And, with StarPets, as with human actors, with privilege and a spotlight in the public forum come responsibility. More than ever before, we have become a celebrity-focused, media-driven society. Stars understand that, by virtue of their celebrity, they are in a unique position to set standards, become responsible role models, and facilitate care and understanding for those less fortunate than themselves. Some fail miserably, of course (we're only human, after all, not dogs!).

Still, when celebrities rise to the occasion and raise the bar, there is no greater, surefire way to fundraise for philanthropy in today's society. In fact, my own organization, Paws Across America, has facilitated this for many charitable events and organizations throughout the years, with the cross-marketing and cause-marketing of celebrities and pets together.

And this is what I would encourage you, as I myself do, and as I charge all my StarPet clients to commit to: Pick up the mantle of Pet Laureate. Unlike the Poet Laureate, you don't have to wait to be appointed to take charge of your life! Vow that, as you embark on this wonderful adventure that is StarPets, you and your pet will—as celebrities in all arenas of the entertainment industry do—use your time in the spotlight and public arena to uphold standards and to be a good role model for responsible pet ownership. Because to be a Pet Laureate is to bring the inner, private StarPet within your pet into the public, professional forum, and, together—in whichever avenue of public work you choose—do your best and make a difference!

Indeed, legions of legendary StarPets before us heeded the call to give to those less fortunate and to go to where they were needed. Perhaps it was because so many of the early animal actors had themselves been rescued from the "wrong side of the tracks," or from the trenches and foxholes of war-ravaged Europe (of both World War I and World War II), that, when the going got rough, these "ruffs" got going—leaving their starring roles in the entertainment industry to tour at home and abroad to boost the morale of servicemen and women and visiting army hospitals and platoons, behind the scenes and on the front lines.

And oftentimes, costarring with their on-camera, studio costars, these plucky and patriotic pooches also gave selflessly to their canine combat counterparts: the war dogs.

In fact, in 1917, two of the biggest film stars of the day—Mary Pickford, "America's Sweetheart," and Teddy, the Great Dane, "America's Hero"—gave up films altogether, toiling ceaselessly in several back-to-back tours to drum up support and funds for the Red Star Animal Relief. The Red Star Animal Relief was a relief service for army dogs, organized by the American Humane Association and dedicated to aiding the injured animals involved in warfare. It served as a kind of canine Red Cross.

With Mary Pickford and Teddy in the lead, countless celebrities and their canine counterparts quickly followed. Daisy, the delightful dog star from the old *Blondie* motion picture series, selflessly gave blood time and again to the Red Star Animal Relief for the benefit of wounded war dogs—and the legendary Lassie criss-crossed the country countless times, visiting army hospitals and logging grueling, dawn-to-dusk hours performing for and visiting with the wounded troops.

But it was the inimitable Strongheart who was one of the first to balance a film career with philanthropic efforts, both at home and abroad, using his celebrity to illuminate and benefit those philanthropic and charitable causes. He brought the inspiring story of "Buddy," the first guide dog for the blind, to the silver screen, and his stirring portrayal of the hero dog raised the public's awareness of these remarkable service dogs. Not content to just "stick to the script," however, Strongheart also became the guide dog's symbol and lead fundraiser, stumping tirelessly to raise funds for the dogs' training and placement, as well as for their rightful and legal acceptance in all arenas.

And while these selfless StarPets were risking their lives in service on the front lines, two very special guardians—Pet Laureates—were working tirelessly to safeguard their lives when they returned home.

J. Allen Boone and Richard C. Craven were contemporaries in Hollywood's growing Golden Era. Movers and shakers both, they were without peer in both their careers and their chosen philanthropy. In fact, the welfare of Hollywood's animal actors became their lives' work, indeed, their mission, and, thanks to their tireless, selfless work, the Golden Era of Hollywood glowed—for pets and people alike—a whole lot brighter!

Known, respectively, as Hollywood's Albert Schweitzer and Hollywood's St. Francis of Assisi, J. Allen Boone was an accomplished journalist and close friend of Larry Trimble and Strongheart, and Richard C. Craven was the director of the Hollywood branch of the American Humane Association.

An erudite, insightful, and respected reporter, J. Allen Boone chronicled much of the glory years of the entertainment industry, as well as, with a rare combination of cunning and compassion, exploring the lives and loves, talents and testimonials, of the rare breed of animal actors and trainers whose hearts and souls and talents, when brought to the silver screen, uplifted audiences everywhere.

But this talented writer (whose book *Kinship with All Life* reverently explored the human/animal bond and, much like Albert Schweitzer's famed *Reverence for Life,* earned him his honorary mantle) believed his greatest byline was caring for, promoting, and chronicling for the ages the gift that was Strongheart.

Indeed, so great was Boone's love for his friend Trimble's dog that his vocation gave way to his avocation, as caretaker to the great furry film star. Sharing the care of Strongheart with his longtime friend, Trimble, and his wife, playwright Jane Murfin, Boone was with Strongheart right up until the final curtain. Indeed, it was Boone's love letter to Strongheart—*Letters to Strongheart,* a book written and published *after* the great dog's death—that, in an exquisite marriage of bereavement and beatitude, posthumously continues to garner legions of new fans who have never even seen the films of this incredible dog, and to shape and influence the views of those who work, or aspire to work, in the world of Star-Pets!

And Richard C. Craven more than earned his noble nickname, Hollywood's St. Francis of Assisi! As director of the American Humane Association's Hollywood branch, Craven was a strong and steadfast sentinel in safeguarding Hollywood's sentient screen stars. A diligent watchdog, Craven made certain that, on his watch, at least, no mistreatment or inhumane act ever occurred on the set or on the screen—never hesitating to enact sanctions against any offending individual professionals or company productions.

Like St. Francis, who looked out for even the smallest of his little brothers and sisters, the birds and the beasts, Craven also looked out for the smallest of Hollywood's animal actors. But, in the entertainment industry, that doesn't just mean little creatures, like rabbits and mice and birds (although Craven protected them, as well). No, Craven also looked out for the creatures—big or small—who had small roles in the films!

Believing that by acknowledging the hardy band of animal actors who have no chance for starring roles—animal extras, if you will!—but who excel in ability, talent, and training, Craven felt that a special recognition of these StarPets would foster added assurance of better care and treatment for these animal actors. Thus, after many long years of in-house industry work on behalf of all motion picture animals, a special Patsy Award, named in honor of this great man, is awarded to outstanding company or ensemble animal actors!

So the StarPets of today, our talented tailwaggers and felicitous felines, owe their aspirations and accomplishments, their fame and fortune, to quite a substantial legacy of love—not only to their talented forepaws and their trainers who forged the way, but also to the early Pet Laureates who, through managing and marketing the careers and well-being of animal actors in both film and philanthropy, have made the motion picture world a better place for StarPets.

And now, I would charge all Pet Laureates and their StarPets to continue the twin paths forged by Boone and Craven:

First, as J. Allen Boone did, to aspire, through whatever work you choose with your StarPet, to set an example of the boundless privilege of a beautifully in-sync, symbiotic human/animal bond and the satisfaction of responsible pet ownership.

And second, to emulate Richard C. Craven, by taking personal, responsible pet ownership to a higher, professional level—and carrying it over into the realm of the entertainment industry.

Because now, more than ever before—and it's been a long time coming!—is the time to secure an added level of professional protection to our StarPets. It is time, once and for all, to unionize.

So many animal actors, from so many parts of the country, work in so many different areas of the entertainment industry that it is important to create a collective, united front in regulating not just responsibility for their physical well-being but responsibility for their fiscal well-being.

And, in joining forces for a creative coalition in a new attempt at forming a real animal actors union, who better to lead than Richard C. Craven's animal alma mater, the American Humane Association, which has traditionally been in the forefront of overseeing the care and treatment of animals in the motion picture industry. Today, the AHA continues its legacy of setting guidelines for and monitoring and enforcing film and television units in protecting the animal actors of the entertainment industry.

Still, when it comes to doing the right thing, there can never be enough of a good thing!

Just as the legendary Tallulah Bankhead tried to unionize her animal costars with her Stage and Screen Dogs, so the beautiful and brainy Gretchen Wyler, leading actress and longtime animal welfare advocate, has picked up Bankhead's cerebral, charismatic, and compassionate mantle.

Wyler will always be most remembered for her starring residency in the hit television series *Dallas,* but she now resides at the Hollywood Office of the Humane Society of the United States, where she is working hard to give all animals a new lease on life and to shine a sensitive and savvy media spotlight on the plight of animals.

Toward this end, Gretchen Wyler founded the Genesis Awards, under the aegis of the Fund for Animals (itself founded by the late and legendary television critic Cleveland Amory).

The Genesis Awards pay tribute to the major news and entertainment media for producing outstanding works that raise public understanding of animal issues. As time went on, and Wyler's work for animals began to burgeon, she founded the Ark Trust, Inc., which continued to present the Genesis Awards. And, finally, in 2002, the Ark Trust joined forces with the Humane Society of the United States, becoming the HSUS's Hollywood office. As vice president of this office, the indefatigable Wyler also continues to executive-produce the Genesis Awards television specials.

These are indeed special times for animals in the entertainment industry, and you and your StarPet, as part of this new generation, have a unique opportunity to showcase not just the privilege of your talent but the responsibility of your commitment to the professional treatment of your cat and canine colleagues, the StarPets.

And, as these times have changed and grown and evolved, and we are riding an arc of a combined theatrical and technological revolution, you and your pet, as members of a new generation of the StarPet family, have a unique opportunity, with the guidance and information of this book, to join the growing family of animal actors in print work, advertising, television, and film. And, as you work at developing a body of work, a résumé, and a portfolio, it is my hope that you will also join forces and work at creating and developing new standards for the future of animals within our industry, which will facilitate their growth and work, and will enable them to gain just compensation. Indeed, these professional animals can and should benefit from the kind of personal and professional care and treatment they not only deserve, but have earned.

You, the new generation, are in a unique time and at a unique juncture to help your StarPets in the industry they call home. Just as generations before you, the old guard worked hard to build a foundation of care and recognition for the animal actors, so you, as the new generation, can work to safeguard not only the animal actors' care and recognition, but also their compensation and remuneration. And in today's world of countless television shows and commercials (where animals play a large and lucrative role), reruns mean residuals—but not for the participating pets! Unfortunately, as it stands today, human actors collect residuals for their work, but their costarring StarPets are left in the doghouse!

But you, the new generation, by combining the best of your mentors with the best you have to offer, can also combine the best of both worlds for your StarPets!

In my twin endeavors of film and philanthropy, I have witnessed and worked firsthand with our own close-knit group of generations—the Baby Boomers and Generations X, Y, and Z—and I have never worked with a more earnest, dedicated, and fun-loving group of people.

In fact, it was in marrying and marketing diverse generations for their strengths and contributions in my intergenerational pet therapy programs that the new philanthropic thrust, which Paws Across America employs quite successfully, was born.

I call it Paws Marketing, because animals can be both the champions and the beneficiaries.

Paws Marketing directs StarPets, guided by Pet Laureates, to work to help their less fortunate fellow creatures, whether they be animals or people. And the Pet Laureates are compassionate, like-minded people of all ages, both children and adults, from any generation. Working together, hand to paw, Pet Laureates and StarPets are a winning team for the advancement of philanthropy.

Paws Marketing evolved from the work of StarPets and Paws Across America in promoting the twin endeavors of film and philanthropy. Combining cross-marketing (multimedia, celebrity-driven commercial appeals) and cause-marketing (multimedia, celebrity-driven charitable appeals)—and inviting the pet crowd and StarPet crowd to really liven things up!—you have Paws Marketing, a financial and philanthropic funfest!

Several years ago, when financial and real-estate mogul Donald Trump was flush with his first successes in his phenomenal ascent as the kingpin of New York City real estate, I was called in to train a Trump family dog. This particular dog belonged to his equally savvy businessman brother, Robert, and his wife, Blaine. At the time, the blonde and beautiful Blaine was in the throes of nearly singlehandedly building and guiding God's Love We Deliver—one of New York's most respected charities, which brings meals (à la Meals on Wheels) to home-bound AIDS patients. I was struck by, and never forgot, the enormity of the ability to make both business a success and charity a success.

My hope is that people everywhere will take their knowledge and talents and savvy and success and use those abilities, not just in business, but in whatever philanthropic endeavor they choose, to make this world, for all who share it, a better place.

And for our StarPets, that means turning "dog-eat-dog" business strategy into a "dog-save-dog" charitable appeal! With their winsome and winning ways, our appealing pets appeal to our better selves and can help to make our charitable appeals more successful.

And now, as you and your StarPet embark on this exciting new adventure, and don the mantle of Pet Laureate, whatever script you choose to follow is up to you.

Remember that you are a part of the pioneering youngsters of Hollywood's new Golden Age—so, roll up your sleeves, jump in, and have fun!

Because sometime, somewhere, a director will cry out, "Lights! Camera! Action!"—and the pet that steps into the spotlight and becomes a *StarPet* could be *your* pet!

Directory of Animal Groups and Industry Organizations and Affiliations

Humane Society of the United States (HSUS)
(Hollywood Office)
5551 Balboa Blvd.
Encino, CA 91316
(818) 501-2275
www.hsushollywood.org
www.genesisawards.org

Humane Society of the United States (HSUS)
2100 L St., N.W.
Washington, DC 20037
(202) 452-1100
www.hsus.org

StarPet
3476 Bailey Ave.
Riverdale, NY 10463
(718) 796-4541
www.starpet.com

The American Humane Association Film and Television Unit
(AHA)
"No Animals Were Harmed"®
15366 Dickens St.
Sherman Oaks, CA 91403
(818) 501-0123
(818) 501-8725 (fax)
www.ahafilm.org

The American Humane Association (AHA)
63 Inverness Dr. East
Englewood, CO 80112
(303) 792-9900
(303) 792-5333 (fax)
www.americanhumane.org

American Society for the Prevention of Cruelty to Animals
(ASPCA)
441 East 92nd St.
New York, NY 10028
www.aspca.org

Delta Society
580 Naches Ave., S.W., Suite 101
Renton, WA 98055-2297
(425) 226-7357
(425) 235-1076 (fax)
www.deltasociety.org
email: info@deltasociety.org

Therapy Dogs International
1536 Morris Pl.
Hillsdale, NJ 07205

World Canine Freestyle
P.O. Box 350122
Brooklyn, NY 11235-2525
(718) 332-8336
www.worldcaninefreestyle.org
email: wcfodogs@aol.com

American Kennel Club
260 Madison Ave.
New York, NY 10016
(212) 696-8200
www.akc.org

United Kennel Club (UKC)
100 E. Kilgore
Kalamazoo, MI 49001
(269) 943-9020
www.ukcdogs.com

Paws Across America
3476 Bailey Ave.
Riverdale, NY 10463
(718) 796-4541
www.pawsacrossamerica.com

American Veterinary Medical Association (AVMA)
1931 N. Meacham Rd., Suite 100
Schaumburg, IL 60173
(847) 925-8070
www.avma.org
email: avmaininfo@avma.org

Wild Canid Survival and Research Center
Box 760
Eureka, MO 63025
(636) 938-5900
email: wildcanidcenter@onemain.com

United States Department of Agriculture
Federal Building, Room 565
6505 Belcrest Rd.
Hyattsville, MD 20782
(301) 436-7833

USDA-Forest Service
Public Affairs
201 14th St., S.W.
Washington, DC 20250
(202) 205-1438
(202) 205-0885 (fax)

Actors' Equity Association
165 West 46th St.
New York, NY 10036
(212) 869-8530

American Federation of Television and Radio Artists
260 Madison Ave.
New York, NY 10016
(212) 683-2346

American Guild of Variety Artists
184 Fifth Ave.
New York, NY 10019
(212) 675-1003

Screen Actors Guild (SAG)
5757 Wilshire Blvd.
Los Angeles, CA 90036
(323) 954-1600

International Brotherhood of Teamsters
25 Louisiana Ave., N.W.
Washington, DC 20001
(202) 626-6192

Index

Page numbers in *italics* refer to illustrations.

About the Authors

BASH DIBRA is an internationally acclaimed animal trainer, award-winning behaviorist, and bestselling author of *Cat Speak, Dog Speak,* and many other popular pet books.

Dubbed the industry's "Power Dog Trainer" by *Entertainment Weekly,* and America's "Pet Laureate" by the *Yearbook of Experts,* Bash's clients include Sarah Jessica Parker and Matthew Broderick, Jennifer Lopez, Mariah Carey, Martin Scorsese, Ron Howard, Kim Basinger, Alec Baldwin, Ralph Lauren, S. I. Newhouse, and Henry Kissinger, among others.

The recipient of the New York State Humane Association Award, the Veterinary Medical Association of New York City's Unsung Hero Award, and the North Shore Animal League America's Legendary Bond Award, Bash has appeared in numerous magazines, newspapers, and TV shows, including *Inside Edition, The Tonight Show, Good Morning America,* the *Today* show, *The Early Show,* and CNN.

Bash's own pets are celebrities as well, featured in motion pictures, television, commercials, and advertisements.

You can visit the author's websites at www.bashdibra.com, www.pawsacrossamerica.com, and www.starpet.com.

KITTY BROWN is a writer and broadcast journalist specializing in animals. She has reported for WCBS-TV News, FX-TV's *The Pet Department, USA TODAY, Forbes, Soap Opera Digest, Soap Opera Weekly,* and The American Kennel Club *Gazette*. She and Bash Dibra previously collaborated on *Your Dream Dog*.